Apologetics after Lindbeck

Apologetics after Lindbeck

Faith, Reason, and the Cultural-Linguistic Turn

JEREMIAH GIBBS

☞PICKWICK *Publications* · Eugene, Oregon

APOLOGETICS AFTER LINDBECK
Faith, Reason, and the Cultural-Linguistic Turn

Pickwick Publications
An Imprint of Wipf and Stock Publishers
199 W. 8th Ave., Suite 3
Eugene, OR 97401

www.wipfandstock.com

ISBN 13: 978-1-4982-2497-0

Cataloguing-in-Publication Data

Gibbs, Jeremiah

Apologetics after Lindbeck : faith, reason, and the cultural-linguistic turn / Jeremiah Gibbs.

xvi + 178 p. ; 23 cm. Includes bibliographical references and index.

ISBN 13: 978-1-4982-2497-0

1. Postliberal theology. 2. Apologetics. I. Title.

BT83.595 .G53 2015

Manufactured in the U.S.A.   11/03/2015

Contents

Acknowledgments | vii
Introduction | ix

1 The Postliberal Challenge to Apologetics | 1

2 God of the Beautiful and the Good | 35

3 Rational Justification in a Postliberal Mode | 86

4 Worship, Apologetics, and the Need for Catechesis | 125

Bibliography | 165
Index | 175

Acknowledgments

BECAUSE THIS BOOK IS derived from my dissertation, some of the most influential persons in my young career are due my gratitude. I will be forever grateful to Brent Waters, my doctoral advisor, for giving me the freedom to write my dissertation while working full-time. For the sake of the project, Dr. Waters often made himself available at unusual times to accommodate my odd schedule. More importantly, he has challenged me for many years to write and reason carefully and my scholarship will forever be indebted to his mentoring. During my master's program, D. Stephen Long enabled and coached me to do constructive theology for the first time. His formative influence cannot be understated. E. Byron Anderson welcomed a Pentecostal into his worship classes, one who knew less about liturgy than the average Methodist confirmand. I have come a long way in my liturgical scholarship and formation because of his patience.

The University of Indianapolis's Michael Cartwright, then Dean of Ecumenical and Interfaith Programs, and Deborah Balogh, Provost, arranged for me to have time in the summer of 2013 to finish writing my dissertation. I am very grateful to them. Dr. Cartwright also read and gave feedback on sections that were quite helpful. I am also thankful for my undergraduate research assistant, Joseph Krall, for his careful editing in the final stages of the project. I look forward to reading his dissertation someday in the future.

Finally, I am thankful for my gracious family. My parents, Frank and Penny Gibbs, instilled a deep love of learning in me. My wife, Jenifer Stuelpe Gibbs, is an excellent theological dialogue partner, life partner, and the greatest joy in my life. Her support during this long project has been unwavering. Finally, I am thankful for my son, De'Avalon. He paid a price, too, for this project, though he never understood why I always needed to "work on my book." Thankfully, God's grace has been enough for me.

Introduction

"You really could say that everything I've ever written is apologetics."
Stanley Hauerwas[1]

Can the Christian account of the world be considered true above all others? No matter the extent to which some persons desire to subordinate the possibility, necessity, and role of apologetic discourse, this question persists.

Christian apologetics has been present in every age of the church. For the first sixteen hundred years of church history, the explicit method of apologetics was the "faith seeking understanding" first articulated by Augustine. Apologetic argument was almost always occasional, responding to one or another argument posed to detract from the attractiveness of Christian faith. Though Anselm represents a significant shift toward a more systemic argument for the Christian faith, Enlightenment thinkers were the first to suggest that Christian faith should only be maintained if it could show itself to be reasonable by general standards of rationality. John Locke will serve as my prime example of this in chapter 3. Given that this period was marked by incredibly high standards of proof and evidence, Christian apologetics can generally be said to have followed two different responses. Some apologists accepted that faith could not meet these high standards and endeavored to show that there was no need for Christian faith to meet the standards of proof. In contemporary apologetics, the heirs of the presuppositional apologetics of Cornelius Van Til best represent this position. The second approach, one better known by apologists, is that of attempting

---

1. This was Hauerwas's response to a question about the role of apologetics in the context of his arguing that his theology is a public theology. Stanley Hauerwas, "On Being a Theologian."

to answer the call to such high standards of rationality. Though contemporary Catholics such as Peter Kreeft and Denys Turner could be counted among those who attempt to meet the Enlightenment standards, many contemporary apologists associated with this effort are conservative evangelical theologians, such as William Lane Craig, Norman Geisler, and R.C. Sproul.

Some Christian apologists after the Enlightenment suggested that Christianity was reasonable, but resisted the temptation to accept that this could only be shown by the standards of Enlightenment philosophy. Joseph Butler, John Henry Newman, and C.S. Lewis could be included among these. The postmodern critique of the Enlightenment could have had the effect of reviving interest in these thinkers, but did so in only limited ways. Instead, it has been common to dismiss the possibility of a rational defense of Christian faith.[2] I would suggest that Christians might not do so and remain faithful.

Whether we should consider the postmodern turn to be an intellectual revolution equivalent to that of Copernicus, the Enlightenment, or the medieval revival of Aristotle is a question that can only be definitively answered by future historians. But there has been an undeniable and fundamental shift in this century to a notion of reason that questions the assumptions of foundationalist epistemology. Whatever may be said a century from now, this century demands an apologetic that responds to the intellectual climate of our age.

How might we name this intellectual climate, especially with regard to its implications for theology and apologetics? George Lindbeck and scholars that share conceptual affinity with him have provided an analysis of this question that I find compelling and will use to frame the issues at hand. The focus of chapter 1 will be his analysis of the implications of our current environment for theological reasoning. I will especially focus on those questions most closely related to apologetics: the nature of truth, epistemology, and intelligibility in a pluralistic environment. While Lindbeck's book, *The Nature of Doctrine*, has long been criticized for its brevity and oversimplification of the categories, his categories are nevertheless helpful in diagnosing the issues at hand. While his distinctions are sometimes unhelpful, I contend that he has named the scope of the argument well. And Lindbeck is more nuanced than some commentary would make him out to be.

---

2. The surprising popularity among evangelicals of a recent book by Myron B. Penner is a great example. While Penner believes that Christianity is true in a universal sense, he eschews the possibility of rationally justifying that true claim to another person. Our Christian witness is our only justification of our claims to truth. While I explain the ways in which our witness genuinely matter, no access to rational justification does mark the "end of apologetics" that he heralds. Penner, *End of Apologetics*, 112–34.

Lindbeck picks up an unfortunate phrase, "ad hoc apologetics," from his Yale colleague, Hans Frei. This phrase has largely served to discourage those that accept the postliberal diagnosis of the problem from engaging in the discipline. Considering themselves heirs of Karl Barth, postliberals need no more motivation to question the possibility or logic of apologetics. Central to my argument is the conviction that Lindbeck's conclusions are less novel among those that consider themselves apologists than he and his commentators admit. Many that would consider themselves apologists have already accepted similar challenges posed by pluralistic contexts and incorporated their implications into apologetic method.

Lindbeck contrasts the ad hoc apologetics of postliberal theology with "one that is systematically prior and controlling in the fashion of post-Cartesian natural theology and of later liberalism."[3] Post-Cartesian natural theology is the descendant of modern epistemological certainty, while the latter is the correlational theology and apologetics that are left after the failure of the modern project. Lindbeck is concerned to oppose "later liberalism." As I am a Pentecostal theologian from the conservative Assemblies of God, I can hardly be identified as an historical "postliberal" because I have never been committed to the liberal project. I am more concerned with "post-Cartesian natural theology." Apologetics of this variety has been prevalent among conservative evangelicals, with contemporary examples including those such as Norman Geisler, William Lane Craig, and R.C. Sproul. However, epistemology is not monolithic among evangelicals as some might suppose.

Since the publication of the *The Nature of Doctrine*, evangelical scholars have drawn upon postliberal conceptions of theology to identify a "post-conservative" evangelicalism, most notably Stanley Grenz.[4] He has argued that the central issue for reconsidering evangelical theology is the social dimension of knowledge that is so central to Lindbeck's book.

> Evangelical theologians tend to misunderstand the social nature
> of theological discourse. More than its advocates have cared to
> admit, evangelical theology has been the captive of the orienta-
> tion to the individual knower that has reigned over the Western
> mindset throughout the modern era . . . The revisioning of the
> theological task is dependent on a renewed understanding of
> the role of the community in the life of faith. Evangelicals are
> correct in asserting that the revealed truth of God forms the

3. Lindbeck, *Nature of Doctrine*, 117–18.

4. For a short history of the use of the term see Olson, *Reformed and Always Reforming*, 1–17. Because I appeal strongly to the ecumenical consensus as a locus of authority, Olson would likely include me as a conservative in his own delineation. I prefer Grenz's notion of postconservative.

"basic grammar" that creates Christian identity . . . But this identity-creative process is not an individualistic manner occurring in isolation. Instead it is a development that happens within a community.[5]

As Grenz suggests, evangelical inattention to the social nature of discourse is under revision among these postconservative theologians. Central to the postconservative project is the notion that "traditional evangelical commitment to objectivism and propositionalism has worked against an inadequate understanding of the relationship between theology and culture, even among those who have called for contextualization as a part of the theological process."[6] As I will show in chapter 1, "postliberal" can be summarized as a rearticulation of the nature of theology after the myth of a universal, foundational religious experience. "Postconservative" similarly can be described as postfoundationalist redescription of theology after the myth of objective knowledge. Gary Dorrien argues that postfoundationalism is the future of evangelical theology.[7] While I think the road to a postfoundationist conservative theology is a long one, I agree with Dorrien that the future of evangelicalism is found here. F. Leron Shults describes postfoundationalism as "hold[ing] on to the ideals of truth, objectivity, and rationality, while at the same time acknowledging the provisional, contextual, and fallible nature of human reason."[8] Postfoundationalism is not a rejection of realism, but a critical acknowledgement of subjective epistemology. Postconservative theology and apologetics will necessarily work to rearticulate their tasks in view of this acknowledgement.

This book is a proposal of an apologetic method in a postconservative mode. After investigating Lindbeck's postfoundationalist conception of truth and religion, I will propose three related implications for the apologetic task. First, a more holistic conception of metaphysics after modernism will entail appeals to the Beautiful and the Good in addition to the True. In chapter 2, I will make and defend the contentious theological claim that the traditional transcendental predicates are interdependent. The Good,

---

5. Grenz, *Revisioning Evangelical Theology*, 73.

6. Franke, *Character of Theology*, 90. Franke's example of one who calls for contextualization is particularly telling. Millard Erickson calls for theology that "strives to give a coherent statement of the doctrines . . . placed in the context of culture in general, [and] worded in contemporary idiom." This presumes that doctrine is the proposition that exists independently of an articulation of it in a contemporary idiom. Cf. Erickson, *Christian Theology*, 23. Roger Olson traces postfoundationalism through the evangelical movement in Olson, *Reformed and Always Reforming*, 125–52.

7. Dorrien, *Remaking of Evangelical*, 201–3.

8. Shults, *Postfoundationalist Task of Theology*, 58.

Beautiful, and True are three different ways of talking about the same quality: that which is most real. Apologetic method should therefore argue that Christianity is not only true, but is also the most beautiful and ethical account of the world. It is then argued that both aesthetics and ethics are ontologically grounded and pragmatically reliable.

The second implication of postfoundationalism upon apologetics is a different notion of rational justification than previously imagined. In the opening section of chapter 3, I review a number of conservative apologists that reject foundationalism. While Lindbeck is largely right about the social nature of knowledge, he misunderstands or does not pay attention to the state of conservative apologetics in the late twentieth century. I will explain two different notions of apologetics that reach conclusions similar to Lindbeck and yet proceed with apologetics unabated. After arguing that Lindbeck's position is not unique among professional apologists, I will situate Lindbeck within a particular school of apologetics known as "cumulative case apologetics." These cumulative case apologists have proposed a set of guidelines for reasonable judgment between competing idioms, given the unique case that they make about epistemology and justification. I will describe this process of judgment and justification, suggesting that post-conservative apologetics will necessarily make judgments between religious idioms in this way.

The final implication for apologetics is a heightened awareness of the need for a new catechesis in post-Christian context. Lindbeck suggests that theology and the telling of the Christian Gospel will be unintelligible in a culture where Christian language and grammar has long since disappeared. Therefore, Christians will need to teach this language and the related practices to potential adherents. This analysis can be significantly contrasted with that of Karl Barth's suggestions about apologetics:

> [Theology] may bring the *fides* before those who happen to come to its notice in its inner consistency as the *intellectus fidei*, thus making its own contribution to the presentation of the likeness of the kingdom of God. Since it cannot do more than this, it will spare both the world and itself the pain of a specific apologetic, the more so in view of the fact that good dogmatics is always the best and basically the only possible apologetics. Those who are without or partly without hear theologians best when these do not speak so ardently to them but pursue their own way before their eyes and ears. Correctly conceived and executed, theology

will present itself even to the community and its members in such a way that it cannot fail to be noticed.[9]

Barth rightly understands the challenge and task of apologetics as training in the use of Christian language, specifically training by observation. It is easy to misunderstand Barth and think that this task is primarily a cerebral one, particularly since Barth is the author of one of the most extensive theological treatises in the history of the church. But although Barth does not often speak of the teaching and transformative aspects of liturgy, a curious passage late in the *Church Dogmatics* shows that he, too, sees that catechesis is sometimes best done in everyday practice of Christian worship.

> I must interpose at this point a small but sincerely grateful tribute. It is to a theologian who cannot be called great, but to whom I am greatly indebted. I refer to Abel Burckhardt, who a hundred years ago—a contemporary of the more famous Jacob Burckhardt—was the second pastor at the minster here in Basel. He composed and edited a collection of songs for children in the local dialect. This was the textbook in which, at the beginning of the last decade of the last century, I received my first theological instruction in a form appropriate to my then immaturity. And what made an indelible impression on me was the homely naturalness with which these very modest compositions spoke of the events of Christmas, Palm Sunday, Good Friday, Easter, the Ascension and Pentecost as things which might take place any day in Basel or its environs like any other important happenings. History? Doctrine? Dogma? Myth? No—but things actually taking place, so that we could see and hear and lay up in our hearts. For as these songs were sung in the everyday language we were then beginning to hear and speak, and as we joined in singing, we took our mother's hand, as it were, and went to the stall at Bethlehem, and to the streets of Jerusalem where, greeted by children of a similar age, the Saviour made His entry, and to the dark hill of Golgotha, and as the sun rose to the garden of Joseph. Was this *representation*, like the unbloody repetition of the sacrifice of Christ in the Roman doctrine of the Mass? Was it the kind of faith which in that rather convulsive doctrine is supposed to consist in a re-enactment of the crucifixion of Christ in our own existence? Again, no. It was all present without needing to be made present. The yawning chasm of Lessing did not exist. The contemporaneity of Kierkegaard was not a problem. The Saviour Himself was obviously the same yesterday and today.

9. Barth, *Church Dogmatics* IV.3.2, 882.

All very naïve, and not worth mentioning at all in academic circles? Yes, it was very naïve, but perhaps in the very naivety there lay the deepest wisdom and the greatest power, so that once grasped, it was calculated to carry one relatively unscathed—although not, of course, untempted or unassailed—through all the serried ranks of historicism and anti-historicism, mysticism and rationalism, orthodoxy and liberalism and existentialism, and to bring one back some day to the matter itself.[10]

In this passage, more so than his extensive writings typically reveal, Barth shows that he understands that some of the most important theological understanding is developed without theological instruction. Good theology has a way of enveloping a worshipper over time through acts as an informal and deeply formative catechesis. This is entailed in the social understanding of knowledge implied by postfoundationalism and is a consistent theme in much postmodern literature. Therefore, chapter 4 of this book will argue that the central practice of Christian public worship is the way that Christians must "pursue their own way before [the non-Christian's] eyes and ears." It is here that Christians and apologetic interlocutors will encounter the paradigmatic use of Christian language and practice.

While the task of apologetics is markedly different for postconservative theologians than for a previous generation of evangelicals, Lindbeck and his postliberal colleagues grossly overstate the limits of apologetics. Though Stanley Hauerwas is another postliberal that has sometimes been skeptical of the possibility of apologetics, the quote with which I began this "Introduction" is evidence that Hauerwas recognizes that a clear articulation of theology is its own apologetic. Like Barth, even as he protests apologetic method, his massive articulation of theology and its ethical implications leaves a great apologetic legacy. It is my hope that *Apologetics After Lindbeck* will provide guidance for how the church might similarly articulate her theology well as she carries out her mission.

---

10. Barth, *Church Dogmatics IV.2*, 112–13. I am grateful to Michael Cartwright for turning my attention to this passage as quoted in Ford, *Barth and God's Story*, 16.

1

The Postliberal Challenge to Apologetics

INTRODUCTION

Postliberal Christian theologians have been largely skeptical of the
possibility of a coherent apologetic method. It is not too much to say that
they have often been dismissive of both its task and necessity. To understand
why this is the case, this chapter will explain the theological prolegomena
proposed by George Lindbeck with regards to the concerns that the construal raises for apologetics. I am not arguing that Lindbeck's proposal has
no implications for apologetics. But I want to explain those implications
without dismissing the necessity and possibility of the discipline as postliberals are tempted to do. Therefore I will pay close attention to Lindbeck's
proposal that I might show in later chapters how we might develop apologetics in ways that are more consistent with postliberal concepts.

Summaries of what is cohesive about postliberal theology are available.[1] For my purposes, I need not reformulate these summaries. James
Fodor's summary is widely accepted and sets the cohesive aspects in just
nine interrelated concepts. The problems for a postliberal apologetic method are found in the final three points of Fodor's summary. Apologists of a
correlationist perspective will find his seventh point problematic: postliberal approaches deny the existence of a universal "core" of all religious experience of which Christianity is only one example among many. Postliberals

---

1. Fodor, "Postliberal Theology," 229–24; Placher, "Paul Ricoeur and Postliberal
Theology," 35–52; Dehart, *Trial of the Witnesses*, 57–100; Goh, *Christian Tradition To-
day*, 172–216; Michener, *Postliberal Theology*, 1–18; Pecknold, *Transforming Postliberal
Theology*, 19–34.

think that the idea of a single phenomenon called "religion" is a creation of the modern age that cannot withstand scrutiny. Apologists of a more evidentialist stripe, or those who understand natural theology to stand on its own without dependence upon biblical revelation, will take issue with his eighth point: postliberal theologians share a commitment to nonfoundationalist epistemological posture. I will take up this aspect of postliberal thinking through much of this chapter. Postliberalism's nonfoundationalism is the most controversial aspect for conservative apologists and for those conservative theologians that dialogue with postliberalism.[2] If I am to describe something like a "postconservative" apologetic method, I will need to be clearest at this point. Fodor's final point in the survey flows naturally from the others: postliberals explain that the primary task of theology, therefore, is descriptive rather than apologetic. Christian theology is called to describe the internal consistencies and structures of Christian thinking and avoid trying to translate these into universal religious experience, on the one hand, and universal "objective truth" on the other. As Fodor explains, postliberal theologians have almost universally accepted the early conclusion that this results in apologetics proceeding "in a non-systematic, *ad hoc* fashion—as the occasion arises, in connection with a particular issue, relative to a specific context, with respect to particular interlocutors."[3] The postliberal theologians themselves recognize that this designation has different meanings among them.[4] In this chapter, I will evaluate the seminal work of George Lindbeck as a way of outlining the problem for apologetics that is posed by this conception of theology. While postliberalism has developed in many different directions since the explosion of literature following the publication of *The Nature of Doctrine*, Lindbeck organizes the postliberal impulse in the most systematic way and therefore provides the clearest explanation of the impact on apologetics, even if not the most nuanced. A postliberal proposal with a concept of truth more amenable to conservative apologetics, that of D. Stephen Long, will be explained in chapter 2.

---

2. For a good critique of the foundationalism of evangelical theology, see Clapp, "How Firm a Foundation," 81–92. Nicholas Wolterstorff and Alvin Plantinga are Reformed evangelical theologians that have extensively argued against foundationalism, as I will show in chapter 3.

3. Fodor, "Postliberal Theology," 231.

4. For the variety of uses of the phrase "ad hoc apologetics," see Placher, *Unapologetic Theology*, 167–68.

GEORGE LINDBECK

Lindbeck famously begins his *The Nature of Doctrine* by delineating three conceptions of church doctrine that he regards as being independent of the Christian religion in particular, such that he can identify them as theories of religion generally. The propositionalist conception is closely aligned with American Christian analytic philosophy. A doctrine is thought to function as a truth claim regarding unchanging and objective reality. "God is good" is not dependent upon anything to be regarded as truth except whether it is the case that God is indeed good and that the words in the statement are defined and used in a clear way. The doctrine is true if the content of the proposition that it expresses accords with the thing as it is; alignment with classical conceptions of the correspondence theory of truth is obvious.[5] Grenz and Franke tell a humble version of the story of the "eclipse of biblical narrative" within conservative evangelicalism by suggesting that conservative evangelicals exchanged the authority of the Bible as the community's text for the Bible as a "storehouse of theological facts." They claim that the conservative evangelicals then "set out to amass the true statements or factual propositions they believed were taught in the pages of scripture."[6] Propositions about God take the authoritative role in governing speech about God.

The "experiential-expressivist" conception of doctrine assumes that doctrines do not actually speak definitely about how the world is, but rather express the inner feelings, emotions, and intuitions of those who ascribe to them. This does not mean that the doctrinal statements are not true in some sense. But truth is not primarily about correspondence with reality, but instead refers to the ways in which the doctrine explains the world to its adherents. Doctrines are therefore symbols that can assume multiple meanings for multiple individual adherents. These doctrines can be true in an experiential-expressivist sense for many different interpreters and many different interpretations. The doctrine itself takes on different meanings, and "truth" in this sense is multiple. In a similar way, very different religious doctrines can be taken to mean the same thing and can still be considered to be true, respectively. For example, a Hindu conception of karma and a Christian conception of sin may be taken by a single individual or many

5. For more on the inadequacy of Lindbeck's account of propositions, see Vanhoozer, *Drama of Doctrine*, 88–92.

6. Grenz and Franke, *Beyond Foundationalism*, 62. Nancey Murphy also surveys some conservative articulations of propositionalism. Murphy does not tell the story of the rise of propositionalism, but she represents the defenders of it well. Murphy, *Beyond Liberalism and Fundamentalism*, 42–46.

different persons as interpreting the same experience or concept. From a propositionalist perspective this is not possible without distorting one or both of the doctrines. Because doctrines in this framework can assume multiple meanings for different persons, Lindbeck says that they are not crucial for either religious agreement or disagreement for theologians of this second type.[7] Lindbeck argues that doctrine matters little in ecumenical discussions of persons who adhere to this theory of religion. Since ecumenism is his purpose for writing, he is critical of the inadequacy of this method. For those of the first type, experiential-expressive thinking clearly spells the end of any version of apologetics that seeks to defend the truth of a particular religious doctrine over another. Multivalent meanings leave adherence to one doctrine or another insignificant for apologetics of the first type.[8]

Disappointed that theology of the first type prevents ecumenical reconciliation without capitulation and that theology of the second type makes doctrine insignificant for ecumenical discussion, Lindbeck discusses a third type that proposes that religion functions more like a culture or language. This "cultural-linguistic" type claims that doctrines function as "rules" which govern the proper use of language and action. To be a Christian of a certain kind is to be defined by adherence to the doctrinal positions of that community and the practices associated with them. Rather than allowing doctrines to interpret religious and non-religious experiences as in the experiential-expressivist type, the third type claims that religions actually govern what types of experiences that a person can have. For example, while two religious communities may be eating similar meals of similar contents in similar settings, one may understand themselves to be eating a celebrative meal of fellowship with the god while the other understands itself to be sharing in the god's suffering by consuming his body. The meal is itself a different thing, whether the content and setting remain the same or not. And the doctrines that govern these practices limit the kinds of experiences possible within them, for to celebrate while partaking in suffering, for example, is to be doing something other than simply participating in the meal of the

---

7. Lindbeck, *Nature of Doctrine*, 3.

8. Tracy rightly criticized Lindbeck for the ways that his summary of "experiential-expressivism" caricatured the position such that it did not describe any actual theologians. Undoubtedly, my summary here has likely done so even more dramatically, if only for its brevity. But the reader should not mistake my brevity for an actual maligning of the position. I agree that these theologians have indeed answered many of Lindbeck's challenges even before he issued them. Nevertheless, I will not be engaging these theologians significantly, given that my primary concern is dialogue between conservative apologetics and postliberalism. See Tracy, "Lindbeck's New Program for Theology," 463–5. Dehart has summarized the more extended debate between Lindbeck and Tracy. See Dehart, *Trial of the Witnesses*, 161–71.

latter community. Of course, the example is particularly poignant for Christians because the notion of the Christian Eucharist actually contains both of these concepts simultaneously. This, therefore, opens another set of possible experiences that are not present in either of the first two conceptions.

Lindbeck immediately turns to the implications for varying religious communities when he introduces this concept. He is primarily interested in the concept's usefulness.[9] He explains that if doctrines function as rules which govern a religious culture, it is not difficult to see how those rules may or may not apply in various times and places. The doctrine is not therefore dependent upon whether and how a person interprets it and uses it to give meaning to his or her life. Rather the doctrine functions as a rule that is authoritative for all adherents, but may not be authoritative in the same way in every historical situation or every location. Lindbeck uses the example of "drive on the right side of the road," which is not applicable in England or even in the United States under some unusual circumstances that re-route traffic to the left. Lindbeck's intentions regarding ecumenism are helped by this limit to the rules. Apologists of the first type still find this explanation problematic, as we will see, because there appears to be no appeal to a stable referent outside of the cultural system that can be authoritative. I will explain below that this is not what Lindbeck intends, but the critique has been common.[10]

Lindbeck is far more concerned in *The Nature of Doctrine* with contrasting a postliberal cultural-linguistic conception of doctrine with the experiential-expressivist conception. This is primarily due to his being located within both a liberal Protestant denomination and within an institution dominated by liberal Protestant perspectives. For the experiential-expressivist, apologetics, and theology more generally, is primarily about articulating doctrine in such a way that it is helpful for individuals to give meaning to the experiences, religious and otherwise, of their lives. When doctrine is articulated such that persons find it helpful in giving meaning to their lives, it has achieved an apologetic purpose. In fact, for correspondence theologians such as Tillich, for whom the experiential-expressivist mode is primary, one could rightly say that all theology is apologetic. Theology's primary purpose for these persons is providing meaning to life; aiming at

---

9. Pecknold argues that Lindbeck's postliberalism is a distinct kind of pragmatism (Pecknold, *Transforming Postliberal Theology*). Jackson summarizes why Lindbeck's proposal is problematic from a pragmatist's perspective in Jackson, "Against Grammar," 140–45.

10. Hensley summarizes a few of these in Hensley, "Are Postliberals Necessarily Antirealists?" 71–72. Cf. Bloesch, *Theology of Word and Spirit*, 30; Bloesch, *Holy Scripture*, 208–18; Morris, "Introduction," 6–7; McGrath, *Genesis of Doctrine*, 29–32.

declarative or doxological statements about the personhood and nature of God are not primarily in view. This is apologetics of a distinctly liberal sort. This liberal theological type is the primary aim of Lindbeck's polemic, as might be assumed from the name that he gives the movement: "postliberal."

My concern in this project is not resolving the tensions between postliberal understandings of theology and this sort of liberal apologetics. I share the concerns of Lindbeck, Barth, and others that this sort of apologetics is little more than nihilism with Christian ornamentation.[11] Rather, I hope to resolve tensions between postliberal theological construal and apologetics of a more traditional and conservative type. The reader should not overlook this significant difference between the aims of this project and that of the postliberal theologians. Postliberalism intends to take aim at the liberal impulse and is constantly contrasting itself with this impulse. My aim throughout this book is to appropriate the theological construal of the postliberals, but to do so in a way that addresses the concerns of the conservative theologians from which I come. This has also been attempted by Kevin Vanhoozer, Stanley Grenz, and in the edited volume by Timothy Phillips and Dennis Okholm, but without explicit concern for apologetics.[12]

There is no need to be particularly precise with a definition of the kind of apologetics of which I am concerned. The differences between the correspondence mode of apologetics of experiential-expressivist theories of religion and the conservative mode of apologetics consist of what is taken as the primary task. Avery Cardinal Dulles classifies these two schools by saying the conservative mode of apologetics follows fundamentalist B. B. Warfield by aiming to "establish the truth of Christianity as the absolute religion, directly and as a whole."[13] He calls that of the liberal theologians an "apologetics of accommodation."[14] The latter presumes that the primary issue is explaining Christianity such that someone can see that Christianity *matters*. The former presumes that the primary issue is explaining Christianity such that someone can see that Christianity is *true*. As a recent book on apologetic method defined it, "Apologetics is concerned with the defense of the Christian faith against charges of falsehood, inconsistency, and credulity . . . [It] has to do with defending, or making a case for, the truth of

---

11. "What Lindbeck finds objectionable in the [liberal] foundationalist approach to theology is that this approach contributes to the erosion of Christian identity: as it measures the intelligibility of the Gospel message by bringing the criteria of the larger culture to bear, the natural outcome is a loss of Christian particularity" (Goh, *Christian Tradition Today*, 178–79).

12. Vanhoozer, *Drama of Doctrine*; Phillips and Okholm, *Nature of Confession*.

13. Dulles, *History of Apologetics*, 229.

14. Ibid., 230.

the Christian faith."[15] This definition is neither definitive nor unique, but is representative of a great deal of conservative apologists[16] that presume that the issue of the truthfulness of Christian faith and communicating that truthfulness in a compelling and clear way are the essence of the discipline. The experiential-expressivist mode of apologetics is so foreign to this perspective that it is not even included in this book that outlines five apologetic methods. In fact, I can find no mention of experiential-expressivist or correlationist type apologetics in the book. The definition of apologetics from a conservative perspective directs us toward two concerns: 1) Is Christianity true and can this be shown? 2) What is required to demonstrate the truthfulness of Christianity to an interlocutor?

Lindbeck and the Question of Truth

If anyone could be taken as typical of the conservative theologians of whom I am speaking, the evangelical Alister McGrath is as good as any. McGrath is a very balanced, well-spoken and considered theologian and, in my judgment, a generally good reader and interpreter of theology. His critique of Lindbeck's notion of truth is, however, quite ungenerous and fails to get to the very heart of Lindbeck's argument. His assessment is nonetheless typical of evangelical critiques.[17] In short, he claims that

> Lindbeck thus appears to suggest that the cultural-linguistic approach to doctrine may dispense with the question of whether the Christian idiom has any external referent. Language *functions* within a cultural and linguistic world; it does not necessarily, however, *refer* to anything. Doctrine is concerned with the internal regulation of the Christian idiom, ensuring its

15. Cowan, "Introduction," 8.

16. When the terms "conservative apologists" or "conservative apologetics" are used in this book I mean only to refer to the apologetic disposition toward defending the faith in this way. I do not mean that all of these apologists will necessarily be theological conservatives. I take this to be a sociological identifier with a tradition of apologetics most closely associated with those on the conservative side of the Modernist/Fundamentalist controversies of the twentieth century. The method that I will describe could be used by theologically liberal persons as they attempt to show that their theological vision is the most truthful one available. The identification of this intellectual community as "conservative" is really just to contrast with Lindbeck's self–identification of "postliberal."

17. For a summary of evangelical critiques, see Hensley, "Are Postliberals Necessarily Antirealists?" 71–72.

consistency. The question of how that idiom relates to the external world is considered to be improper.[18]

It seems that the rather narrow way in which Lindbeck is speaking of the concept of "doctrine" as a concept that has regulative function for the community, whether officially as in doctrinal statements or unofficially as it does in many non-creedal communities, has been conflated in McGrath. Lindbeck would say that doctrines *as doctrines* only serve to form the community such that it is possible to make truthful statements and cannot themselves be truthful. McGrath is concerned that Lindbeck does not believe that doctrines can in fact refer to some outside referent.[19] William Placher gives an important distinction that makes sense of McGrath's confusion. Placher claims that one can read Lindbeck as saying that all religious speech is culturally-linguistically defined or he can be read as saying that only doctrine *as doctrines* are culturally-linguistically defined.[20] Placher thinks the latter reading is the correct one. There are obviously some aspects of cultural-linguistic thinking that do apply to all religious speech (for example, the *meaning* of all religious speech is determined by its use in the community). So I think that Placher is making a distinction between the aspects of religious speech that are judged intrasystematically. Doctrines are self-referential according to Lindbeck; other kinds of religious speech are not. As explained by Hensley,

> When the statement "Jesus Christ is fully human and fully divine" functions as a first-order statement uttered in the context of worship, it makes a truth claim concerning the nature of the person Jesus of Nazareth. But as a second-order statement uttered in an academic lecture on Christology, it states a rule about the limits of christological discourse. According to Lindbeck, the latter use of the statement as doctrine does not make a truth claim per se, but rather governs or regulates what truth claims are appropriate for Christians.[21]

18. McGrath, "Evangelical Evaluation of Postliberalism," 36. Much of this quote and the argument of the aforementioned article is a revision of his earlier *Genesis of Doctrine*, 28–30. See also Dulles, "Postmodern Ecumenism," 57–61.

19. Though appreciative of Lindbeck's overall project, Wainwright also criticizes Lindbeck for putting too much distance between doctrine as regulative rules and claims to truth. Wainwright, "Ecumenical Dimensions of Lindbeck's 'Nature of Doctrine,'" 121–32. Though he does not claim that Lindbeck is eschewing truth, Fackre argues that a lack of clarity on reference to "objective reality" is Lindbeck's great weakness. See Fackre, *Christian Story*, Vol. 2, 219.

20. Placher, "Paul Ricoeur and Postliberal Theology," 46.

21. Hensley, "Are Postliberals Necessarily Antirealists?" 78.

As can be seen from this summary, Lindbeck would respond that only the actual statements of living and breathing Christians can "refer" to an outside referent. That is to say, "doctrines" are only those official and quasi-official regulative rules, the product of secondary theological dialogue. But "language" for Lindbeck does in fact "refer" to objects and realities, but only when certain conditions are met and "doctrines" do not meet these conditions in the rather narrow way that Lindbeck defines them.[22] This conflation leads McGrath to believe that the only thing that actually matters for Lindbeck is the consistency of the Christian idiom.

Though I have no intentions of following an argument in this direction, I agree with David Tracy's intuition that the cultural-linguistic aspects of Lindbeck's theory and his regulative theory of doctrine are not inseparable. It is worth noting that Tracy, one of Lindbeck's chief opponents, is one of the few scholars that noticed that these theories need not be taken as a single proposition.[23] Tracy also states that Lindbeck fails to make the case for their link.[24] I mention his comments only to suggest that much of my assessment of Lindbeck avoids the questions regarding whether doctrine does or does not make first-order truth claims. Lindbeck famously argues that doctrine is only second-order speech and therefore cannot be true or false and rather functions as communally accepted "grammatical" rules. I think Lindbeck has stated his case too strongly, as doctrines are, even if only in a weak way, grounded in a particular community and form of life—the one that authorizes them. I want to suspend judgment about the regulative theory of doctrine for the purposes of evaluating the truth claims of Lindbeck's cultural-linguistic model. Regardless of whether the authorized doctrines of a community do or do not make truth claims in themselves, it is agreed that the people that make up these communities do make such truth claims. Assessing their truth claims is the more important matter for apologetics. Conflating Lindbeck's theory of doctrine with his contextualizing of truth claims is part of what has led McGrath and others to ungenerously critique Lindbeck as relativistic.

22. Hensley summarizes well: "Theology and doctrine, in Lindbeck's words, 'assert nothing either true or false about God and his relation to creatures, but only speak about such assertions.' But note Lindbeck's careful wording of this passage. Theology and doctrine, he claims, *to the extent that they are second-order activities*, have no truth value. Here Lindbeck is making a claim about theological utterances functioning *as doctrines*, as second-order statements or rules that govern Christian discourse, and not about theological statements functioning *as first-order assertions*, as, for example, in cases of catechetical or doxological utterances" (ibid., 78).

23. Dehart, *Trial of the Witnesses*, 33.

24. Tracy, "Lindbeck's New Program for Theology," 460–72.

McGrath therefore claims that the postliberal approach to theology "entails the abandonment of any talk about God as independent reality and any suggestion that it is possible to make truth claims (in an ontological, rather than intrasystemic, sense) about him."[25] One can hardly imagine an evangelical theology (in the contemporary American sense) that does not adhere to a correspondence theory of truth.[26] And this is what McGrath believes that Lindbeck has sacrificed for the sake of intrasystematic truth. The project that I have identified as conservative apologetics would therefore be rendered illegitimate since this project primarily is an effort to show that the claims that Christians make about God and the world do indeed correspond well to God and the world.

The centrality of the concept of intratextuality likewise led some interpreters to conclude that Lindbeck was unconcerned with a correspondence theory of truth. But this too is largely due to a misunderstanding of what Lindbeck means be intratextuality. In a Wittengenstinian sense of "meaning is determined by use," intratextuality is an emphasis upon the way the cultural use of a word or phrase and the way in which it is embedded in an entire semiotic system is determinative of its depth meaning. When this idea is applied to religious language the effect is increased by the comprehensive nature of religious speech. Unlike math, which only seeks to describe systems of equations and their use, religious idioms describe not only religious life but also every aspect of reality. While the experiential-expressivist takes biblical language as a metaphor or figure that describes realities that stand outside of it, Lindbeck claimed with Hans Frei that "it is the religion instantiated in Scripture which defines being, truth, goodness, and beauty, and the nonscriptural exemplifications of these realities need to be transformed into figures (or types or antitypes) of the scriptural ones."[27] When the religion of Scripture is determinative of the definitions of such transcendental predicates, one might easily presume that the inevitable result is either a relativistic, "self-enclosed and incommensurable intellectual ghetto" or a fideistic and arbitrary choice between competing religious idioms.[28] Lindbeck's critics presumed he was posing just such a dilemma and opting for the fideistic option. His now famous description of intratextuality sounds

25. McGrath, "Evangelical Evaluation of Postliberalism," 36. Though he does not himself seem to share a commitment to propositional theology, Jackson summarizes the problems from a propositionalist's perspective as a philosopher. See Jackson, "Against Grammar."

26. This point is obvious from the prominence of these questions in the various articles in Phillips and Okholm, *Nature of Confession*.

27. Lindbeck, *Nature of Doctrine*, 104.

28. Ibid., 114.

like an imperialistic version of fideism: "Intratextual theology redescribes reality within the scriptural framework rather than translating Scripture into extratextual categories. It is the text, so to speak, which absorbs the world, rather than the world the text."[29] Critics often missed the point made by Placher that Frei's was not a theory of truth but of *meaning*. While Lindbeck does offer an account of truth as I will show below, intratextuality in Lindbeck is most appropriately pertaining to the meaning of the text just as it was for Frei.[30] So the circularity implicit in intratextuality places no limit upon the possibility of rational justification. Lindbeck's own concerns about relativism and fideism led him to respond to these concerns explicitly.

Lindbeck's programmatic book was not intended to be a book about philosophy of religion. Lindbeck understood the difficulties that this proposal would cultivate, given that Hans Frei had already engaged in some of the same arguments with Carl F.H. Henry, who had summarily dismissed Frei's arguments.[31] Lindbeck attempts to preempt these concerns with the brief excursus on "Religion and Truth" in *The Nature of Doctrine*. His attempt is obviously not thorough enough, and it is imprecise as well. But Lindbeck provides enough to readers that those who share McGrath's critique and that of other evangelicals should be satisfied that Lindbeck has not negated the need for ontological truth or correspondence. "In order for constructive dialogue to occur on this issue, it is important to realize that it is not truth that is denied or devalued in postliberal theology, it is the question of how truth is obtained and what we promote and define as 'truth.'"[32]

In the twenty-five years of interpretation and engagement that have followed the publication of Lindbeck's book, critiques such as McGrath's have been commonplace. The problem originates with Lindbeck himself when, in his excursus, he tries to delineate three senses in which something can be said to be true.[33] I am concerned with what he called "intrasystematic" truth and "ontological" truth. Lindbeck acknowledged that these two concepts were not significantly different than those identified as coherence and cor-

29. Ibid., 104. While Lindbeck defended himself against fideism in the original text, his defense against charges of imperialism comes in the updated edition (134–37).

30. Placher, "Paul Ricoeur and Postliberal Theology," 47.

31. See Henry, "Narrative Theology: An Evangelical Appraisal," 9–19; Frei, "Response to 'Narrative Theology: An Evangelical Appraisal,'" 21–24. For a summary of the debate see Hunsinger, "What Can Evangelicals and Postliberals Learn from Each Other?, 134–50.

32. Michener, *Postliberal Theology*, 96.

33. Though Lindbeck actually had three categories for truth, "categorical truth" is for our purposes not different than intrasystematic truth as both are simply preconditions for ontological truth.

respondence, respectively, in philosophical literature. Intrasystematic truth is the condition of being in right relationship with other sets of propositions, descriptions, and practices that give a particular statement or concept meaning. Without this full instrasystematic sense of truth, the statement not only is not true, it is meaningless.[34] It has no content and no meaning, because it does not have a full context that renders the statement intelligible. Coherence is a necessary condition for something to have a claim to truth at all. Lindbeck goes on to say that this does not mean that the statement is therefore true. Intrasystematic truth or falsity is fundamental in the sense that it is a necessary though not sufficient condition for the second kind of truth: that of ontological correspondence. A statement, in other words, cannot be ontologically true unless it is intrasystematically true, but intrasystematic truth is quite possible without ontological truth."[35] Elsewhere Lindbeck further clarifies that ontological truth (correspondence) is the "primary" notion of truthfulness.[36]

Charles Wood challenges the idea that Lindbeck's notion of intrasystematic truth is a *necessary* condition for ontological truth (correspondence). He claims that requiring a statement to be consistent intrasystematically gives religion inappropriate "veto power" over truth claims that are inconsistent with the system. For example, Christianity would be "vetoing," in Lindbeck's often repeated example, the crusader's "*Christus est Dominus*" proclamation because the notion of lordship to which the crusader holds is inconsistent with a Christian notion of Christ's lordship as suffering servanthood. Consistent with Wood's critique, it may in fact be the case that the crusader is correct in his particular way of proclaiming Christ's lordship (i.e. while cleaving the infidel's skull), therefore giving Christianity or any other religious system "veto power" regarding inconsistent truth claims is illegitimate. Wood rightly notes that this becomes even more problematic when interreligious matters are in view. Wood prefers to suggest that the crusader's proclamation is false, not because it is inconsistent with the Christian narrative of Christ's lordship, but rather because of the meaning of "*Dominus*" in the crusader's usage, the statement is not ontologically true. Wood suggests another possible way of explaining this: the crusader's proclamation is indeed true (i.e. the crusader does understand lordship in a basically Christian sense), but he is making improper use of it or drawing the wrong implications when he cleaves the infidel's skull.[37] Much of Wood's

---

34. Lindbeck, *Nature of Doctrine*, 51.
35. Ibid., 50.
36. Lindbeck, "George Lindbeck Replies to Avery Cardinal Dulles," 15.
37. Wood, "Review of Lindbeck, *The Nature of Doctrine*," 237.

critique is dependent upon his concern that intrasystematic consistency is a measure of truth or falsity. As I stated above, Lindbeck explicitly says, even if only briefly, that "intrasystematic truth" is a necessary condition of ontological truth because statements that are inconsistent, or "intrasystematically false," are *meaningless*. There is not sufficient narrative context for the utterance to have meaning such that it can be true or false. As I will explain below, Lindbeck later clarifies that his naming coherence as a type of truth was improper and confusing. To return to our example, the crusader is not uttering an ontologically false statement because his notion of lordship is inconsistent with that which is ontologically true of Jesus. Rather his statement is incomprehensible and meaningless from a Christian perspective. To turn this back upon the crusader and critics such as Wood, the crusader's statement may actually be "intrasystematically true" within a system of thinking aligned with the crusader's worldview and narrative, and yet be ontologically false because Christ is not in fact that kind of lord.[38] This is an example of Lindbeck's claim that some systems can "be intrasystematically true, but this in no sense assures their ontological truth or meaningfulness."[39]

As Lindbeck later clarified, he would have done his readers a favor if he had referred to "intrasystematic consistency" or "intrasystematic coherence" rather than "intrasystematic truth." The "truth" which results from such coherence does not meet the demands of even popular notions of truth, which Lindbeck rightly acknowledges as correspondence.

It would be easy to dismiss the interpretation of Lindbeck that I have given here had Lindbeck not clarified himself in just such a way. Avery Cardinal Dulles leveled similar criticisms to those of Alister McGrath in his review of *The Church in a Postliberal Age*, which was as much a critique of *The Nature of Doctrine* as it was of the later book. In response to Dulles' charges of relativism, Lindbeck explained that his own tripartite division of truth was confusing. He now prefers to clarify that "intrasystematic truth" should be referred to as a condition for truth and not itself a kind of truth. Rather Lindbeck admits that truth is in actuality a propositional and ontological matter.[40] The cultural-linguistic theory is not an attack on ontological notions of truth as many assume. "A corrected formulation, in contrast, simply notes that special attention to the intrasystematic (and categorical) conditions for affirming ontological *truth* is inseparable from a cultural-lin-

---

38. Marshall would argue that the statement has therefore failed the precondition of categorial truth because there is an improper alignment of meaning and truth. See Marshall, "Aquinas as Postliberal Theologian," 365–66.

39. Lindbeck, *Nature of Doctrine*, 51.

40. Lindbeck, "George Lindbeck Replies to Avery Cardinal Dulles," 15.

guistic perspective on a religion such as Christianity."[41] Lindbeck explicitly says that the referent to which all theology and doctrine refers is not in any way intrasystematic. In a rather candid way, he insists that his theory "most emphatically does not imply that the realities which faith affirms and trusts are in the slightest degree intrasystematic. They are not dependent on the performative faith of believers (as if, for example, Christ rose from the dead only in the faith of the church), but objectively independent."[42] It is understandable that some readers have mistaken his emphasis on intrasystematic consistency for a lack of concern for objectively true referents. Nevertheless, their interpretation is mistaken.

Bruce Marshall has done an even better job than Lindbeck himself by explaining that both "categorial truth" and "intrasystematic truth" are conditions of ontological truth. He explains that these conditions for truth are closely aligned with categories that philosophers call by others names:

> On this point Lindbeck's language has no doubt contributed to the confusion about his views. In *The Nature of Doctrine* he speaks of "truth" in three different ways: there is "categorial" truth, "intrasystematic" truth, and "ontological" truth. Lindbeck is in favor of all three, and not only, as critics have alleged, of the first two. As Lindbeck conceives them, the last of these concepts lines up directly with traditional notions of truth as correspondence to reality or *adequatio mentis ad rem*. But categorial "truth" has to do with what contemporary philosophy of language and epistemology usually think of as matters of meaning and reference, and intrasystematic "truth" has to do with warrant or justification—what we think entitles us to hold some beliefs and reject others. It was therefore misleading for Lindbeck to speak as though where were three different kinds of truth; it would have been clearer to speak of meaning, warrant, and truth.[43]

In his later article, "Aquinas as Postliberal Theologian," Marshall has additionally argued that these two conditions for truth are not only necessary for truth, but that the two together are also sufficient condition for truth. Lindbeck enthusiastically affirms Marshall's argument.[44] The brevity of Lindbeck's response makes it impossible to know if he affirms every aspect

---

41. Ibid., 15.

42. Ibid., 15.

43. Marshall, "Introduction," xvii.

44. Marshall, "Aquinas as Postliberal Theologian," 353–402; Lindbeck, "Response to Bruce Marshall," 403–6.

of Marshall's argument, but it seems that Marshall's thesis that these two together are sufficient conditions for truth is not consistent with Lindbeck's insistence on the need for correspondence.

In a later article, Marshall explains his thesis by suggesting that "the coherence of sentences . . . with the plain sense [of Scripture] is at least necessary, and in some cases sufficient, criterion of their truth. This test will tend to be not simply necessary, but sufficient, to the degree that the discourse in question is directly tied to the characteristic 'categories' of the community." He adds, "[M]ore coherence with the plain sense of the text will tend to be the decisive test of its truth."[45] If Marshall is correct that categorial adequacy and intrasystematic coherence are together sufficient conditions for truth, then he is the antirealist that some feared Lindbeck to be. Marshall says nothing of correspondence with the world, but only correspondence with the plain sense of Scripture. In spite of Lindbeck's overall affirmation of Marshall's interpretation, this notion is inconsistent with Lindbeck's own insistence that truth as we normally speak of it demands correspondence with "God's being and will."

As can be seen from this confusion, a thorough argument regarding what constitutes ontological truth would have been helpful, but Lindbeck does not make such an argument. He only says that "if the form of life and understanding of the world shaped by an authentic use of the Christian stories does in fact correspond to God's being and will, then the proper use of [Christian confession] is not only intrasystematically but also ontologically true."[46] This is not, strictly speaking, the traditional notion of correspondence. There is an additional pragmatic step inserted. The traditional notion of correspondence would simply require that the "Christian stories [do] in fact correspond to God's being and will." By adding that the additional notion that the truthfulness of the Christian's confession is dependent upon the "form of life and understanding of the world" being properly shaped in accordance with God's being and will, Lindbeck has attempted to account for the cultural-linguistic turn which he is suggesting. This does not mean that a particular failure of a particular community to actually form Christians well in accordance with the story disqualifies that community's narrative as truthful, even in Lindbeck's configuration. Failure to adhere to the formation entailed in the stories would at least fail under the category of "authentic use" suggested by Lindbeck. That is, a community may be telling a truthful story but has failed to enact that story well. Lindbeck argues that "Christ's Lordship is objectively real no matter what the faith or unfaith of

45. Marshall, "Absorbing the World," 73.
46. Lindbeck, Nature of Doctrine, 51.

those who hear or say the words," but that "the only way to assert this truth is do something about it, i.e., to commit oneself to a way of life."[47] In this sense, the pragmatic step in Lindbeck's theory is aimed at the conditions required to make a true statement, not whether there is such thing as true statements.[48]

Taking this a step further, the failure to form persons well with the Christian story is actually accounted for by the story itself, under the notion of sin and the lasting effect of sin. But it would make a difference if generations of living in accordance with the story and being formed by it actually created persons who were far from being in accordance with the being and will of God. McClendon and Smith's colorful suggestion that justification of worldviews is best done over centuries is helpful here: "We humans are a classroom of children learning to express happily our deepest prehensions—our generation (in Lessing's metaphor) a single school-day in the education of the human race."[49] This pragmatic step must be made humbly, because the Christian stories of the pervasiveness of sin give good reason to doubt the trustworthiness of individual Christian confession. People simply do not adhere very well to the stories that they most claim to believe and trust. But this is not a formal problem for Lindbeck's thesis, even if it challenges the practicalities of his pragmatism.

If Lindbeck can assuage these fears that he is arguing for relativism in a strong sense, then maybe it is not difficult to reconcile his theory with the correspondence theory which conservative apologetics seems to require. At least as far as truth is concerned, it would seem that apologetic method would only be affected in this: special attention must be paid to the cultural-linguistic conditions necessary for truth.

To put this in quite simple terms, we may consider the popular apologetic arguments for the resurrection of Jesus or the ontological argument for the existence of God. Assuming that the argument is made convincingly, the former argument is often taken to be self-evident as evidence that a person should become a Christian. It is presumed that if Jesus were indeed raised from the dead, it would be foolish to not take up worship of him as a lifestyle. This argument and the supposed conclusions assumes the rest of the Christian narrative—prophecy predicting the resurrection, Jesus' own claims about himself, and the predicted resurrection of all—are presupposed. Otherwise all of the evidence for the resurrection of Jesus proves nothing more than that something quite odd happened in the life of a first

---

47. Lindbeck, *Nature of Doctrine*, 52.
48. Marshall, "Aquinas as Postliberal Theologian," 364–5.
49. McClendon and Smith, *Convictions*, 153.

century Jewish man. The philosophical ontological argument for the existence of God entails an even more foreign assumption. Who would assume that the definition of God would be "that-than-which-nothing-greater-can-exist," that the fact of existence would improve upon this being's greatness, or that existence could be necessitated by the definition of a thing? This is all contingent upon logic that is internal to a particular tradition of metaphysical rationality. For those who no longer are formed by this mode of rationality, Anselm's argument is nonsensical.

Lindbeck suggests that correspondence is better thought of in relation to the entire system of thought associated with a religious tradition. "Propositions" are spoken of pejoratively in most of the book, but are spoken of positively with a qualification:

> A religion thought of as comparable to a cultural system, as a set of language games correlated with a form of life, may as a whole correspond or not correspond to what a theist calls God's being and will. As actually lived, a religion may be pictured as a single gigantic proposition. It is a true proposition to the extent that its objectivities are interiorized and exercised by groups and individuals in such a way as to conform them in some measure in the various dimensions of their existence to the ultimate reality and goodness that lies at the heart of things.[50]

The notion of correspondence here is not opposed to notions of correspondence taken up by other apologists. Rather, Lindbeck is only insisting on a consistency of logic and context appropriate to making judgments about an entire system of thought and not only single propositions extracted from that system. Any particular truth claim is embedded in a larger narrative matrix that renders it intelligible. Coupled with the notion that these various truth claims form a web of belief that is consistent, we have a clear understanding of what Lindbeck confusingly calls "intrasystematic truth" and could better be called, as the philosophers do, coherence.

This is generally accepted as a precondition for a truth claim in those schools of apologetics which focus on the conversion of a worldview, especially that of the presuppositionalists.[51] These apologists have long argued that Christian truth claims require entirely accepting or entirely rejecting

50. Lindbeck, *Nature of Doctrine*, 37.

51. Edgar summarizes: "Presuppositional apologetics asks that we but recognize that all ideas and arguments come within a basic arrangement, a framework within which they make sense . . . To use one of [Cornelius Van Til's] favorite illustrations, unbelievers construct their world by wearing colored glasses. Everyone 'sees' through a lens. There can be no neutrality, because everything in our awareness flows out of some kind of presupposition" (Edgar, "Introduction," 5.).

the entire system of thought within which those claims are embedded. Presuppositionalists are often criticized by other apologists, but not because of this aspect of their apologetic method. Presuppositionalists are criticized because "[Presuppositionalism] commits the informal fallacy of *petitio principii*, or begging the question, for it advocates presupposing the truth of Christian theism in order to prove Christian theism."[52] Since similar claims are leveled against Lindbeck in the following section, the pragmatic measure that he suggests here is particularly important for him, and I would suggest for the presuppositionalists as well. We will return to the virtues and challenges of the pragmatic measure below.

What would this mean for a Christian apologist in a world where a great deal of the audience for apologetic arguments, both those who profess to be Christian and those who do not, have been formed by traditions of rationality that are inconsistent with those of Christian theology? An extensive answer to this question will be the subject of chapter 4. Here it is enough to gesture at Lindbeck's answer: Lindbeck is suspicious that apologetics in any traditional sense can be done among those who do not share the narrative that informs the tradition of rationality. But he recognizes that people can be converted to Christian thinking by a process of catechesis. I am going to suggest that this process of catechesis that transforms the mind and the affections is the process that is required for a postmodern apologetic. This catechesis can and will happen in formal settings in preaching, church membership/baptism classes, and confirmation classes. It will also happen in the concrete practices such as prayer, compassionate service, worship, and advocacy for the poor. But a good deal of it will happen in more informal ways. These may include some of these concrete practices, whereby a skeptic participates in prayer, worship, advocacy and service with those who do so as an act of faith. Christians should pray for unbelieving friends that they find these faithful Christian practices compelling. But a great deal of this catechesis will happen in everyday conversations between those who have been well formed by the Christian faith and those who have not had as extensive formation. These will not likely take the form of traditional apologetic arguments, but will resemble a kind of informal catechesis as the Christian explicates the logic of their own belief and faith in God. Where this explication is compelling, an apologetic argument for Christianity may convince some of its truthfulness. The following chapters are intended to extend the implications of Lindbeck's nod toward catechesis as an apologetic necessity.

52. Craig, "Classical Apologist's Response," 232.

Avery Cardinal Dulles is satisfied with Lindbeck's clarification about correspondence as the primary notion of truth.[53] I have no doubt that other conservative critics would not be as generous in accepting Lindbeck's clarification. But I consider his concessions regarding the possibility of making and assessing ontological truth claims to be enough to satisfy the requirements of the apologetic enterprise. Lindbeck's notion of truth does not limit apologetics in this way, other than to provoke the apologist to be attentive to the ways in which apologetic claims are embedded in and dependent upon the larger narrative. Critiques of Lindbeck's program are more often aimed at a perceived relativism that stems from the above emphasis on intrasystematic coherence. Apologists of a conservative theological bent are often trying to sniff out hints of relativism wherever they can find it. I hope that I have shown that this is not a primary issue for apologists in adopting Lindbeck's construal. But there is a significant issue internal to Lindbeck's argument which Lindbeck himself regards as the critical problem with apologetics as a discipline.

Lindbeck and the Question of Intelligibility

Lindbeck thus describes the more serious problem for apologetics in the opening paragraph on "Intelligibility as Skill" as having two sides: "First, intratextuality seems wholly relativistic: it turns religions, so one can argue, into self-disclosed and incommensurable intellectual ghettoes. Associated with this, in the second place, is the fideistic dilemma: it appears that choice between religions is purely arbitrary, a matter of blind faith."[54] Lindbeck admits that either of these options becomes a fatal flaw in a pluralistic world. When real engagement with a variety of theological and religious perspectives is inevitable, so is real disagreement and real decision about one's fundamental commitments.

In Lindbeck's terms, the most pressing issue for the Christian apologist, and it pertains to all of theology and not only apologetics, is the incommensurability of religious systems. Returning again to the language metaphor, understanding how religious systems reason is not learned through translation. No neutral "language" exists in which persons of one religious system can dialogue with persons of another religious system without imposing at least some of their own framework-dependent reasoning upon the "translation."

53. Lindbeck, "George Lindbeck Replies to Avery Cardinal Dulles," 15.
54. Lindbeck, *Nature of Doctrine*, 114.

Before proceeding, we must admit that discussions surrounding post-liberal notions of incommensurability are prone to devolve into nonsense. Incommensurability is always a matter of degree. The strongest notions of incommensurability would imagine that persons from different traditions would share nothing in common and would therefore not even recognize that their systems of reasoning are incommensurable. There would be no common ground to even recognize the discontinuity. This is Donald Davidson's argument against these strongest forms of incommensurability.[55] Lindbeck is most certainly not arguing for these strongest versions.[56] He "cautioned against laying too much weight on the 'incommensurability' or 'untranslatability' subsisting between Christian claims and other cultural configurations."[57] Rather, Lindbeck is arguing that there is no neutral, framework independent idiom into which religious systems can be translated without equivocation or remainder for the purpose of measuring the adequacy or accuracy of their claims. Similarly, the actual questions and problems that need to be resolved will not be the same across these idioms.

This claim, as can be seen in his explanation of experiential-expressivism, is a thinly veiled attack on the theology of correlation. David Tracy responded by saying that Lindbeck is ignoring a great deal of revisionist theological discourse on this matter. Revisionist theologians now understand the relationship between experiences and religion to be dynamic.[58] Presumably this overcomes the critique that experiential-expressivists understand "experience" to be the underlying framework by which theologies can be compared, by recognizing the role that religious systems have in shaping experience. This role is precisely what Lindbeck's cultural-linguistic theory is trying to define and would therefore seem to mitigate a need for the methodological work that Lindbeck has done. Tracy may be right to criticize Lindbeck for not engaging this modification of the tradition. But Lindbeck is not primarily concerned with the experiences of persons and their expression of them; even a modified revisionist theology is still primarily anthropocentric. Lindbeck is trying to provide a conception of theology that accounts for the development and use of a religious tradition and that avoids anthropocentrism. While this understanding does not exclude the role of privatized experience, it does make it secondary. If theology is to be concerned with truth claims, anthropological issues can never take a pri-

55. Davidson, *Inquiries Into Truth and Interpretation*, 183–198.

56. See Lindbeck, "Gospel's Uniqueness," 428–29. This article was republished in Lindbeck, *Church in a Postliberal Age*, 223–52. All my references to this article will be to the earlier printing.

57. Dehart, *Trial of the Witnesses*, 42.

58. Tracy, "Lindbeck's New Program for Theology," 460–72.

mary role; even revisionist theologies now recognize that the "experience" is not a universal one.

As conceded above, Lindbeck rarely makes an argument for the complex issues that he summarizes in *The Nature of Doctrine*. Lindbeck's book is criticized by many for its brevity in addressing such breadth and complexity.[59] And, as Lindbeck has continued his career as an ecumenist, comparatively little of his subsequent work has been concerned with theological prolegomena. This makes sustained engagement on the issue of untranslatability difficult. He provides two examples of untranslatability in "The Gospel's Uniqueness." The first example concerns the lack of the concept of zero being available in the Roman numeral system as compared with the Arabic system. The Arabic system thus has a concept that is untranslatable to the Roman system. He claims that this parallels biblical untranslatable concepts such as the Tetragrammaton and the Trinity, which are basically unavailable to those who do not embrace those scriptures.[60] This is not an issue of untranslatability of the whole of the system, however. This kind of example would suggest that most of a particular system could be translated with little or no equivocation and only particular concepts would be left as remainder. This is a much weaker notion of untranslatability than is originally suggested by Lindbeck's comparison of the concepts of size to concepts of color with his nonsense example of "the red flag is larger than the Red Square in Moscow because it is redder."[61] He seems to be indicating that one idiom pertains to a wholly other matter than the other idiom, and therefore those who ascribe to one idiom take affirmations of those from the other as nonsense. This stronger notion of untranslatable concepts is actually a category mistake. An analogous example would be to say that some Christians deny evolution as an account of human origins because we are justified by faith. The doctrine of justification does not pertain to the scientific account of evolution, at least not in a straightforward way. But that does not preclude aspects of Christian doctrine that do pertain to notions regarding evolution, such as the doctrine of *creatio ex nihilo* or the Genesis account from Scripture. I think at least some interpreters understand untranslatability in Lindbeck to pertain to this latter example as well (creation vs. evolution, and not only justification vs. evolution). This is what is at stake in Kuhn's example of Einsteinian and Newtonian physics, but is not at stake in comparing "redder" and "larger."

59. Goh has an extensive list of adjectives that scholars have used, sometimes pejoratively, to describe the brevity of *The Nature of Doctrine* (Goh, *Christian Tradition Today*, 12).

60. Lindbeck, "Gospel's Uniqueness," 429–30.

61. Lindbeck, *Nature of Doctrine*, 34.

So to return to Lindbeck's much weaker example, the Roman numeral systems is incapable of translating the concept "zero" into its own terms and therefore is limited in many ways with regard to mathematics. This notion of zero is not, however, so utterly foreign that a person only equated with the Roman system could not be explained the concept and then taught the usefulness of it. Presumably, the Roman numerical system could even create a symbol that would stand in for the concept and then be capable of using it. This in fact does happen as one system engages another that does not have particular concepts available to it, as we will see below. This example is more relevant for a discussion of unsurpassability, a concept that Lindbeck thought was quite important in comparing idioms. The ability to absorb concepts from other idioms is considered to be the measure of unsurpassibility from a cultural-linguistic perspective. So we might say that the Arabic numeral system is superior to the Roman system because of its concept of zero, especially if the Roman system is unable to absorb this concept into its system.[62]

Lindbeck raised another analogy for untranslatability, this one comparing "literary" and "botanical" interpretations of a poem by William Blake ("O rose, thou art sick . . ."). He readily admits that the botanist reading such a poem would be making a "category mistake" to read such a poem literally as if it pertains to the science of botany. He thinks this is the same as "translat[ing] the Bible into an alien conceptuality." The problem here is not that translation has distorted meaning, but that there has been no such effort to translate at all. Presumably the poet could teach the botanist to read the poem appropriately and the botanist could then, able to understand both idioms, begin to make judgments about the truth content from within her own idiom. So if Blake's poem "The Sick Rose" is not about botany but love that suffers decay, this latter concept is actually what pertains and is the concept that the botanist must consider. Again, I suppose that the botanist would have little to say to the matter. Nevertheless, that Lindbeck compares the literal mediating language of this comparison, ordinary English, to the metaphorical "language" of the biblical idiom is yet another category mistake. The biblical idiom is, in fact, translatable into English, at least without formal or theological objection. Similarly, other religious idioms would also be translatable into English, with some possible exceptions. Actual language translations of the metaphorical "languages" of idioms are not his concern.[63] So the concern is not that Buddhism and Christianity cannot both be faith-

---

62. In this case, it seems that Roman system could in fact absorb the concept by creating a signifier as I suggested above.

63. Lindbeck, "Gospel's Uniqueness," 428–29.

fully translated into a literal language such as English for comparison. The concern is that such idioms cannot be translated into a neutral third idiom.

So when Lindbeck finally does get around to comparing an entire idiom with another and the concepts which it contains in concrete ways, he moves to an entirely theological argument for untranslatability, rather than a strictly cultural-linguistic one. He claims that "Everything is clarified when looked at through biblical lenses . . . and is distorted without these lenses."[64] Here he references Barth specifically, though he thinks his own argument is more conceptually adequate. Unsurprisingly, Lindbeck goes on to argue that the same kind of untranslatability claims will be made by other competing idioms. Though the situation may seem a "Darwinian-free-for-all," only one of these idioms can indeed be ultimately successful: "the prize winner stands alone."

Here, as in the case above, Lindbeck is not arguing for untranslatability in the sense of properly relating concepts from one idiom into the concept of another (or translating both into a third). He is arguing for unsurpassibility, that the ultimately successful idiom will assimilate all others without itself being assimilated. I will take up this concern under the criteria for comparing idioms below. But first we must concern ourselves with the more comprehensive account of untranslatability that pertains to the entirety of one idiom being translated into another idiom.

Though Lindbeck only rarely refers to him, Alasdair MacIntyre's notion of "second first language" is particular helpful on this matter and is consistent with Lindbeck's proposal.[65] For MacIntyre, learning a language and the difficulties of translation are not the same as incommensurability. Incommensurability and untranslatability are at least in principle separable. MacIntyre imagines that two idioms could basically agree on the subject matters which are to be addressed and share such concepts which make comparison and contrast a possibility, and yet not share the measures by which truth or falsity are measured and thus be incommensurable. This occasion would open the possibility of what MacIntyre calls "translation-plus-explanation." Macintyre concludes that this would entail a rejection of such a tradition's beliefs, based on the criteria of one's own tradition, but would nonetheless be an informed rejection. Presumably the person rejecting such beliefs could even recognize the incommensurability entailed.[66]

64. Ibid., 429–30.

65. Lindbeck, "Gospel's Uniqueness," 429. MacIntyre is very influential on other postliberals. For a summary, see Goh, *Christian Tradition Today*, 39–64.

66. MacIntyre, *Whose Justice? Which Rationality?* 380.

To be able to have this depth of understanding, a person must acquire the competency of a "second first language." When a person undertakes to learn a new language, he or she begins by learning roughly equivalent vocabulary and grammatical rules. They practice hearing and speaking words and phrases with an accomplished bilingual person. For a significant time, even a relatively accomplished bilingual person will still translate the foreign language into their native language in their mind. They have not yet gotten very far into learning language. Only after extensive time of learning and using grammatical rules and vocabulary is a person able to use the language without "translating" into their first language in their mind. They begin to inhabit the grammar and vocabulary in a new way. But MacIntyre has something more than this when he speaks of a "second first language." Even this deep learning of a second language requires acquiring an understanding of culture closely coupled with it.

> Anthropologists have for a long time insisted that no alien culture can be adequately characterized, let alone understood, without actually living in it for a certain length of time . . . understanding requires knowing the culture, so far as is possible, as a native inhabitant knows it, and speaking, hearing, writing, and reading the language as a native inhabitant speaks, hears, writes, and reads it.[67]

To learn language in such a way, MacIntyre suggests that a person is better to return to the way that a child learns language. Children do not a have a prior language to translate their concepts into, so they absorb language and culture together without distortion. So, those who would learn a "second first language" must also immerse themselves just as an anthropologist in training does. "The characteristic mark of someone who has in either of these two ways acquired two first languages is to be able to recognize where and in what respects utterances in the one are untranslatable into the other."[68] These persons are specially qualified to compare these idioms, each standing on their own merit and, at least potentially, incommensurable with those of the first language. For these reasons, MacIntyre insists that there is no such thing as "ancient Greek" or "modern English." There are only instances of one or another language inseparable from a particular time, place, and culture: Latin-as-in-the-Rome-of-Cicero or Greek-as-in-the-Asia-Minor-of-St. Paul.[69] This emphasizes the way in which language is embedded in culture. Being a part of that culture, as deeply as is possible for

67. Ibid., 374.
68. Ibid., 375.
69. Ibid., 372–73.

non-natives, enables a person from outside of it to inhabit the logic of the culture as well. These persons are then able to carry out a process of comparison between these cultures and are only then able to provide translation. This translation may be a clunky "translation-plus-explanation," which enables the audience to recognize where untranslatable aspects lie. Thus the equivocation is named as such and the dissimilarity of the analogies used in speaking of it is taken to be greater than in other parts. Similarly, the person who knows both idioms well should be able to name those parts where the idioms actually do share significant similarities, analogous to an instance of "same saying" within the process of actual language translation. I do not know that Lindbeck engages this material exegetically anywhere, so we cannot know how he regarded MacIntyre's conclusions on all these matters.[70] He is able to cite MacIntyre approvingly only with regard to his notion of "second first language" acquisition. I have attempted to restrain my summary to the part that Lindbeck cites, but this does not mean that he agrees with all aspects of it.

The apologist is left to conclude that Lindbeck thinks that translation is a possibility, even if only very difficult and without leaving the logic of the original tradition. This answers the first of two questions to which the apologist must respond if we are to mark a way forward for apologetics after Lindbeck: How much equivocation or remainder is the apologist likely to encounter? That is, to what degree and by what means *can* two idioms be correlated or translated such that some understanding is possible? The answer is that a significantly accurate translation can be achieved by an interpreter willing to learn the idiom as if it were a "second first language," so long as the translation does not attempt to leave the originating culture but only illuminate it. So incommensurability still pertains while untranslatability is qualified.

The second question would involve the practical and methodological implications of the answer to the first question. If an apologist accepts the limitations of incommensurability and of this kind of untranslatability, how should he or she make judgments between these idioms that are not irrational, as Lindbeck maintains?

---

70. At least one interpreter would conclude that Lindbeck does disagree with MacIntyre on this point. See Goh, *Christian Tradition Today,* 49–50, n. 86. Lindbeck only says that he thinks MacIntyre's conception is unsatisfying but does not doubt the reasonableness of the proposal. Lindbeck, "Gospel's Uniqueness," 429.

Making Judgments between Competing Idioms

While Lindbeck argued significantly throughout the book against neutral languages, he insists that he is not arguing for irrationalism. Reasonableness is better judged by its aesthetic qualities, which do not admit of formal proof or refutation, but can be rationally judged based on verifiable criteria. But he resists the notion that these criteria can be defined in advance in some universal way.[71] Probably because of his reliance upon philosopher of science Thomas Kuhn, Lindbeck claims that this testing of religious claims is subject "to rational testing procedures not wholly unlike those which apply to general scientific theories or idioms (for which, unlike hypotheses, there are no crucial experiments)."[72] Put in those terms, the General Theory of Evolution is not tested by laboratory testing of genetic familiarity and difference in two species thought to share an evolutionary history. The findings of such an experiment are just one piece of data. These findings must be combined with all of the other relevant experiments and discoveries, and the sum of these is used by scientists in making a judgment about origins.[73]

Religious idioms are judged similarly. An expert practitioner of religion embodies the logic of the religious idiom in such a way that he or she is able to discern if and how the idiom does or does not account for the information and experiences relevant to it. Some of these will be the same bits of information that are relevant to the evolutionary scientist in the proceeding example. An expert practitioner of a religious system can evaluate the findings regarding genetic similarities of two species and their supposed relationship, and make judgments about whether such data affirms their theological commitments regarding the narrative and doctrine of creation or whether it introduces dissonance into the system. Similar judgments will need to be made about data that is wholly different than the scientist's concerns as well. Though no formal proof is possible,

> Confirmation or disconfirmation [of the idiom] occurs through an accumulation of successes or failures in making practically and cognitively coherent sense of relevant data. . . [This] does provide warrants for taking reasonableness in religion seriously, and it helps explain why the intellectual labors of theologians,

71. Lindbeck, *Nature of Doctrine*, 116–17.

72. Ibid., 117. Basil Mitchell, whom Lindbeck often cites on this matter, also relies upon Kuhn (Mitchell, *Justification of Religious Belief*, 75–98.).

73. Actually, origins is not a great example here, but one with which much of my audience will be familiar. I suspect that the Newtonian and Einsteinian physics which Kuhn and Lindbeck discuss is a better example that avoids the cross-disciplinary judgments necessary for a scientist to make a judgment about origins.

though vacuous without corresponding practice, do sometimes make significant contribution to the health of religious
traditions.[74]

This likely is a bit unsettling for some conservative apologists, but it is not
inconsistent with the judgments of most contemporary apologists regarding certainty. Basil Mitchell, one of the philosophers to whom Lindbeck appeals, is known as a "cumulative case" apologist. Though Lindbeck endorses
Mitchell's argument, he never acknowledges that this is an establish school
of thinking among apologists. Some very well known apologists belong to
this school: G. K. Chesterton, C. S. Lewis, Richard Swinburne, and William Abraham.[75] As with Lindbeck's proposal, for many "cumulative case"
apologists the entire religious idiom is to be judged as one giant proposition
which can be neither affirmed nor denied formally.[76] But the criteria for
judgment are nevertheless rational. Since Lindbeck explicitly says that he
depends upon Mitchell at this point, it will help to summarize the tests for
truth among cumulative case proponents.

Consistency is the first test and is the same as Lindbeck's intrasystematic truth criteria. Like Lindbeck, cumulative case apologetics assumes that
a consistent account of all relevant data is necessary before truth claims
can even be assessed. The second test for these thinkers is *correspondence*.
While this is related to a philosophical notion of correspondence, it has a
decidedly more empirical and pragmatic edge. Lindbeck seems to appeal
to the former kind of correspondence when he talks of the narrative corresponding to "God's being and will" as the measure of ontological truth.
This is in contrast with cumulative case thinking which claims that what
does not accord with experience cannot be true. This is measured primarily with concrete empirical testing. Take the Christian doctrine of sin as
an example. Do human beings act toward one another in the way that the
system explains that they will interact? If in fact people never or rarely act in
ways that are destructive and hurtful toward one another, then the Christian
doctrine of depravity does not correspond with our experience of reality.

The third test of truth is *comprehensiveness*. The system that explains
most or all of the relevant data well is thought to be most truthful. If an
observer continued to see that persons do harmful and destructive things
to one another and his or her idiom had no explanation to account for this

74. Lindbeck, *Nature of Doctrine*, 117.

75. See Swinburne, *Existence of God*; Abraham, "Cumulative Case Arguments for
Christian Theism."

76. As we will see in chapter 3, Richard Swinburne is an exception in that he argues
for a cumulative case formally.

behavior, then the idiom would be considered less truthful. This is what Lindbeck calls "unsurpassibility" and is a concern of a great deal of his writing as I explained above.[77]

Simplicity is the fourth test and is the classical Ockham's razor argument. The test of simplicity may be problematic for Lindbeck given that narratives are a primary category for him and narratives are by nature complex sorts of things. He explicitly uses an Ockham's razor argument in arguing against pre-linguistic experience, but that still does not mean that he would imagine the argument to be helpful in comparing religious idioms.[78] I think we can suspend judgment about this aspect of cumulative case arguments.

The final two tests are both pragmatic in nature. If a person who claims to prescribe to an idiom is unable to live according to its prescriptions, it is said to fail the *livability* test. I think Lindbeck is claiming this and even more than this when he wrote:

> A religion thought of as comparable to a cultural system, as a set of language games correlated with a form of life, may as a whole correspond or not correspond to what a theist calls God's being and will. As actually lived, a religion may be pictured as a single gigantic proposition. It is a true proposition to the extent that its objectivities are interiorized and exercised by groups and individuals in such a way as to conform them in some measure in the various dimensions of their existence to the ultimate reality and goodness that lies at the heart of things.[79]

It is important to suggest that Lindbeck does not argue that a community failing to enact the narrative well counts against it as a claim to truthfulness. I would take his "in some measure" qualification as a recognition that sinfulness, finitude, and a host of other human weaknesses will inevitably mean any narrative will fail at forming some and maybe most of its adherents. But Lindbeck is suggesting that a narrative that does not form its adherents to the goodness and truth of God cannot correspond with God's being and will. Adding to the pragmatic category of whether an idiom can be lived truthfully, Lindbeck thinks a test for truth includes whether living just this way brings you into alignment with God's being and will. This is closely related to the final test.

77. See for example Lindbeck, *Nature of Doctrine*, 33–38; idem., "Gospel's Uniqueness."

78. Lindbeck, *Nature of Doctrine*, 24.

79. Ibid., 37.

Fruitfulness is the test of how a person or society living according to the system will live.[80] An example arises from applying this test to my own Pentecostal tradition. Some Pentecostals have avoided modern medicine when sick or injured and have died as a result. The *fruitfulness* test would suggest that this doctrine cannot be part of the most truthful idiom because it leads people to make decisions that lead to their own death.[81]

I suspect that Lindbeck would not object to these criteria as all six criteria here are mentioned by Lindbeck explicitly throughout *The Nature of Doctrine*, but never as clearly as this. As can be seen from this summary, deciding between various idioms is not an arbitrary choice, even if it is not a straightforward proof.[82] The truthfulness of the Christian narrative "will come to seem persuasive only if and when we find that the world [it] characterize[s] makes sense of the whole of our experience and enables us to get on with the living of our lives."[83] This is why Lindbeck claims that "a postliberal approach need not exclude an ad hoc apologetics, but only one that is systematically prior and controlling in the fashion of post-Cartesian natural theology and of later liberalism."[84] What is often taken as an objection to apologetics entirely is actually an objection to two particular notions of apologetics. As I began this chapter, he wants to reject the notion that Christianity can be translated into a neutral framework. As MacIntyre's notion of acquiring a "second first language" explained, this does not mean that translation is impossible, but does limit translation in certain ways. The entire discussion about a tradition-bound and yet rational judgment of competing idioms is an attack on the notion of post-Cartesian natural theology. As I have shown, Lindbeck thinks that arguing for the Christian idiom simply is less formal than these kinds of arguments and does not therefore constitute a proof.

When asked by Alister McGrath how a Christian could commend the Christian narrative as having merit over other religious narratives, Lindbeck responds with the following description of ad hoc apologetics:

> The slogan that has become popular among postliberals is the
> slogan of ad hoc apologetics . . . why Christianity rather than

80. This summary is taken from Feinberg, "Cumulative Case Apologetics," 153–56. Though this list is not explicitly from Basil Mitchell, Mitchell is the most referenced author in Feinberg's article. Mitchell approvingly mentions the same list in Mitchell, *Justification of Religious Belief*, 81–2.

81. Gibbs, "Medicine Is a Good Thing," 178–79.

82. Abraham calls this a "soft rationalism" and the term seems appropriate. Abraham, *Introduction to the Philosophy of Religion*, 104–13.

83. Placher, "Modest Response to Paul Schwartzentruber," 199.

84. Lindbeck, *Nature of Doctrine*, 117–18.

another faith? The answer depends upon the character of the questioner and the character of the questions he or she raises. In regard to some Muslims you might say, Look, this is why I recommend Christ rather than Muhammad to you. To other Muslims you might present a different set of reasons. As Hans Frei expressed it, there is no single logic of coming [to faith]. There is a logic of belief. There is a structure of Christian faith. But the ways in which God calls us through the Holy Spirit to come to believe are so varied that you cannot possibly make generalizations.[85]

I think two thousand years of apologetic and evangelical discourse and method would respond with a complete acceptance of his argument. At the least, we might imagine that some small portion of Christian apologists have thought that a method similar to that of natural theology might convince persons of Christianity's truthfulness and elicit a response for Christian faith.[86] Apologists have not typically thought in this way, however. Rather, apologetics has always been *ad hoc* in the way that Lindbeck describes.[87] So this "limit" which Lindbeck has placed on apologetics is really only a limit on a very narrow brand of apologetics. The Reformed epistemologists (Plantinga, Wolterstorff, etc.), the cumulative case apologists, and the presuppositional apologists (Van Til, Frame, etc.) have all placed similar limits on formal proofs in their own ways and yet proceed with apologetics, albeit in a way that Lindbeck would call ad hoc. Comparing the methods of these other apologetic approaches to postliberal conceptions of reason will be the subject of chapter 3. Lindbeck's notion that apologetics must at some point in the process include a catechetical element is a more significant contribution than his ad hoc limit to apologetics. But this will be the subject of this book's final chapter.

OTHER POSTLIBERAL ACCOUNTS OF APOLOGETICS

Postliberal theologians have said a great deal that might have implications for apologetics. Lindbeck's book is the most programmatic of these, and

85. Phillips and Okholm, *Nature of Confession*, 252.

86. I had a personal encounter at an academic meeting in which Norman Geisler, an esteemed evangelical apologist, claimed that this kind of argumentation is both possible and effective at convincing interlocutors. Even other apologists in the room that agreed with the formal logic were surprised to hear someone say that persons often come to faith in this way. Apologetics rarely makes converts and even more rarely through systematic argument.

87. Kallenberg, "Strange New World in the Church," 197–217.

so serves as a primary specimen. Hans Frei is very critical of apologetics, especially in his assessment of biblical hermeneutics.[88] But Frei is little interested in the theological method involved with apologetics except that those theological types that Lindbeck called cognitive-propositionalist and experiential-expressivism both threatened a narrative reading of the plain sense of Scripture. On this point I can agree with Frei, but will maintain that apologetics can proceed in a cultural-linguistic framework of intratextuality and avoid these errors by maintaining the ad hoc nature that Frei thought they must. Unlike Frei, I do not think "ad hoc" is a condemnation of postliberal apologetics. As I will show below, the limits of the postliberal notion of ad hoc apologetics are simply how other notions of apologetics are intended to proceed.

Stanley Hauerwas has also written much that is relevant for apologetics. While his work is referenced at several places, assessment of his work would require another book. Two comments should suffice. First, the quote which opened this book's "Introduction" situates Hauerwas in the very heart of my argument. Hauerwas understands his work to be a kind of apologetic theology, but like Lindbeck he maintains that this is not publicly accessible in a straightforward way. The second comment is really a reiteration of the first: Brad Kallenberg has made an assessment of Hauerwas similar to the one I have made of Lindbeck.[89] I don't think that Hauerwas and Lindbeck are the same, but at least my initial evaluation is that an extensive interpretation of Hauerwas's work would lead us to a very similar place, in spite of his oft-cited criticism of apologetics.

William Placher would also be an obvious choice for discussion here, given that he published a book called *Unapologetic Theology*, in which he explains a great deal of the postliberal implications for apologetics. But Placher does not add very much to what Lindbeck has already said, except *clarity*. Lindbeck gets caught in offering sweeping generalizations on notions of religious justification because that was not his primary intent in writing. Placher helps clarify Lindbeck considerably, and helps relate Lindbeck to Hans Frei. Lindbeck largely does not explain his relationship to Frei, so Placher's analysis is helpful in this regard as well. Placher sometimes quipped that he was the unofficial (and unwilling?) historicist of the postliberal movement. In part because of his own penchant for writing book reviews, popular theology articles for the *Christian Century*, and participating in journal article forums, he serves as a window into the movement without contributing significant change or innovation to it. Placher is first

---

88. Frei, *Identity of Jesus Christ*, xi–xii.
89. Kallenberg, "Strange New World."

and foremost a teacher, as exhibited by his significant work in founding the Wabash Center for Teaching and Learning in Theology and Religion. If I may get ahead of the explanations of paradigm shifts in science that I will discuss in chapter 3, we might say that Lindbeck (and Frei, et al.) introduce a paradigm shift in theological prolegomena. Placher is the one that is contributing to the "problem solving" of normal science. He is working out the clarifying questions introduced by the model. For different reasons than Hauerwas, I have not treated Placher on his own terms but as commentary on the proposal of George Lindbeck.

In the following section I assess the arguments of one other candidate for a postliberal apologetic method. In significant ways William Werpehowski builds upon and agrees with Lindbeck. Therefore I will not repeat the arguments but only show where he supplements Lindbeck's construal.

William Werpehowski's "Ad Hoc Apologetics"

Werpehowski begins his article with a basic summary of Lindbeck's thesis, which is without significant commentary. The theological move that begins to set him apart is his notion that the "common ground" with which an apologist must start in an explanation of the Christian idiom is that of their common status as creature. While this is not an identification that the interlocutor is likely to share initially, this identification is what makes the apologetic efforts theological.[90] Werpehowski says that this identification as creature "must be seen to sustain and nurture the non-Christian in some particular area of belief or practice."[91] After establishing some common commitments between Christian and non-Christian, the Christian can presumably show the non-Christian the ways in which the Christian way of arriving at this shared commitment is both consistent with the Christian idiom and at least potentially more satisfying than the way in which the non-Christian arrived at such commitments.

He uses two examples as case studies for the kind of proposal that he is suggesting. The first case study involves some questions from medical ethics in a book by William F. May related to the trend among medical practitioners to treat disease rather than treating patients, resulting in paternalism toward patients, an unrelenting war against suffering and death to the exclusion of all other concerns, and a fascination with technique in which patients become objects on which to "practice." Not surprisingly, Mays argues that Christian theology limits death and suffering to something less

90. Werpehowski, "Ad Hoc Apologetics," 287.
91. Ibid., 287.

than ultimate while elevating the power of love of a particular kind within the patient-physician relationship.[92] He presumes that at least some non-Christian persons would agree that these are deficiencies with undesirable consequences in the current state of medicine. So presumably an apologetic exchange is possible whereby the Christian suggests that the Christian theological refutation of these deficiencies is more reasonable and has greater explanatory power than those previously held by the non-Christian objector. Like Lindbeck, he contends that the moral sensibility of those concerned will appeal to their "considered judgments. Lindbeck considers these judgments to have an "aesthetic character."[93] Both "judgments" and "aesthetics" are subject to criticism and not subject to rational proof. This is unsatisfying for some, but does not mean that these judgments are illegitimate or lack a claim to truthfulness. Here Werpehowski makes a distinction between rational comparison and commensurability that explains Lindbeck's trajectory more adequately. He contends that an interlocutor can engage comparison while not yet accepting the presuppositions implicit in the other's argument. "In that case, the non-Christian adopts what can only be an *approximation of the Christian belief.* If the apologetic is to proceed, conversation would have to move to another level, one concerning the warrants for the background belief just found helpfully to order our moral sensibility about medical healing."[94]

This second level of the argument is to push one's interlocutor back to a comparison of presuppositions and their warrant and is the subject of Werpehowski's second case study. At this level, he suggests that a similar kind of comparison without neutral grounds is applied to the presuppositions. Oddly, he suggests that one of the primary tasks at this level is to accommodate the challenges of the other, even if not conceding the other's position. That is, the challenges that the other's presuppositions pose to that sensibility which they share are to be used as a corrective for one's own theological articulation. He assumes that neither party will in fact change their beliefs, at least not in a straightforward way. Each side will resist the challenge to give up their beliefs but will accommodate that which they learn from the engagement and the objections posed by the other. This improvement of their own position can then be tested in subsequent theological engagement on this topic and others. I do not deny that this kind of revision does in fact happen and can improve Christian theology. But it is unclear to me how this can be considered an apologetically aimed dialogue. It is

92. Ibid., 289–90.

93. Lindbeck, *Nature of Doctrine*, 116.

94. Werpehowski, "Ad Hoc Apologetics," 292–93.

also difficult to see how even the improved articulation of the internal logic of the faith can avoid pandering, but this is a practical rather than formal problem. At other points in this essay I have assumed that something being difficult, such as making difficult judgments between competing paradigms, does not imply that it should not be done. Even if it can be done well, I am not sure that there is anything particularly apologetic about the task. Even if it results in theology that is somewhat more tenable for the interlocutor, if one has conceded that the interlocutor did indeed have a better argument for this or that presupposition then it is unlikely that they can be convinced of the rest of your idiom's truthfulness. In spite of this, I think this likely is Werpehowski's version of what Lindbeck regarded as an idiom's "assimilative powers."[95]

Each of these case studies represents a step in the apologetic argument for Werpehowski. He seems to think that these are not only logical steps but are also presumably sequential steps as well.[96] Presumably each step could go simultaneously. I think this is what Barth and Hauerwas are doing by constantly describing and redescribing the same dogmatic arguments in each discussion and context they enter into dialogue.

While Lindbeck is vague about how an ad hoc apologetics might proceed, Werpehowski proposes one possibility for what this might mean. Specifically, he suggests that apologetics would proceed from moral and intellectual commitments that the apologist shares with the interlocutor. In the following chapter I will suggest that the categories for thinking about the shared commitments of Christians and interlocutors are those identified with the traditional transcendental predicates of being. For example, while Werpehowski argues that interlocutors will find the Christian conception of death and hope to be preferable, it is not too much to say that this conception is in fact *good*. While there is no single path by which persons come to faith, few would suggest that the true, the good, and the beautiful are not desirable. The cultural-linguistic turn will suggest that each of these notions will find a particular context within a variety of traditions. In that sense the criteria are not independent and prior to the traditions. Nevertheless, I will argue that they are transcendental categories to which apologists can appeal in the same fashion that Werpehowski has suggested is ad hoc. This is the first implication for apologetics of Lindbeck's construal of theology to which I now turn.

---

95. Lindbeck, *Nature of Doctrine*, 117.

96. ". . . conversation would have to move to another level . . ." Werpehowski, "Ad Hoc Apologetics," 293.

2

God of the Beautiful and the Good

INTRODUCTION

I SUGGESTED IN THE last chapter that apologetics of the kind with which I am concerned has two questions that drive methodology and other meta-questions: 1. Is Christianity true and can this be demonstrated? 2. What is required to demonstrate the truthfulness of Christianity to an interlocutor? This chapter will attempt to answer the former question by supplementing the minimal arguments of George Lindbeck with that of another postliberal, D. Stephen Long. The result will be a broadening of the relevant criteria for apologetic argument to include not only concern for the truth of Christian theology, but also its ethical and aesthetic dimensions. This is the first impli-cation of postliberal construal of theology for postconservative apologetics.

Generosity is a Christian virtue, and for theologians this must ex-tend to a hermeneutic of generosity. Authors should not be criticized for the book that they did not write or the argument that they did not make. Similarly, if a theologian is among the best educated and published in the world, it should be assumed that they are aware of the basic challenges to the position that they are proposing. The problem with some of the treat-ment of Lindbeck's work and that of other postliberals by McGrath and some other conservatives is a failure to extend that hermeneutic generosity. George Lindbeck never set out to write a book on epistemology or ontology. Rather he intended to clarify a program, which he imagined to have some traction already in his theological circles, such that this program could be used to make sense of ecumenical discussions in which doctrine matters but does not require participants giving up traditional commitments in order to enter into dialogue. As I explained in chapter 1, McGrath is representative of a number of interpreters who imagine Lindbeck to be writing a book about truth and therefore hold him to rigorous standards regarding epistemology. The book is actually about the rules that govern the speech and actions of religious communities. It is not surprising that such a book would be epistemologically and metaphysically unsatisfying.

I examine the work of Long in this chapter because he makes explicit the metaphysical assumptions that I believe Lindbeck shares. As I showed above, Lindbeck's six and one-half page "Excursus" makes references to a need for an idiom to have ontological correspondence with that which is "Ultimate." But we must turn elsewhere if we are to find the robust metaphysics necessary to answer questions about how we must regard truth claims in a postliberal mode. As I explained in the previous chapter, Lindbeck's "Excursus" and other occasional comments in *The Nature of Doctrine* open the door for an explication of metaphysics that he does not himself provide.[1]

As Sue Patterson rightly recognizes, the postliberal insistence on intrasystematic consistency means that the ambiguity about truth with which postliberals are attributed is excluded by the content of Christian doctrine. Christian doctrine does not claim that Christians *say* that Jesus is the Way, the Truth, and the Life, or that God created the heavens and earth. Christian doctrine, confession, and proclamation are that these claims are actually and really (ontologically) true. "Such [an intrasystematic] criterion requires postliberal theology to accept the claim, central to Christianity's central logic, of an *absolute* truth revealed in Christ and therefore within Christianity."[2] In *Fides et Ratio*, Pope John Paul II argues similarly when he says that "Holy Scripture always insists that man, however prone he may be to falsity and deception, can always reflect on and comprehend clear and simple truth."[3] Since the postliberal project demands that an idiom must maintain internal consistency as a necessary condition for ontological truth claims, Christian doctrine cannot give up claims to metaphysical realism and the possibility of comprehension.

As I argued in the last chapter, Lindbeck regards what he calls "ontological truth" as the primary notion of truthfulness and defines this as what is typically known as correspondence. A notion of truth that is explicated ontologically is necessary when the subject is itself metaphysical. Long

1. And I have also shown that Lindbeck made some effort to clarify himself regarding ontology and truth in the years after writing *The Nature of Doctrine*, as the book took on significance as a book about religious epistemology.

2. Patterson, *Realist Christian Theology in a Postmodern*, 37.

3. Pope John Paul II, *Restoring Faith in Reason*, 135.

approvingly quotes philosopher William Desmond who argues simply that all thinking, whether acknowledged or not, presupposes some account of what it means "to be."[4] In the same article quoted by Long, Desmond goes on to say

> One can live, more or less, without being a metaphysician in the explicit sense, but one cannot be a good philosopher without being more or less a metaphysician, in the sense of bringing to bear on what is at play in being an attentive mindfulness for the basic presuppositions, sources, and orientation towards the "to be." One does not have a choice about being an *animale meta-physicum*. The issue is not being a post-metaphysician but being a good metaphysician—under the call of truthful fidelity to the sourcing powers of the "to be."[5]

It would be easy to presume that postliberal thinkers would be troubled by such an insistence upon metaphysics, given the inheritance of Karl Barth. In response to Desmond, Barth would likely have responded that a theologian need not become a philosopher or metaphysician to be faithful to the Gospel—and in fact to do so might hinder one's ability to be faithful. Barth only critiques metaphysics and refuses to give a positive account. But contemporary postliberal theologians realize that this does not enable the theologian to avoid ontological questions. Desmond's quote above seems to encapsulate a notion that the Barthian postliberals have embraced in the years since the publication of Lindbeck's book. Postliberal theologians understand the implication of eschewing metaphysics such as Barth explicitly does in his constant invective against it. Therefore many have engaged a program to reinterpret Barth such that he is not seen as opposing all metaphysics. Long insists that Barth "clearly gives attention to metaphysics. Theologians who suggest otherwise are wrong."[6] Stanley Hauerwas demonstrates this when he makes Barth the hero of his Gifford lectures and the unique kind of "natural theology" which Barth represents for him there.[7] Similarly, Hans Frei claimed that "Barth sounds like a traditional metaphysician who wants to make theological information do service for what in the eighteenth century used to be the duty of school metaphysics."[8] Long is not alone among postliberals when he insists that metaphysics simply is necessary

---

4. Long, *Speaking of God*, 8.

5. Desmond, "Neither Servility nor Sovereignty," 154.

6. Long, *Speaking of God*, 102.

7. Hauerwas, *With the Grain of the Universe*, 141–204.

8. Frei, *Types of Christian Theology*, 45.

when questions of truth and existence are either presupposed or explicit to theology's concerns.

Long claims that there are five different uses for the term "metaphysics" in modern theology. His delineation is helpful to understand what is and is not problematic for postliberals regarding metaphysics. Metaphysics 1 is what Long describes as "a philosophical invective used against an imprecise use of language, which speaks of being or beings for which there can be neither verification nor falsification."[9] Long is referring to the ways in which "metaphysics" is the derogatory label that many modern thinkers apply to any speculation which is not verifiable by modern epistemological standards. Long says that this is in fact a form of metaphysics: nominalism.

Metaphysics 2 is "a totalizing discourse that presents Being as origin, cause, and goal and thinks everything within its structure."[10] Long claims that Barth's opposition to metaphysics is primarily an opposition to this kind of metaphysics.[11] While Long never explicates the concerns with this kind of metaphysics, they are closely tied with the concerns surrounding ontotheology that he does describe.[12] The problem with ontotheology (and metaphysics 2) is the way in which God becomes an object within the world. Like all beings, God becomes an object that is univocal with Being/being itself. Furthermore, God becomes but one being in a chain of causal relations, reducing God to the first cause. But God is not a cause like other causes. God does not create the world as a first cause, but as one who "speaks" creation into existence with a "let there be." While speaking of God as "first cause" is not strictly prohibited, to do so is to speak analogously to the way causes are normally spoken of, because God does not exist within the same causal scheme as other causes. God stands apart from creation. Long claims that the great failure of Metaphysics 2 is due to its inability to recognize that all God speech is dependent upon analogy.

Metaphysics 3 and Metaphysics 4 are nearly inseparable in Long's description. Metaphysics 3 is the "inevitable opening of a sign that exceeds its context." Metaphysics 4 is the "beyond that interrupts immanence 'in the

---

9. Long, *Speaking of God*, 9.

10. Ibid.

11. Ibid., 103.

12. Before introducing the five types of metaphysics, Long explains the concerns of Kevin Hart regarding metaphysics, which he describes as "that [which] totalizes texts within a philosophical account of origin, ground, and source" (*Speaking of God*, 5). He goes on to suggest that theology must "avoid the totalizing claim of metaphysics that inevitably lead to ontotheology." It is the "totalizing" nature of this talk of "Being/being" which are most concerning for Long and those he engages (Barth, Hart, etc.).With) with such talk, ontotheology is inevitable.

middle."[13] Like the definitions of the other uses of metaphysics, Long does little to explain these complex and vague sentences. But he clearly thinks that these are the Christian notions of metaphysics.[14] This is metaphysics that will open the possibility of meaningful God speech that does not fall prey to the (supposedly premodern) naiveté of Metaphysics 2. "Metaphysics, then, is less a totalizing whole within which everything can be asked and answered and more a 'way' that opens language up, pointing beyond itself to something profound, something mysterious."[15] The ultimate example of this metaphysics is the incarnation. Jesus is the "visible face of invisible God."[16] Jesus is not only "like" God or is some "part" of God. Jesus is fully God incarnate. Jesus is God fully present but does not fully exhaust all that God is. God is both seen and yet exceeds that which is seen. Though the incarnation is the archetypal example, all speech about God and theology has a similar participation in a reality that exceeds itself. Consistent with a notion of analogical speech, speech about God is in fact truthful speech, but God speech never exhausts truth. For Long, this notion of metaphysics is closely tied to the tradition of the divine names to which I return below.

Long describes Metaphysics 5 as a "beyond that secures the presence of any sign such that the sign is unnecessary. It is an objective, universal validation where a sign corresponds to a reality such that the reality could be known without the sign. In fact, the reality secures the sign and not vice versa."[17] Long further describes this notion as a "cartoon Platonism." Being is something that exists beyond eminent objects and realities. In fact, the ontological realities are only barely accessible to us via the sign. For this reason, Long thinks that Metaphysics 5 and the nominalism of Metaphysics 1 share many similarities in spite of their appearance as opposites. Both presume to have a comprehensive view of reality and the function of theological speech.

This fifth notion of metaphysics is the one most heavily critiqued by deconstructionist and post-metaphysical theology. This is the metaphysics upon which a great deal of contemporary conservative Roman Catholic and evangelical theology depends. Long insists that this metaphysics is "a greater threat to a proper relationship between faith and reason than Barth's critique of metaphysics." While Barth threatens to ignore the necessity of philosophy

---

13. Long, *Speaking of God*, 9.

14. Hence, "This is metaphysics." Ibid., 226.

15. Ibid., 150.

16. Ibid., 226.

17. Ibid., 9.

in theological thinking, Metaphysics 5 and its objective realism threatens to ignore the necessity of the incarnation for theological thinking.[18]

It is the incarnation which Long claims is the archetypal example of the Metaphysics 3 and Metaphysics 4 for which he provides a defense. "The incarnation is the Christian metaphysics."[19] This is not a reductionism, however. Long thinks that metaphysics is illumined and determined by the logic of the incarnation, but he similarly thinks that the incarnation is illumined by metaphysics. Barth's disdain for metaphysics is a mistake. Even Barth has an implicit metaphysics of the incarnation.[20] The incarnation is the archetypal example of Metaphysics 3 and 4 because in the incarnation God is authentically revealed but illumines that which is more than that which is revealed. Jesus truly reveals God but does not reveal all that God is.

Long argues that the incarnation can only be regarded as revelation, however, because of a prior revelation, that of God's revealing God's own name to Moses. We only recognize Jesus as God because God has already revealed God's own being to humanity. Jesus is recognized as God because of the prior revelation of God's self in Exodus 3: "He Who Is." Jesus's "I am" statements in the Gospel of John allude to that which his incarnate life and resurrection reveal: Jesus is the one who reveals himself to Moses. Jesus is the one who can only be properly called by a name without reference to creation or other beings. The divine name "He Who Is" sets God outside of the framework of created beings as the one being that simply is. For Long, and his interpretation of Aquinas, the revealing of the divine name in Exodus 3 cannot be interpreted well without reference to metaphysics because it reveals God as that being which exists entirely independent of other beings.

LONG, AQUINAS, AND THE TRANSCENDENTAL PREDICATES (PROPERTIES) OF BEING

At several points, Long insists that the attention to metaphysics that he believes theology demands will necessarily involve the recovery of the traditional transcendental predicates of being. Though Long never systematically explicates the implications of this, he mentions it often in his writing. Furthermore, his earlier *The Goodness of God* and *Speaking of God* should be regarded as the first two parts of a trilogy that he intends to write, with the two former books treating the Good and the True respectively and a

---

18. Ibid., 10.

19. Ibid., 85. See also Long, *Goodness of God*, 22.

20. Ibid., 85.

future book working through the implications of Beauty.[21] This would be consistent with Kant's *Critique* trilogy and Balthasar's trilogy, each of which were structured around these three transcendentals. Both of these thinkers are important to Long, the former as a critical opponent and the latter as a critical hero of Long's theology. So it should not be surprising when he mentions these transcendental predicates at critical points.

Long's treatment of ethics begins with a critique of an often-cited postmodern description of ethics: "All moral norms are social constructions and subject to revision." His response to this statement begins with an insistence on the existence of God who is transcendentally good, and an attempt to explain the concepts of being which make this concept intelligible. *Being* is that metaphysical concept which describes a thing at its most basic. But this is not a "mere existence" says Long, but one which is in so far as it participates in those predicates which relate beings to ensouled bodies like ours. Of course, *being*, and especially God, is not dependent upon their relationship to ensouled bodies. But beings have certain predicates that are true of all beings insofar as they exist, and the relationship between ensouled bodies and beings is described by these transcendentals. Therefore the transcendentals serve as a benchmark for apprehending a thing's ontological existence. Truth is the correspondence of a thing to a mind. This correspondence with a mind occurs when the subject perceives harmony between a thing and its *telos* via an aesthetic judgment. Goodness and beauty are the aspect of being in which we take delight. To say that all things that are created are necessarily good and beautiful in so far as they fulfill their *telos* is a theological claim grounded in the goodness of creation. That which God creates conforms to the intellect (truth), delights the appetite (good), and delights the intellect (beauty) or it does not exist as God created it to exist.[22]

Long explains that these transcendentals are necessarily subjective, because they describe being's relationship with ensouled bodies,

> The "fittingness" of being with our appetite depends upon and affirms the good. The "fittingness" of being with our intellect depends upon and affirms the true. But goodness and truth are not simply cognitive faculties in the subject; they are also in the things themselves . . . Thus truth, goodness, and beauty are neither merely objective nor subjective, they are both simultaneously.[23]

---

21. His intentions are known from personal conversations that I have had with him.

22. The above is a summary of Long, *Goodness of God*, 20–21.

23. Ibid., 21.

The apprehension of the truth, goodness, or beauty of a thing is significantly subjective. But the observer is only apprehending what exists previous to the event of apprehension. Persons observe the good, beautiful, and true in particular things not only because of subjective categories, but also because these are the objective, ontological predicates of the things themselves. As Aquinas argues, these categories are not prior to God, but proceed from God who is good, beautiful, and true and creates things that are good, beautiful, and true.[24] The ancients understood the transcendental predicates of goodness and beauty to be objectively based in ontology, though subjectively apprehended in observation.

Thus Christian theology must assert that the transcendental predicates of being are simultaneously perceived because they are necessarily predicates of a God who is beautiful, good, and true simultaneously. They are necessarily simultaneously observed because they are "conceptually distinct but ontologically identical and interchangeable with Being Itself/God."[25] Modern theology has largely ignored the beauty and goodness of God because modernity separated the true as a superior category to the good and beautiful. Good and beautiful have been viewed as purely subjective categories, while true was an objective category. Premodern Christian thought avoided this dualism because of its theological methodology. When the transcendental predicates are understood to be ontological categories, then one cannot relegate any of them to purely subjective status. Postmodern deconstruction of truth claims have shown us what we have known about beauty and goodness all along. The True, Good, and Beautiful have a subjective element in observation. But against postmodernity's nihilism, they are also properly ontological categories. Christian theology finds the source of the good, beautiful, and true to have a stable source in the immutable character of God. However, any Christian epistemology must also account for the infinite difference between Creator and Creation that cannot be overcome in the subjective moment. Christian epistemology must argue both for a stable meaning (contra postmodernism) and a *necessarily* partial and subjective apprehension (contra modernity).[26] This subjective space has been traversed by the Christian doctrine of analogy.[27]

24. Aquinas, *Summa Theologica* I, q. 5, a. 2.

25. Navone, *Toward a Theology of Beauty*, 77.

26. Much of modernity would recognize that we currently do not know all that is to be known. But scientific methodology assumes that all knowledge is attainable by rational means.

27. For more on the importance of analogical thinking, see Long, *Goodness of God*, 22.

With this we can understand Long's close affinity with Lindbeck. Lindbeck argues that truth and the standards by which our reason perceives truthfulness is socially conditioned and, in the case of Christian faith, is conditioned by the narrative of Christian faith. As I explained in chapter 1, Lindbeck does not imagine himself to be writing a sustained account of truth such as Long's. When a postliberal such as Long articulates the subjective and socially constructed nature of truth, he does so paired with a substantial explanation of the transcendental nature of truth. Though his comments about the transcendentals in *Speaking of God* are usually only in passing reference, he does not lose sight of this earlier insight.

Long claims that one of the common themes of "modern theology's discontents," the "discontent" describing the theological heroes of *Speaking of God*, is the move these theologians make beyond epistemology and toward recovering ontology. This is a move closely related to a decrease in the concerns of political power and recovering the transcendental predicates of being—truth, goodness, and beauty.[28] And he ends *Speaking of God* with Balthasar representing the account of the transcendental predicates that Long is commending. For Balthasar, the transcendental predicates arise from being itself and are not categories that have a mastery over being. To define these predicates finally is a mistake for Balthasar. "Neither goodness nor beauty nor truth is exhausted by any definition."[29] Truth, Goodness, and Beauty always exceed our explanations, but that does not mean that they are inexpressible. Worldly beauty, goodness, and truth are all around us and our experience of them is not an illusion. Worldly experiences of the transcendentals are an encounter with beings' participation in God's good, beautiful, and true creation.[30]

Both Balthasar and Long depend upon Aquinas for their understanding of the unity of the transcendental predicates. As explained above, Aquinas understands these transcendentals to be "convertible"; that is to say that, they are not identical but are dependent upon one another to be understood. Put quite simply, truth and existence (being) are two ways of naming the same aspect of being. Existence names being as it is. Truth names being as it relates to the intellect. Aquinas claims that all being is knowable, so truth names the degree to which being is known by an intellect.[31] Good describes being insofar as it delights the appetite. This too does not add anything to being, according to Aquinas, because all things that exist are created by

28. Long, *Speaking of God,* 91–92.

29. Balthasar, *Theo-Logic, Vol. I,* 17.

30. Long, *Speaking of God,* 313.

31. Aquinas, *Summa Theologica* I q. 16, a. 1 and 3.

God and are therefore good. Good only names that being is desirable and is pleasing to the appetite. Aquinas says that some things are said to exist in reality which are not normally called good, but this is only because any participation in being at all is generally credited as existence, whereas something has to participate in the perfection of being to a greater degree to be considered good.[32] Aquinas is naming the phenomenon whereby everyday speech names things that participate in very low levels of being's perfection as in fact existing; the threshold for calling something good in everyday speech requires a higher threshold of perfection of being. "Existence" and "good" in everyday speech are imagined to be categorically different attributes, but in Aquinas's account they are merely different degrees of perfection. Therefore good names the ability of those things that have some high degree of perfection of being to satisfy desire. Good and beauty name the same quality of being, but each in a different aspect. While good delights the appetite, beauty delights the intellect. Beauty is the aspect of being that gives joy to the intellect that apprehends it.[33] I will say more about each of these transcendentals below, but this introduction is enough to explain that in this concept the nature of truth, beauty, and goodness are fully dependent upon one another because each of them names differently the existence and perfection of being.[34]

Nietzsche had little patience for the argument that Aquinas, Balthasar, Long, and I share: "It is unworthy of a philosopher to say 'the good and the beautiful are one'; if he has the audacity to add 'so is the true,' he should be soundly beaten."[35] Long references Balthasar when he argues that "'modern rationalism' makes us choose truth against beauty or goodness."[36] Specifically, Balthasar claims that, "Modern rationalism, attempting to narrow the range of truth to a supposedly isolable core of pure theory, has exiled the

32. Aquinas, *Summa Theologica* I, q. 5, a. 1, obj. 1.

33. Aquinas, *Summa Theologica* I–II, q. 27, a. 1, obj. 3.

34. Montague Brown argues for a similar unity of the transcendental predicates, but does so on the opposite of the basis that I have traced through Long, Balthasar, and Aquinas. Rather than the unity resting in being itself, and each of the transcendentals being different in the way that they relate to the subject, Brown argues that the transcendentals are significantly different objects. Each pursues a different matter, but he maintains the unity of these aspects in the reason of the subject. Brown arrives at this conclusion through what I consider a misreading of Aquinas. Brown, *Restoration of Reason*, 237–42.

35. From Nietzsche, *Werke*, 3:832. As quoted in Balthasar, *Theo-logic I*, 15.

36. Long, *Speaking of God*, 312–13. Brown also thinks modern rationalism precludes the possibility of ethics or aesthetics, but he says this is so because of modernism's empiricism. Neither beauty nor goodness can be empirically verified. Therefore they are both entirely subjective. Brown, *Restoration of Reason*, 42–45.

good and the beautiful from the domain of the rationally verifiable, relegating them to arbitrary subjectivity or to a world of private belief and personal taste."[37] The consequences of this "narrow range of truth" to the field of apologetics have been inattention to ethics and aesthetics. With an effort to broaden the view of apologetic's interest in ethics, Brad Kallenberg argues that Stanley Hauerwas, the great ethicist of postliberalism, is actually himself an apologist. He claims that the earliest apologists' goal was to simply explain Christianity in its own terms while pointing the ethics of the Christian community as "proof" of the truth claims. "At the end of the day, the [early] apologist's trump card was to point to the Christian [community's ethics] while describing it in Christian terms. For the truth of Christian speech supervenes on descriptions of their practices. This interplay between speech and practice makes possible communication with outsiders."[38]

For Kallenberg and the early apologists[39], the evidence for Christian truth is the results of the community that is formed by it. C. C. Pecknold argues that this is implicit in *The Nature of Doctrine* as part of Lindbeck's distinct kind of pragmatism, though I am not convinced that this label is adequate.[40] But Hauerwas's quote with which I began, Kallenberg's analysis of Hauerwas, Long's *The Goodness of God*, and Pecknold's explanation of Lindbeck all bring ethics back to the forefront of the Christian witness. Kallenberg and Hauerwas recognize that the recovery of ethics is an aspect of apologetics. Long and Balthasar also recognize the role of beauty in the recovery of a more robust kind of reasoning.

The good and the beautiful have played a minor role in modern apologetics. I will argue below that aesthetics and ethics have the potential to display the persuasive aspect of the Christian story. Postliberals do not normally argue this way, as they typically resist the idea that a category can transcend the individual narratives of a particular tradition. As we have seen from Long, postliberal theology can make space for such a notion of the transcendental predicates.

---

37. Balthasar, *Theo-logic I*, 29.

38. Kallenberg, "Strange New World in the Church," 213.

39. By "early apologists" Kallenberg especially means the apologists of the second century who were answering accusations concerning the Eucharist, "brotherly" love, and insurrection.

40. Pecknold, *Transforming Postliberal Theology*.

BEAUTY AS CRITERIA AND THE CRITERIA OF BEAUTY

One must ask whether a category as seemingly subjective as beauty can carry the weight of theological reasoning and apologetics. The question is justified, especially if beauty were to be proposed as a category independent of the other transcendentals. But I contend that beauty must be pursued as apologetic criteria if theology is to be called evangelical and therefore apologetic. If humanity's true end is to glorify God and enjoy him forever, then our concern is not only that a person intellectually assents to Christian truth. Rather, Christians must pray that the person falls in love with the beauty and glory of God. While Balthasar begins by saying that God's truth is "great enough to allow an infinity of approaches and entryways," he *decides* to begin with beauty.[41] Later Balthasar admits that beginning with aesthetics is "comparable to what was once called apologetics, or, if you will, fundamental theology."[42] Like Balthasar, because I am suggesting a method for apologetics, I *must* begin with beauty. It is beauty that will cause a person to choose Christ rather than the multitude of other "gods" which summon her. While Balthasar contends we could begin elsewhere if doing theology of another kind, apologetic concerns must start at the beauty that will draw all people to God. We begin with beauty because it is beauty that gives us a taste for the good and the true.

> In a world without beauty . . . the good also loses its attractiveness, the self-evidence of why it must be carried out. Man stands before the good and asks himself why it must be done and not rather it's alternative, evil. For this too, is a possibility, and even the more exciting one: Why not investigate Satan's depths? In a world that no longer has enough confidence in itself to affirm the beautiful, the proofs of the truth have lost their cogency. In other words, syllogisms may dutifully clatter away like rotary presses or computers that infallibly spew out an exact number of answers by the minute. But the logic of these answers is itself a mechanism that no longer captivates anyone. The very conclusions are no longer conclusive.[43]

Without a proper understanding of beauty, the good appears to be nothing more than choice or preference. For Nietzsche's nihilism, claims to the "good" are simply an expression of the will to power, a usurpation of the

---

41. Balthasar, *Glory of the Lord*, 17.

42. Balthasar, *Theo-logic I*, 20.

43. Ibid., 19.

powerful by the "priests."[44] The good has no persuasive power. Likewise, truth *qua* truth has no persuasive power. Therefore every truth claim is subject to deconstruction without love to motivate its defense. When truth claims had the false certainty of "objectivity," it was possible to appeal to submission to this "self-evident" truth. But the *zeitgeist* of the postmodern turn insists that knowledge is located within presuppositional frameworks. As such, Christianity can embrace the postmodern claim.

Patristic and medieval theology was always a "faith seeking under-standing" and not a supposedly apologetic "understanding seeking faith." For example, Anselm claims that his *Cur Deus Homo* is not intended to attain faith by reason. Yet he is clear that it is a thoroughly apologetic work.

> They ask, not for the sake of attaining to faith by means of reason, but that they may be gladdened by understanding and meditating on those things which they believe; and that, as far as possible, they may be always ready to convince anyone who demands of them a reason of that hope which is in us . . . and though it seem very difficult in the investigation, it is yet plain to all in the solution, and attractive for the value and beauty of the reasoning.[45]

Anselm recognizes that a person must presuppose faith if his "proof" is to make rational sense. However, he also claims that the "proof" will be "plain to all in the solution. "For Anselm it is possible for those outside of faith to recognize the logic of faith if they are willing to presuppose it. Most importantly for my purposes, Anselm maintains that even those outside of faith will be drawn to faith for the beauty of faith's reasoning. The truth of Christian faith is not "self-evident" because it requires presupposition. But the beauty of the Christian narrative will be evident to all who encounter it within its given presuppositions. For Anselm, beauty has a kind of univer-sality that truth does not. While unable to attain faith by reason, Anselm assumes one is able to recognize the beauty of reason. "The beautiful brings with it a self-evidence that en-lightens without mediation."[46]

Therefore, beauty serves as an entry into the contemplation of the real. One first recognizes the beauty of an argument and is drawn to tithe beauty is not independent of truth or goodness, but it enables the observer to rec-ognize the others. Aquinas makes comments regarding the good similar to Anselm's comments about truth. For Aquinas, beauty is the cognitive fac-ulty that enables one to see the good. Put briefly, the good is an end that is

44. Nietzsche, *On the Genealogy of Morality*, 9–34.

45. Anselm, "Cur Deus Homo," I, 1.

46. Balthasar, *Glory of the Lord, Vol. I*, 37.

desired or enjoyed; the beautiful is that which is desired or enjoyed through contemplation. The good is the end; the beautiful is the faculty by which we recognize and desire the good.[47] But this distinction is too clean to be considered final. What seems consistent in Aquinas is that beauty has logical priority in causing a person to be drawn towards a thing. While the good and true serve as love's final causes, beauty is love's efficient cause.

> Good is the cause of love, as being its object. But good is not the object of the appetite, except as apprehended. And therefore love demands some apprehension of the good that is loved. For this reason the Philosopher (Ethic. ix, 5, 12) says that bodily sight is the beginning of sensitive love: and in like manner *the contemplation of spiritual beauty or goodness is the beginning of spiritual love.* Accordingly knowledge is the cause of love for the same reason as good is, which can be loved only if known [emphasis added].[48]

Both goodness and knowledge (truth?) are apprehended by contemplation of beauty. Like Anselm, Aquinas understands beauty to have a persuasive power that makes apprehension possible. Plato puts a similar view into the mouth of Diotima in the *Symposium*, but for Diotima beauty is the object of love the same as the good. Beauty is something that can be possessed as an object of love.[49] Though Plato's view differs slightly, if the transcendental predicates are truly interdependent then reaching consensus on these distinctions is impossible. But the thinkers surveyed generally agree that beauty has a logical priority in desiring the good and true in a thing. This logical priority is only functional, however. No hierarchy should be distinguished.

To say God is beautiful is to say "that God has this superior force, this power of attraction, which speaks for itself, which wins and conquers."[50] While all three of the transcendentals are found equally in God and God's creation, the true and good are less self-evident than beauty. Like the Psalmist, the believer can invite others to "taste and see that the Lord is good" and be reasonably sure that "the glory of the Lord" can be apprehended.

At this point in the argument I think it is necessary to consider the most important objection that this methodology invites. As mentioned above, beauty has often been considered the most subjective of the predicates of being, often taken to have no stable ontology whatsoever. By claiming that beauty does have an ontological referent, I do not deny its

47. Aquinas, *Summa Theologica* I–II, q. 27, a. 1.
48. Aquinas, *Summa Theologica* I–II, q. 27, a. 2.
49. Plato, *Symposium* 204d–205a.
50. Barth, *Church Dogmatics* II.1, 650.

subjective aspect. Like Long, I recognize the transcendental predicates as simultaneously being subjectively apprehended and having objectively and ontologically stable existence. This condition is equally real for truth, goodness, and beauty. Modernity's totalizing epistemology appeared to eliminate truth's subjectivity. But postmodernity's deconstruction of objective truth has opened the door for a fuller account of the transcendental predicates that recognizes simultaneously objective and subjective elements, even if most postmodernists cannot accept this account of ontology.

Already in Plato's *Symposium* there is forceful resistance to a wholly subjective account of beauty.[51] If beauty is not wholly subjective in Plato's metaphysics, then Christian metaphysics need not relegate beauty solely to the preference of the subject either. Like Plato, Christian theology's metaphysics depends upon an immutable God. Beyond Plato, Christian theology can assert that the redemption of creation proceeds analogically from God. Therefore creation and God can be described to varying degrees with the transcendental predicates of being because of their "objective" referents. Beauty is an ontological category proper to speech about God and Christian witness and should not be subordinated to the concept of truth. Beauty and goodness are no more subjective than truth as ontological categories, though all have subjective aspects in apprehension.

In spite of the questions regarding the subjective perception, we cannot avoid beauty as a key apologetic category precisely because it is the persuasive category of God's being. Beauty is the efficient cause of love.[52] If we are to love God, then we will finally be persuaded to love by God's beauty. But we should not make beauty alone central to our doctrine of God or finally even of our apologetics. This is not only because the transcendentals are necessarily interdependent, but also because a single concept of being cannot carry the weight of the whole doctrine of God. Beauty is not central or finally the whole of apologetics; it is only the entry point into the apprehension of God. Barth cautions against making beauty or any other concept key to our doctrine of God; to do so is idolatry. Barth also warns that a totalizing aestheticism is no more dangerous than a totalizing logism, moralism, or intellectualism. All of these must be avoided for the sake of more fully apprehending God. But Barth concludes that beauty must be the final statement in our doctrine of God, because "with the help of it we are able to dissipate even the suggestion that God's glory is a mere fact . . . It is not this. It is effective because and as it is beautiful. This explanation as such

51. White, "Plato's Metaphysical Epistemology," 283.

52. Plato, *Symposium* 209c–211a.

is not merely legitimate. It is essential."[53] The beauty of God is that aspect of God that draws all people to himself. "Objective" truth is mere fact, but God is also beautiful. Therefore where Barth concludes his doctrine of God, apologetics begins. Presuppositional knowledge requires that a person be formed in its logical framework if they are to comprehend. But how can one be formed in that knowledge if one is not first captivated by it? God's beauty captivates even before God's truth becomes evident. Once the beauty of God and his redemption captivates a person, more complete apprehension becomes possible as that person is formed by the beautiful object of his love.

Universal Aesthetic Criteria

Thus far I have argued that all things really exist in so far as they participate in the good, beautiful, and true. Really-existing things participate in all three as necessary predicates of being. While reality has this objective referent, it is subjectively dependent on the observer's conceptual framework. Truth, beauty, and goodness can only be observed in a thing according to the presumed framework of the observer. Therefore Christian apologetics cannot assume modernity's totalizing epistemology that gave truth a universal objectivity. In spite of beauty and truth's simultaneously subjective and objective elements, beauty has a kind of persuasiveness which truth does not. Therefore, if Christian apologetics hopes to persuade persons to faithfulness to God and Christian faith, then presentation of Christian dogma must attend to aesthetic criteria. If the subject of Christian dogma (i.e. God and God's redemption of creation) is itself beautiful, then it is objectively so, and the apologist need not "make" the presentation of Christianity aesthetic. Aesthetic apologetics is not just rhetoric or sophistry. But apologists must present the beautiful story of God's redemption with beautiful reasoning if those outside of Christianity will be drawn to it. Therefore we must ask, "What is beautiful reasoning?" What aesthetic criteria are relevant for judging an account of the world such as Christian dogma provides?

Before proceeding with aesthetic judgment, beauty must be distinguished from the merely pretty. Barth called aestheticism idolatry. Aestheticism produces art for art's sake. Beauty must refer also to what is good and true. Beautiful objects must point beyond themselves to real Beauty, the essence (or form) of Beauty. Medieval theologians borrowed this concept primarily from the Neoplatonists. But for Christian thought, this claim is dependent upon a theological conception of the transcendentals that conceives of all three concepts as unified in the Creator. God the Creator created

53. Barth, *Church Dogmatics* II.1, 655.

all things in accord with God's own being, which is good, beautiful, and true. Yet God's creation is not the Good, the Beautiful, and the True. Only God can be identified with these transcendentals without qualification.

Therefore all proper speech about God is dependent on some form of analogy. Regardless of one's acceptance of *analogia entis* or its rejection (Barth's "Nein!") in favor of *analogia fides*, the purpose is the same. Analogy opens up the possibility of speech about God without reducing God to a being like us. Analogy preserves the infinity of God and makes knowledge of God possible, avoiding univocity and equivocity. The use of analogy in theological speech helps to distinguish the merely pretty from the beautiful. Pretty things may please the eye. But beautiful things point beyond themselves to the very reality of Beauty, God.

As David Bentley Hart has argued, the doctrine of analogy is the link between the Platonic conception of aesthetics that I have assumed to this point and the doctrine of creation that must ground any Christian ontology. When creation is understood as a finite (and sinful) participation in the transcendental predicates of Being, then all creation can be expressed in terms of greater or lesser participation in God. This is the "principle" of analogy in all its various theological forms.[54] Like art, analogical speech is always an approximation of truth that points beyond itself to truth larger than itself—what Long called Metaphysics 3 and 4. The degree to which something participates in God, Beauty Itself, is the degree to which it is beautiful. But aside from its accord with revelation, Protestants can find little to measure the degree to which something participates in God. A theological aesthetics must provide some principles, if not measures, by which participation in God and therefore the Good, the True, and the Beautiful can be recognized. Natural theologies or existential projection (Feuerbach) will inevitably lead to a vision of God dependent on something lower than God. This was Barth's fear of his (mis)understanding of the *analogia entis*, and every Protestant must affirm his fear.[55] However, it is this doctrine of analogy that opens up aesthetic possibilities for apologetics. Some ways of telling the story of God's redemption will point beyond themselves to redemption itself. All those who can accept these stories' presuppositions will find them beautiful. Therefore, the apologist must ask how she can tell the story in accord with the reality of God. How can the story be told such that it opens up the possibility of encounters with God and redemption that go beyond the story itself?

54. Hart, *Beauty of the Infinite*, 241–49.

55. Though I do not think the *analogia entis* should be equated with natural theology, some Roman Catholics and especially those associated with Vatican I (Denys Turner) have a form of natural theology that Barth and all Protestants must oppose.

Aquinas named three aesthetic criteria that are well accepted in aesthetics universally: unity, harmony or proportion, and brightness.[56] Taken as a whole, "fittingness" describes the degree to which the theological or aesthetic point beyond themselves well. Are the specific elements held in proper proportion, such that each element is expressed to its proper intensity? Is the representation sufficiently rich, such that it portrays seemingly disparate concepts with proper harmony or dissonance? Is the unity of the whole called into question by a significant concept's overemphasis or omission? Although the overarching concept of "fittingness" is helpful to understand participation, analysis of the individual criteria provides guidelines for forming a beautiful apologetic witness.

Unity primarily concerns the coherence and completeness of the aesthetic object. Nicholas Wolterstorff explains that, as an artistic criterion, unity is based on the formal concept of unity inherent to particular art forms.[57] When measuring the unity of a conception of the world's reality, the formal concept is reality itself. Therefore, unity of the Christian story or any other worldview will be the extent to which every area of reality is included in the conception. For example, Christianity's failure to convincingly account for or provide alternative visions for evolutionary theory has arguably been a lack of unity in contemporary Christian witness. Christian apologetics will need to account for these widely held beliefs, or apologetically reveal evolutionary theory's presuppositional grounds (as false?) to maintain the Christian story's own unity. Likewise, if a theory's internal coherence breaks down at significant points as Newtonian physics was known to do, then unity is lacking.

Proportion speaks of the relationship of one element to another. Doctrines of God which emphasize either mercy or judgment (or Oneness and Threeness) without the other are recognized as out of proportion. Likewise, harmony speaks of the beauty of varied elements when spoken of together, therefore holding such diverse concepts as mercy and judgment as mutually dependent. Contemporary evangelical theologies have often emphasized the grace and mercy displayed in sacrificial atonement without the ethical implications of incarnation. When both atonement and incarnation are given their proper place, Christian doctrine will proclaim forgiveness and also take up the social responsibility inherent in Christian faith. Outsiders will be able to acknowledge this as a beautiful way of life.

Harmony also speaks of the richness of an account. A single musical note has unity, but it lacks the richness of harmony. The popular "Romans

---

56. Aquinas, *Summa Theologica* I, q. 39, a. 8.

57. Wolterstorff, *Art in Action*, 164–65.

Road" or "Four Spiritual Laws" approaches to evangelism serve as an example here. When an account is reduced to a single concept without the tensions of other "dissonant" concepts, it lacks beauty. As Don Saliers says about praise without lamentation, a theology that lacks richness may turn out to be simply a cheap imitation.[58]

Aquinas named the third criteria "brightness." Wolterstorff identifies this criterion with what he calls "fittingness-intensities."[59] By this he means the degree to which an aesthetic object achieves the character to which it is intended. If the Christian story is intended to be a redeeming story, then its "brightness" will be measured by the depth of its redemption. Is every area of a person's life redeemed, including the physical, emotional, and spiritual parts? Is creation itself redeemed? Can social entities, artistic forms, and academic disciplines (to name just a few examples) be redeemed? Does redemption mean a complete break from that which was held bondage (i.e. does the alcoholic ever return to the drink, and if so, does redemption even extend there)?

The similarities between these aesthetic criteria and the truth criteria explicated by cumulative case apologists bear some striking similarities. We would expect this if in fact truth and beauty were different ways of speaking about the perfection of being, or, to speak theologically, the perfection of creation. Like the criteria by which one judges truthfulness, the criteria by which one judges beauty help to illuminate the degree to which the Christian vision of the world corresponds, interprets, and makes sense of the world of experience. Similarly, insofar as Christianity is able to show that Jesus and the way of life he demands are good, Christianity will also thereby be shown to be truthful.

APOLOGETICS AND THE DEMONSTRATION OF THE GOOD

The final transcendental predicate is goodness, the object of desire. According to Aquinas, goodness relates to being's "end" and appeals to the appetite. Augustine asserted that all created things are good, which means that all created things have a desirable *telos*. Even the statement that all things are good makes us uneasy because not all things seem good. We immediately question this account of created good because we know of that which is not good. But this actually confirms the existence of the good rather than rendering it an obsolete concept. As D. Stephen Long argues, the ontological

58. Saliers, *Worship as Theology*, 122–55.
59. Wolterstorff, *Art in Action*, 166–68.

reality of the good is verified when someone speaks of a good which we know to have bad ends. If someone says "Slavery was good for the African people" we respond passionately against it. At least, we might conclude that the one who spoke is ignorant. Going further, we may respond with rage or wholesale dismissal of the one who spoke. We may even respond that the statement or the one who spoke it is evil. These responses reveal that the "good" still has an impassioned hold on us, even though popular thought has intended to reduce the good to preference. "Slavery was good for the African people" is a statement about the *telos* of slavery, and this "end" has an experiential verifiability that is (seemingly) universally not true.[60]

But this argument does not yet preclude the possibility that there is such a thing as good, in which not all things participate fully. Augustine's classic account of evil as the privation of good is relevant here. Augustine insisted that all created things are good because their creator is good. Therefore anything we recognize as evil is actually just a corrupted good thing. In its nature it retains its status as good creation and yet in its corruption it is evil. Nothing is radically evil, because evil is no thing; it does not exist. What we call evil are those things that do not pursue their proper *telos* for which God created them, which is good.

Our enchantment with the good should surprise us at the conclusion of modernity. Alasdair MacIntyre insists that the major towers of the Enlightenment project all reject the conception of humanity having a *telos*. Without a human *telos*, there can be no "good" human life. For Kant and Hume, there are no discernible teleological features in the objective universe. These philosophers must therefore give an account of the moral life that is independent of an ontological account of the good. This is due in part to their theological inheritance that demanded such an independent account. For the late medieval Christian theologians who immediately preceded Kant and Hume, "Reason can supply, so these new theologies assert, *no* genuine comprehension of man's true end; that power of reason was destroyed by the fall of man."[61] If the *telos* and the good that depends upon it cannot be known, then ethics must construct an account of the good that will be universal without an ontological basis. This explains the genesis of modern ethics, including Kant's categorical imperative and the utilitarian-consequentialist theories. According to MacIntyre, Kant recognized this failure and thus conceded in the second book of his second *Critique* that "without a teleological framework the whole project of morality becomes unintelligible." Kant then inserted the teleological framework as a presup-

60. Long, *Goodness of God*, 31–32.

61. MacIntyre, *After Virtue*, 53–54.

position independent of reason. Macintyre concludes that Kant recognized something his contemporaries and disciples did not. Kant's social milieu provided a *telos* for humanity that his philosophy could not.[62] In modernity, that teleological scheme which finds its end in God and God's enjoyment has receded to a distant memory, instead being replaced by a vision of happiness constructed by the insatiable desire of consumerism.[63]

Lacking its teleological content, modern ethics has failed to properly justify its account of the good. An ontological account of rationality that presupposes God, the Christian God, can overcome this deficit. Accounting for this deficit is part of the apologetic task. *Persons will find this Christian conception of God, creation, and redemption beautiful because they find the Christian account of the good, creation's telos, to be true.* Now we have a more complete conception of rationality which accounts not only for the truthfulness of a way of life, but also its desirability and reasonableness. Though beauty has a logical priority as the formal cause of a person's desire, the heavy lifting of Christian apologetics in postmodernity is, as it had been until the modern era, an account of ethics. While this philosophical work is primarily a work on apologetic methodology, Christian ethicists who are committed theologians, pastors, and lay persons will carry out the real task of apologetics. Those laypersons will tell of the beauty, goodness, and truth of the Christian story as the make art, tell stories, heal broken families, and set order to broken institutions. As faithful persons interact with their relevant circles of influence, the Christian way will be found to be good or true based on these persons' ability to contribute significantly to the most basic ethical questions of their areas of expertise. Christian ethics is its own postmodern apologetic. Apologetics can appeal confidently to the Good because an ontological construal of reality affirms its objective grounding in Truth and Beauty.

This apologetic emphasis on ethics was a concern for Karl Barth, as it should be for us if Barth's assessment is truthful. Thus I think it is necessary to contend with Barth's concerns if we are to approach ethics as a form of apologetics. Apologetics sometimes concedes a general conception of ethics that can be deduced from any number of philosophical inquiries. The apologetic task within this framework is to validate a theological account of ethics by justifying according to presumed conclusions of the logically prior general conception of ethics.[64] Therefore general ethical inquiry determines the questions that theological ethics must ask and answer, and also

62. Ibid., 56.

63. Žižek, "'Thrilling Romance of Orthodoxy,'" 56–60.

64. Barth, *Church Dogmatics* II.2, 520.

determines the criteria that constitute an adequate answer for the question. The only possible reason for an apologetic of this nature is the conviction that a general ethics exists which is prior to theology. Of course, this conclusion is problematic for Barth and should be for any Christian theologian. Christian theology and apologetics are accountable to none but God. A human or an entire human community working together can gain no vantage point higher than God from which they may judge a theological ethics appropriately.[65]

Barth admits that the Roman Catholic conception, which is very close to the ontological construal of reality that I propose here, is a helpful alternative, though he concludes that it too finally fails. The Roman conception avoids surrendering theology to a controlling general ethics. It also avoids the strictly voluntarist ethics which can easily result from specialized dogmatic theology which distances itself too completely from general ethical inquiry. Barth's explanation of the Roman moralists is quite helpful. He explains that the Roman construal places the two ethical sciences within distinguished realms that cannot be separated, moral philosophy and moral theology. In a classic "grace perfecting nature," moral philosophy depends upon moral theology and *vice versa*. Though they are connected in an inseparable union, they are not considered equal. Barth describes moral theology as the pivot of a wheel on which moral philosophy turns and is thus dependent. Likewise, moral theology is the upper story and moral philosophy the lower story of one and the same structure.[66] Thus the task of moral philosophy is a significant one: it recognizes the principles of moral behavior as experience and history have taught them using the light of human reason. Following rational principles it can go a long way in apprehension, just as it is capable in apprehending logic *a priori*. However, it can also go far off the path of truth if it does not acknowledge the role of revelation. It can recognize moral virtue as pertaining to reason as a penultimate good, which proceeds from the ultimate good in God. Moral theology is fully dependent upon the revelation of Scripture and the church's tradition. It develops a positive law upon the theological virtues of faith, hope, and love, which cannot be discerned without revelation. Grace perfects nature because it heals nature from the disorder of sin that persists in it. Only faith, hope, and love repair the distance between human justice and abundant life.

Barth insists that this is a significant improvement on the previous apologetic ethics. But Barth insists with most Reformed critiques of Roman doctrine that the *analogia entis* provides too much space for a good

65. Ibid., 522.
66. Ibid., 528.

humanity which seeks after God without need for God's drawing people to himself. Put simply, the Roman doctrine of sin is not thoroughgoing enough for Barth. The communion between humanity and God in Roman thought is too close without the explicit emergence of grace found in Jesus Christ.[67] Indeed, we may accept Barth's critique without forfeiting the classical mode of thinking. The Christian confession of Jesus as the Word made flesh allows no content for revelation if it is not the person of Jesus. Therefore the usefulness of Barth's critique is his insistence that Jesus is the definitive content of revelation. The Roman conception can be affirmed and yet supplemented with Barth's insistence on Jesus. Though Roman ethics and apologetics may be a theological ethics and theological apologetics, it is only a Christian one when it insists upon Jesus as the primary content of theology.

Barth's insistence does not actually preclude the Roman methodology, however. Barth attempts to account for the significant inadequacy of human knowledge by reminding us of the thoroughgoing effect of sin and an insistence upon Jesus as the divine act of grace. Thus Jesus does not destroy the noetic effect of sin but reveals the grace and command of God (the Good). O'Donovan explains that Barth's concerns with natural theology are primarily epistemological, and he therefore fails to recognize the ontological propriety of "Natural Law."[68] The created order is rightly discerned as coming from the logic of the Logos, but this does little work epistemologically, as Barth explained. Therefore Barth criticized a caricature of the Roman *analogia entis*, failing to recognize the principle that governs it in Roman thought. The Roman recognition of "ever-greater dissimilarity however great the similarity"[69] (i.e. the principle of analogy) means that moral philosophy can never gain independence from moral theology. While Barth's reservation puts the reason for the distance in the fall of humanity, Roman thought places the distance in an insurmountable separation between infinite God and finite persons. Both Barth and Roman thinkers thus insist upon revelation's primacy to guide moral thinking.

The distance between the ability of human reason and the conclusion of revelation and theology calls the project of apologetics into question as a whole. Will non-Christian ethicists recognize the good purported from revelation as good within the program of general ethics? Will this not necessarily partition Christian theology into the specialist field of a Christian theological ghetto? Christian theology is not doomed to unintelligibility.

---

67. Ibid., 530.

68. O'Donovan, *Resurrection and Moral Order*, 86–87.

69. See Balthasar, *Glory of the Lord, Vol. I*, 460.

However, it may be that theology must proceed with an "ad hoc apologetics," as George Lindbeck insists.[70]

Unwittingly, Barth has given guidance as to how such an "ad hoc" apologetic ethics should proceed. He describes the relationship of apologetics to general ethics as like that of the Israelites to the Promised Land. Apologetics does not enter the world of general ethical enquiry as a visitor or a participant in a democratic state. Apologetics enters the field of moral inquiry as its rightful heir. Apologetics must deny the independence of general ethics and assert its dependence upon the grace of Jesus Christ. The person of Jesus Christ and the image put on display in his person determines the question and command of moral inquiry. Rather than providing space for humanity to judge both God and the Good, apologetics must insist that even where general ethics succeeds it does so as a result of the grace of God and the determination of humanity's *telos* as the image of God. Humanity only seeks after God because of the gracious orientation of the Creator towards creation. Theological ethics in the mode of apologetics may therefore take seriously the contribution of secular moralists, but must always do so without making treaty with them or their assumptions. General ethics must remain a foreigner and a stranger. This bold alienation is necessary to maintain the potency of theological ethics (Rom 1:16).

On the other hand, in the course of its apologetic witness, theological ethics will encounter many topics to which the revelation of God in Jesus Christ only speaks ambiguously. This is not to say that the silence of Jesus in the Scriptures regarding contemporary concerns (e.g. medical research on human embryos) silences theological ethics as well. Jesus' ethics are not simply historically contingent. But it does mean that moral theology must speak humbly. This humble speech requires that theological ethics does not allow general moral inquiry to determine the questions or the terms of the question. This would be conceding too much even for a humble theological inquiry.

The construal of reality that we have just surveyed goes far beyond Plato, though it presupposes his metaphysics. A Christian account of the transcendental predicates is grounded in a theological claim to the Goodness, Beauty, and Truth of God. As such, Christian apologists can be confidant that an appeal to the universality of goodness, beauty, and truth in God's creation is valid. The effect of sin on our perceptions does not destroy the reliability of the universal nature of the predicates. Paul could exhort the Philippians to think about good things because the good is always grounded in God. "Finally, brothers, whatever is true, whatever is noble, whatever is

---

70. Lindbeck, *Nature of Doctrine*, 129.

right, whatever is pure, whatever is lovely, whatever is admirable—if any-thing is excellent or praiseworthy—think about such things" (Phil 4:8). The good things which the apologist points his interlocutor towards will reliably point her towards God.

Establishing Humanity's Telos

The only ethic that can provide a *telos* for a Christian apologetic must be grounded in the Gospel of Jesus Christ. This already brings into question the entire project of apologetics in this mode, because apologetics in mo-dernity has largely been a project of assimilating theology into the prevail-ing thought forms acceptable to those outside of Christianity. No theology or apologetics can allow secular reason to set the agenda in this way again. Only Jesus Christ can set the agenda for Christian theology and apologetics. If Jesus Christ is the good, beautiful, and true God that the Gospel pro-claims him to be, then Christian apologetics can be confident that the Way commanded by Jesus will be convincing to those who encounter it.

The church's faith in Jesus Christ is faith in Jesus as the One True God. By virtue of his divinity, Jesus is also therefore the embodiment of all that God is, not the least the real Good, Truth, and Beauty. As we shall see, say-ing that Jesus is beautiful, true, and good is not enough. These predicates belong to all that God has created by virtue of their being creatures *of God*. Jesus more than participates in these predicates in the same way creation does. The church's proclamation of Jesus' divinity is not pantheistic. The church's proclamation of Jesus is a different sort of thing. Jesus is *homoousia* with the Father and the Spirit. John's prologue proclaims Jesus as the Word made flesh. Put simply, Jesus is not just good but is the Good.

Jesus is Good not only as a matter of declaration. Barth begins his *Doctrine of Reconciliation* with the dogmatic proclamation, "The faith and love and hope of the Christian community and the Christians assembled in it live by the message received by and laid upon them, not the reverse."[71] The church is not the church simply because they proclaim a message of God's goodness. God, in his goodness, has made God's self present to the church in the person of Jesus Christ so that good would no longer be only a principle which guide their lives, but would instead be a person who could be received and proclaimed. God has claimed humanity, not the reverse.

Much of contemporary ethics claims Jesus as the image of goodness for which it strives. Kant makes Jesus into a moral hero, a concrete embodi-ment of the categorical imperative. In the face of the grandest of evils, "this

71. Barth, *Church Dogmatics* IV.1, 3.

good man did not sway from his mission and did not sully the purity of his will."[72] Kant thereby reverses the logic of faith. He moves from an image of the *a priori* known good (the categorical imperative) to its embodiment in Jesus. The church moves from the revelation of the ultimate Good in the person of Christ to the content of the ethical life. For Kant, Schleiermacher, and much of contemporary theology, Jesus makes the good tangible by embodying the ideal (Kant) or the *pathos* (Schleiermacher) of "good" humanity well. This is not the church's proclamation. In fact, Kant finally rejects the church's proclamation of Jesus as the incarnate Word because Kant thinks that the incarnation meant Jesus had some kind of moral superpower by which he lived his life of obedience and sacrifice. So Kant finally rejects the incarnation to keep Jesus as an archetypal human that was finally willing to go even to the cross to suffer the loss of his own self-interest.[73] The church does proclaim that Jesus is the archetypal human, but in a way very different than Kant would allow.

Jesus is revealed as the "image of the invisible God, the first-born over all creation" (Col 1:15).This is implicit in much of the New Testament's proclamation of Jesus' lordship. In the words following this opening phrase of the Christological hymn, the author of Colossians declares that Jesus is the image of God in a way that makes him equal to God. He is the "first-born" of creation, and himself Creator. He has dominion over creation, and "all God's fullness dwells in him."

An earlier Pauline passage carries this same theme in a less developed way. In Second Corinthians 4:4–6, Paul proclaims Christ as the image of God and his glory. This knowledge of God is given to humanity so that it will no longer be ignorant of God's glory. The content of the Gospels is the revelation of God's glory in Jesus. Jesus as the image of God's glory is likewise picked up by the author of Hebrews. Jesus reveals the "radiance of God's glory and the exact representation of his being" (Heb 1:1–3).Unlike in the Pauline passages, the Hebrews passage refers to Jesus as the *charakter* of God and not the *eikon* as we would expect. *Charakter* is related to the image that is made by a stamp upon a coin. *Eikon* referred to the image made by a sculptor or painter in reproducing an original. Though *eikon* is generally accepted as an exact reproduction, it could be that the author of Hebrews intends an even stronger connection with the unique word usage. Jesus is an image formed by God's very own impression.[74] The very "high" christolo-

---

72. Barron, *Priority of Christ*, 25.

73. Long, *Goodness of God*, 110.

74. For this discussion see pages on Hebrews 1:1–3 in "Barnes's New Testament Notes."

gies of these various passages is clear. Jesus is true God made present in the incarnation of the Logos, the truest *imago Dei*. Jesus is thereby established as the *telos* for which all humanity aims. In Long's words, "Jesus reveals to us not only who God is but also what it means to be *truly human*."[75]

Stanley Grenz has argued that these very high New Testament christologies actually presuppose Old Testament anthropology. This is most obvious with Hebrews where the "glory and honor" anthropology of Psalm 8:4–6 is refocused upon Jesus alone. God had intended glory for humanity that was eclipsed only by the angels. This universal anthropology is only complete in Jesus, however. Jesus is what humanity was intended to be; the image of God according to Genesis 1:26. The glory of Christ is connected to the image of God language in Second Corinthians 4:4–6 as well. The Greek *eikon* of the relevant Pauline passages (2 Cor 4, Col 1:15) is the same word used of humanity's creation according to God's image in the Genesis account in the LXX (Gen 1:26). In the Greek sense *eikon* is not completely separate from the original that it imitates, but participates in the real thing.

In Second Corinthians 4 as well as Colossians 1:15, the "text embodies an implicit allusion to the creation of humankind in the divine image narrated in Genesis 1:26–27 which is now understood through the lens of Christ as the Second Adam."[76] This is explicit in the Colossians Christ-hymn, as the image of God language is juxtaposed with "firstborn over all creation." Christ is the Second Adam because he is what Adam was intended to be, the image of God, even before Adam was created. In other Pauline texts, Christ as the Second or Last Adam is even more explicit. In these texts, however, Christ's obedience is set over and against Adam's disobedience and reverses its effects (Rom 5:14–17, 1 Cor 15:21–22).[77] Adam is the insufficient man because his sin prevented him from accomplishing all that Christ did. Jesus is the fulfillment of all that Adam was intended to be, the *imago Dei*.

The earliest expositor of this Jesus-as-the–*imago Dei* theology was Irenaeus. He makes the Jewish anthropology of Genesis 1:26 even more explicit to his Christology than Paul did. This is in part due to his reaction to Gnostic anthropologies that gave primacy to certain "pneumatic" people who could be saved when "sarkic" persons could not. Irenaeus argues that all people were created with the same value and *telos* before God, the *imago Dei*.[78] This presupposes his insistence that God is Creator, again against

---

75. Long, *Goodness of God*, 106.

76. Grenz, "Jesus as the Imago Dei," 619. For this connection, Grenz refers the reader to Ridderbos, *Paul*, 70–76.

77. Kärkäinen, *Christology*, 49.

78. Wingren, *Man and the Incarnation*, xii–xiii.

the Gnostics. His anthropology therefore presupposes Jesus as the incarnate Logos who also created man that he became.[79] From this position he argues that "the Son of God, who was made man in Jesus, exists *before* man, and, indeed, when man is created he is created through the Son and *for* the Son, so as to reach his destiny in the Son, his Saviour."[80] Therefore, for Irenaeus Jesus is more than the archetypal man who fulfills man's *telos*. Jesus is the very basis by which man is created as man. He is the Logos through which everything is created; most specifically humanity was created in his image. "For He made man the image of God; and the image of God is the Son, after whose image man was made: and for this cause he appeared in the end of times that He might show the image [to be] like unto Himself. According to this covenant the race of man multiplied, springing up from the seed of the three [sons of Noah]."[81] Irenaeus makes this concise restatement of his Christology and anthropology on the occasion of the story of Noah's covenant. His "mention of the original identity of man comes as a reminder that all this history, of which a new era here [at the flood] begins, is still linked inseparably to, and profoundly bracketed with, the one who, as the Son of God, is Himself the Image of God."[82] This is necessary because the "Son will, at the end of all the times—of which the covenant is a significant and determinative part—demonstrate that humanity was made to be conformable to the image which the Son is."[83] God intends creation and especially humanity to conform to the logic of the Logos. This is its proper *telos*. This *telos* is not only fulfilled by Jesus, but is predetermined by creation's existence through the Logos that is made incarnate in Jesus. The end of the story is determined before the story begins. In a real sense, that story's end, chronologically and teleologically, is in Jesus. Creation was formed according to the Logos. Additionally, humanity was not only formed according to the Logos, but was intended to become like God, to become the very image of God.[84]

The close link between the *telos* of humanity, Jesus, and creation allows for at least two significant theological groundings for ethics. First, because humanity was created in God's image and Jesus brings humanity to its fulfillment, Christian ethics is summarized by conformity with the life

79. Irenaeus, *Demonstration of the Apostolic Preaching*, 43.

80. Wingren, *Man and the Incarnation*, 5.

81. Irenaeus, *Demonstration of the Apostolic Preaching*, 22.

82. Mackenzie, *Irenaeus' Demonstration*, 135.

83. Ibid.

84. Wingren, *Man and the Incarnation*, 20. See also Grenz and Franke, *Beyond Foundationalism*, 198–99.

of Christ. Thus Grenz describes "the Christian ethical task as that of living out our destiny as the *imago Dei*."[85] As we will see, this is not as simple as asking the question "What would Jesus do? "We do not want to reduce Jesus and his ethics to an exemplarist doctrine of the atonement.[86] The historical contingency of Jesus' life limits his example to a particular social context. The limited scope of Jesus' teaching means that many contemporary questions are left unanswered. But the task of "living out our destiny as the *imago Dei*" provides a concrete and objective grounding for the goodness of God and the ethical life.

Secondly, because creation is formed in and through the Logos, the orders of creation provide significant resources for Christian ethics. This explains why we are not surprised by pagans and persons of various religious traditions being good spouses, neighbors, employees, and parents. Creation and humanity is infused with a logic that gives some access to the good which is God. As we will see, the distinction between Creator and creation limits the reliability of any good that can be known *a priori*. Additionally, the noetic effect of sin requires a significant humility towards any kind of natural theology. This does not preclude any appeal to an ethic grounded in creation. Rather, the teleological connection of creation in and through the Logos provides significant objective grounding for Christian ethics.

This objectively grounded *telos* is not self-evident, as some apologists have argued. Therefore, the content of the good revealed in Jesus and creation becomes particularly important for apologetics. If the logic of this presupposition were self-evident, then the correct estimation of the content of the good is unnecessary for apologetics. Showing that Christ is the objective grounding of the good would preclude any necessary judgment on the part of the hearer. All persons shown that Jesus is good would certainly desire to follow his good Way. In contemporary culture, claims that Jesus is good are often met with the objection that he was no better than other great religious geniuses such as Moses, Muhammad, or Gandhi.

Therefore, the content of the good becomes essential for apologetics when the theologian recognizes that the good is not self-evident but requires a presupposed theological claim. The role of the good for this apologetic construal is not simply the content of the Way that is proclaimed. The good persuades others because it is the way that they too were intended to be. It appears universally to be a good way of life. Proclamation of a message that claims to be good and is not persuades no one. All claims to truth and goodness require presuppositions. Thus the apologist recognizes the

85. Grenz, *Moral Quest*, 290.
86. Gunton, *Actuality of Atonement*, 157–59.

limitations of his claim to truth and goodness. Its persuasiveness is not in its objectivity. The good's persuasiveness is in the *a posteriori* perception of the experience of the good Way. Grounding the content of the good properly comes to the fore of this apologetic intention.

With these two ways forward — creation ethics and conformity with the *imago Dei* — I begin some preliminary suggestions on how Christians may proceed with their apologetic witness. In the next section I discuss the mode of thinking which creation ethics requires. The question of apologetic witness must always remain at the fore even while the mode of thinking does not seem explicitly apologetic, but rather dogmatic. Proceeding in this fashion is necessary because, as I suggested above, the apologist can be confident that a bold proclamation of the good will be received as such because the good has an undeniable draw upon those who were made in God's image. Though sin has a hold upon humanity that can only be broken by the grace of Jesus Christ, the very fact of our creation in the image of God suggests that we desire the Good which we were created to be.

In the section following the discussion of creation ethics, I will explain the mode of thinking required by the call of conformity with Christ's image. As discussed, this means more than simply asking the question "What would Jesus do?" Christians do not merely repeat the story of Christ in the Gospels; rather, they go forward in conformity with the character of Christ which the story of Christ in the Gospels' forms.

Grounding the Good: Creation Ethics

As we have seen from our analysis of Irenaeus, humanity is redeemed in and through its recapitulation in Jesus. Jesus fulfills the intention that God had for humanity. He is the incarnate grounding of the Logos. As such, the incarnation of the Logos necessarily makes Jesus the most fully human, the Last Adam. Jesus cannot become human as the Logos which created humanity without being the most fully human of all. For Irenaeus, "the conflict which Jesus had to undergo for His life to be fully human and the reverse of Adam's embraced the Resurrection also, and not merely the period up to his death."[87] The resurrection is the victory over death that came through Adam. In the recapitulation of man, creation, too, is restored to its proper *telos*. This is our first justification for a basis in creation, the teleological basis of creation. Creation has found its end in glorifying God.

---

87. Wingren, *Man and the Incarnation*, 127.

Jesus is also the ontic basis of the knowledge of creation.[88] This is the affirmation of Jesus as the divine Logos, which is the ontological basis for creation's ordering. This is what Barth describes as the covenant (the Word) as the "internal basis of creation."[89] "[God] created the universe in Jesus Christ. That is, Jesus Christ was the meaning and purpose of His creation of the universe. The latter [creation] was only the external basis, as it were, to make the covenant of grace technically possible."[90] Creation is such because God made a stage on which to display his glory and grace in the election of Jesus Christ. Therefore, creation in its very existence is consistent with the logic of grace that it puts on display. To be an appropriate place for the staging of God's redemptive story, creation was created consistently with the goodness of God.

On the basis of this ontic existence, Jesus is the noetic basis of creation. As the love of God is known in Jesus Christ, the Creator himself is known and creation is known in abstraction from the Creator's love. As we know God in Jesus Christ, creation "springs to meet us."[91] Because Jesus is known as Christ, God is known as Creator. Of these three bases, none can be known or helpful without the other two. Where we speak of one, the others lie behind it, analogous to the way all three persons lie behind speech of the works attributed individually to God the Father, Son, or Spirit.

The epistemic priority[92] of Christ, which springs forth from his position as the ontological and teleological basis of creation, requires dependence upon Christ for the ethical quest. The role of the philosophical quest for the good is thus subordinate to what has been revealed in Christ regarding creation. Paul claims that "since the creation of the world God's invisible qualities—his eternal power and his divine nature—have been clearly seen, being understood from what has been made, so that men are without excuse. For although they knew God, they neither glorified him as God nor gave thanks to him, but their thinking became futile and their foolish hearts were darkened" (Rom 1:20–1, NIV). Though certain achievements are made in the quest for knowledge of God, these are limited. Paul claims that power and divinity can be known, but also that those who gain this knowledge can still be considered foolish.

A stronger charge can be brought against general ethics than that of Paul: it simply is not Christian ethics. All foundation for general ethics is

88. Barth, *Church Dogmatics* III.4, 39.

89. Ibid.

90. Ibid., 40.

91. Ibid., 39.

92. I borrow this terminology from Barron, *Priority of Christ*, 133–90.

flawed by all-pervasive anthropocentricity.[93] General ethics is anthropo-centric because it "presupposes a human-centered understanding of the distinguishing characteristic of the human person . . . [which] lies in some dimension of human existence (e.g., the experience of being moral agents) or in some power that humans supposedly possess (such as rationality)."[94] In other words, general ethics assumes that the reason humanity must be moral is because it has some innate quality which enables its moral agency. Likewise, the end of general ethics is the betterment of humanity, personal or social. Neither of these anthropocentricities is Christian because the foundational basis for Christian ethics must be that God is glorified.[95]

Admittedly, some general ethical programs have significant appeal to Christian ethics. Most notable among these is what Grenz calls naturalism. Natural ethics appeals to the way things are (ontology) to derive the way things should be (ethics).

> Viewed from a Christian perspective, naturalism has much to commend it. More readily than intuitionism, naturalism makes ethical judgments a topic for discussion and deliberation, thereby opening the door (at least theoretically) to the develop-ment of a consensual ethic, an understanding of the ethical life born of the give-and-take of life together. In contrast to its other rival, noncognitivism (or emotivism), naturalism presupposes the fundamental objectivity of ethical assertions. In arguing that moral judgments have as their basis what is built into our humanness or in the nature of the world, naturalism assumes that moral judgments have some link to the world beyond the subjectivity of the speaker.[96]

In spite of its advantage of providing an objective grounding for ethics, its anthropocentricity makes naturalism untenable as a Christian ethic as well. Rather, naturalism requires a transformation to genuinely be called Chris-tian. Christian ethics are not founded on how things are, but how God wills them to be. Naturalism's appeal to the way things are is muted by Chris-tian eschatology. Though a look towards creation is helpful in determining what God's will is, creation is not all that God has called it to be. Therefore, Christian ethics must look towards the world as *creation*, not *nature*. As such, creation has no authority in itself to make claims upon what is good because its authority lies only in the divine will. In naturalism, nature claims

93. Grenz, *Moral Quest*, 216. On this subject, Grenz sounds a great deal like Barth.
94. Ibid., 217.
95. Ibid., 218.
96. Ibid., 222.

authority based on its own propriety. True authority for how things ought to be is found in God's will. To view creation as creation is to recognize that its role in ethical reflection is not primarily epistemological, though some insight might be gained from this inquiry. What persons recognize as good among creation is, however, based upon the goodness of its Creator.

Like Irenaeus before him, Oliver O'Donovan focuses significant grounding for special ethics on the idea that Jesus does not just vindicate humanity, but all creation. Jesus was not "resurrected" to a disembodied Gnostic escape from the present world. Neither did God redeem humanity by destroying his creation into which Jesus entered. Jesus entered creation as Creator. As O'Donovan explains, to confess the "natural" world as creation is already to proclaim its order. Because it is order based on a Creator and not randomness, that order reliably points towards that to which it is ordered, God.

O'Donovan goes on to explain that this teleological ordering can be observed in creation, though it is not self-evident. As Aquinas explained, to say something is good is to say that it has a desirable end. The only pure teleological ordering is creation to Creator.[97] All orderings within creation itself are to some extent an ordering alongside, because each shares at least the similarity of being created beings. God's radical transcendence prevents this kind of ordering alongside. God is not a being like other beings. Therefore any analogy between created things and God will be only analogy. Creatures share both generic relations and teleological relations, however. The generic relations, while important, are not our primary concern in discerning the Good. They nevertheless aid in discerning teleological ordering.

One of O'Donovan's examples is that vegetables are ordered to humanity as food.[98] This may appear self-evident at face value. But how does one discern the teleological difference between an oak tree and a carrot? The generic similarities of vegetables, which taste good and provide nutrients, assist our judgment. We can also properly observe other creatures and their common use of vegetables for food. These things taken together help us identify food as the proper *telos* of vegetables. Unfortunately this revelation is not clear from Scripture and does not seem to be written in a hidden "read-me" file in the carrot's DNA. Rather, we discern from these mixed sources its proper use. Barth's discussion of vegetarianism is telling in this regard. Barth, drawing upon Scripture, insists regarding vegetables that "man may and should exercise his creaturely and relative sovereignty by using them as

97. O'Donovan, *Resurrection and Moral Order*, 33.
98. Ibid.

food." He describes such as the "sensible use of its superfluity."[99] At the same time he reservedly allows the death of animal for human use, but equates it to something close to homicide and reserved for necessity.[100] As with most things, though animals are not intended to be killed for meat, this may be an acceptable use, a secondary good. This is how the generic relations of things help us to discern their proper *telos*. Vegetables' proper ordering as food means that using them as food is good. We can, of course, only make this claim presupposing that God who ordered them in such a manner is good. Once presupposed, this ordering provides significant guidance in determining the ethical use of a class of created things. To use vegetables as food is good, but to use animals as food is, at best, a less bad choice than a person starving. This teleological ordering provides guidance for ethical use.

This ordering also helps discern that for which vegetables may not be used. If vegetables are to be used as food, then persons must ask whether it is good to use them for something else. Technology allows the creation and use of alternative fuels from foods such as corn. Does vegetables' teleological ordering as food preclude their use as fuel? This is not necessary. As discussed above with eating animals, a thing may have more than one good use. But the apparent oddity of using vegetables as fuel should surprise us. Additionally, the relatively new phenomenon of corn-based alternative fuels has artificially inflated the price of this vegetable in world markets. The use of vegetables as fuel paired with the large amount of vegetables and grains consumed in using animals as food has caused a worldwide inflation of food prices.[101] Though a teleologically astute person may or may not have discerned the consequences of using vegetables as fuel prior to the shortage, he could have discerned it as an improper use and predicted that it was not properly sustainable. Of course, ethics may allow for the use of something outside of God's intention for it because of necessity, but this does not make it good. Determining whether a thing is being used in conformity with its *telos* or some other acceptable use requires discernment. To be able to discern conformity of a thing with its *telos*, one must know its purpose and be able to make a judgment regarding conformity. This is what it means to be wise.[102] Therefore testing truthfulness requires knowledge of a thing's *telos*, what God intended it to be.

This extended discussion of God's purpose for vegetables is but a single inquiry into how the orders of creation provide an entry point to

99. Barth, *Church Dogmatics* III.4, 351.

100. Ibid., 352–55.

101. Pimentel, "Ethanol Fuels," 131–32.

102. For a discussion of wisdom as judgment, see Vanhoozer, *First Theology*, 347–50.

an objective grounding of the good. Apologetically, this argument would function by providing guidance to environmental and political ethicists concerning the possible evils of improper use of vegetables. The Christian ethicist and apologist can have confidence that when she does her ethics well, the consequences of unethical action and the benefits of her ethical suggestions will become clear to the world, which may or may not be listening. Of course, discerning the will of God for vegetables is not certain even with the help of the orders of creation and the revelation of Scripture. But the ethicist's apologetic witness relies upon the proper ordering of creation to the good, which is reliable because it is found in God. Therefore, any humble contribution to the discussion of proper use of corn can be made with some confidence that improper usage will inevitably result in consequences that are not good. Apologetic arguments will be successful where the Christian account of proper uses of vegetables proves to be truthful. Apologetic arguments will fail where the Christian account of proper uses of vegetables is inadequate or socially and environmentally destructive.

This may at first glance appear to be a type of Pelagian heresy: "When Christians propose a proper ethic, then they will earn favor with God and with humanity." Or, it may appear to be naive: "When Christians get their theology correct, all kinds of people will want submit to Christ." While these errors are real for some, they are not the position of a properly ordered apologetic ethics. Appealing to the orders of creation gives grounding for a confident proclamation of the truth of Christian doctrine in a field hostile to it. If creation is ordered according to the goodness of God, then a proper Christian account of the world will prove to be the most good and true account of the world. This is a reliable apologetic witness.

The Christian account of humanity is the most vital aspect of Christian's apologetic witness. Postmodern culture has accepted the demise of teleological explanations for most things. The scientist does not question the proper use of corn when considering fuel alternatives. Rather, the only question is the feasibility and effects of its use. But the idea of people having a purpose still has a hold on us. The unprecedented success of the recent "Purpose-Driven Life" franchise is but one evidence of this.

To consider humanity's *telos* is to only consider a particular *telos* within the more generic ordering of creation, all of which finds its end in God. Humanity finds itself at the privileged place of responsibility and honor of "naming" the animals, the responsibility of creation's steward. The Old Testament anthropology which considers humanity to be "lacking a very little of God" still recognizes humanity as creation, yet the head of creation.[103]

---

103. O'Donovan, *Resurrection and Moral Order*, 38.

Like all creation, the chief end of humanity is to "glorify God and enjoy Him forever." Humanity's stewardship over creation is primarily a responsibility to direct creation towards, or not prohibit it from, achieving its end in God. Beyond this teleological explanation, little can be said that does not properly belong to Christology. Because Jesus has fulfilled humanity's *telos* as the *imago Dei*, anthropology is properly but one segment within Christology. We have taken this up above and will again below. Within this section regarding the created order it is enough to say that humanity's status is that of being ordered with creation as a creature, but also of having been given the privileged task of ordering creation, with God, towards God.

EXCURSUS: CREATION ETHICS AND NATURAL THEOLOGY

Though this creation ethics insists that it is based upon Christian dogma and not philosophical presuppositions, the functional difference between creation ethics and natural theology may seem unclear. It is a preference for the former over the latter which makes this argument implicitly a postliberal one. The teleological ordering of creation appears to be just one species of natural theology that attempts to discern the "natural" purposes of a created thing. Barth acknowledged that, within the Roman conception, moral philosophy was dependent upon moral theology. He was correct, but dependent for what?

O'Donovan argues that moral philosophy has a place in discerning the good. Creation retains its order in spite of its brokenness. Therefore, revelation is unnecessary to observe the various forms of ordering inherent to creation. Philosophy often discerns virtue, social ordering, duties and the proper response to this ordering independent of theology. However, as Barth explained, moral philosophy will inevitably lose its course without the help of moral theology. But why is this the case? Or, what is the role of moral theology in the task of moral philosophy? The former properly takes priority over the latter, but the latter occupies a proper place.

Theology's task is to provide an overarching intelligibility of the whole. Creation must be known as creation and in relationship to the Creator to be known fully. Philosophy may understand various aspects of the created order, but if creation is not known in its relationship to the Creator, then the whole is misunderstood. "The very contingency of the universe points us beyond itself towards the transcendent Creator on whom its intelligibility depends; so that Paul can say that the invisible God is seen through the comprehension of the things which he has made (Rom 1:20)."[104]

When philosophy identifies a truth, it does so only as a partial truth. Order is not known in pieces, but as a whole.[105] A jigsaw puzzle is extremely difficult to assemble without one's having seen the completed picture as a guide to assembly.[106] Likewise, dogmatic theology provides a framework by which the conclusions of philosophy may be interpreted and properly ordered within creation. "If we know the value of the family, and do not know its relation to individual freedom, then we have misunderstood even the family." Misunderstanding of particular points of the whole is the cause of idolatry in which a part is allowed to interpret the whole.[107]

Therefore knowledge gained from philosophical inquiry need not be denied entirely. Neither can it be built upon as a foundation. The only foundation that can serve the whole is the revelation of God in Christ.[108] Philosophical inquiry can therefore be affirmed for its insights, but itself is dependent upon theology to interpret even its most humble conclusions and properly place them within a more complete understanding of the world. The moral philosopher's conclusions are therefore affirmed for what they are, a limited attestation to the goodness of God revealed in Christ.

> The moral thinker, therefore, has no need to proceed in a totalitarian way, denying the importance and relevance of all that he finds valued as moral conviction in the various cultures and traditions of the world (whether these be 'Christian,' 'non-Christian' or 'post-Christian'). He has no need to prove that anything worthwhile in them has arisen historically from Christian influence. But neither can he simply embrace the perspectives of any such culture, not even—which is most difficult to resist—the one to which he happens to belong and which therefore claims him as an active participant. He cannot set about building a theological ethic upon the moral *a priori* of a liberal culture,

104. O'Donovan, *Resurrection and Moral Order*, 88.

105. Ibid.

106. This analogy is only an analogy. Obviously a puzzle can eventually be completed by trial and error. Philosophy cannot complete its task by a similar method because the "fit" of each piece is not as obvious as a puzzle. The philosopher will often "remove" pieces that seem uncertain and are yet correct and will often "place" pieces where they seem to fit without being able to discern confidently whether the fit is appropriate.

107. O'Donovan, *Resurrection and Moral Order*, 89.

108. Even use of the word foundation here can lead to unfortunate conclusions' do not mean a foundation in the same way Cartesian epistemology means it. Even revelation is not a foundation which can bear the weight of an expansive structure because the human builder of the structure will inevitably make a corrupting error.

a revolutionary culture or any other kind of culture; for that is to make of theology an ideological justification for the cultural constructs of human misknowledge. He can only approach these phenomena critically, evaluating them and interpreting their significance from the place where true knowledge of the moral order is given, under the authority of the gospel. From that position alone can be discerned what there is to be found in these various moral traditions that may be of interest or value.[109]

This construal gives priority to the Gospel in determining the merits of philosophical inquiry but does not give space for philosophy to set the agenda. This is the concern that Barth had with apologetics as a discipline and properly so. In the paragraphs following the above quote, O'Donovan explains that this dilemma is the one in which Barth honed his argument and disagreement with Brunner on the subject of the role of apologetics. Brunner emphasized a scripture-less apologetic.[110] This is acceptable to neither Barth's dogmatics nor my apologetic construal. While the individual accomplishments of philosophical inquiry can be affirmed, these accomplishments require the guiding lens of dogmatic biblical theology to make sense of particular perceptions. The appropriateness of the lens provided is the apologetic witness and defense of the Christian faith.

Conversely, "natural theology" serves as an apologetic by presumably "proving" the truth of Christian faith without recourse to Christian dogma. This position is unsatisfying because it presumes a lack of presuppositions, which is easily deconstructed. The "lens" from which the argument is viewed is that of an objective observer, a myth of Enlightenment discourse.[111] The classification of "natural theology" as a project of Enlightenment rationality should surprise us. Thomas Aquinas is the supposed genesis of this natural theology in the Christian tradition, and he preceded the Enlightenment. However, the type of natural theology that would make this claim is actually that of the nineteenth and twentieth century neoscholastic theologians.[112] If Nicholas Wolterstorff's analysis of Aquinas is correct, and I think it is, then the version of "natural theology" which I have presented here is actually only a caricature of Thomas and at least some Thomists.[113] Aquinas was

---

109. O'Donovan, *Resurrection and Moral Order*, 89–90.

110. Ibid., 90–91.

111. See Wolterstorff, "What New Haven and Grand Rapids Have to Say to Each Other," 257–59.

112. Barron, *Priority of Christ*, 146.

113. Wolterstorff explains that Aquinas' "natural theology" was but the highest of the ways which a well-developed person of faith contemplated Christian truth. This was done primarily so that the one who contemplated nature would have increased

clear in his biblical commentary and in the opening question of the *Summa Theologica* that it was impossible to attain true knowledge of God without revelation. The inquirer's knowledge of God "*such as reason can know it,* would only be known of a few, and that after a long time, and *with the admixture of many errors.*"[114] However, the caricature is not unwarranted, for it is the clear position of some of these later natural theologians.[115] In any case, it is the version of natural theology that Barth critiqued. It shares the key presupposition of the apologetics with which he was concerned, a methodological atheism. The creation ethics I have sketched above, following O'Donovan, avoids these concerns because theology is the guiding presupposition of all apologetic arguments. Rather than arguing that there is good and therefore there must be God, this apologetics argues that there is God and therefore there must be Good, followed by the question, "Do you not agree that this is good?"

GROUNDING THE GOOD: CONFORMING TO THE IMAGE

The ethical framework sketched above declares the primary ethical task of the Christian to be conformity with the image of God, Jesus Christ. Christian ethics that proceeds in this manner has two dangers that must constantly be avoided. The first is characterized by Kant's image of Jesus as the manifestation of universal moral norm. When Jesus is taken only as an archetype of human morality, then the difference between Jesus and humanity is only a matter of degree. This is unsatisfying for Nicaean Christology. A derivative of this Kantian Christology results in an overemphasis upon the historical-critical analysis of the person Jesus of Nazareth. While the former makes Jesus the archetypal man by positing a universal moral norm which precedes Jesus and which he enacts, the latter particularizes Jesus such that Christianity attempts to recover the teaching of a first century Jewish moral genius. His historical particularity therefore prevents speculations regarding the universal effect of the incarnation.

---

joy because of their intellectual accomplishment. However, the grand difficulties with this kind of inquiry make it clear that it was never intended as an apologetic witness in the vein of evidentialist apologetics. Wolterstorff, "Migration of the Theistic Arguments," 56–74.

114. Aquinas, *Summa Theologica* I, q. 1, a. 1. See also Barron, *Priority of Christ,* 146–52.

115. See Long, *Speaking of God,* 68. Long mentions Jean Porter, Romanus Cessario, Linda Zagzebski and, in a "nuanced and qualified way," Denys Turner as contemporary examples of this type of thought.

Robert Barron, a postliberal Catholic theologian, traces these two tendencies and suggests a way forward for a Christian ethic which insists upon Jesus Christ as the true *imago Dei*. Jesus as the manifestation of a universal moral morality is the project of the Enlightenment, and especially Immanuel Kant. According to Barron, Kant imagines the Gospel of Jesus to be "construed as an especially powerful and accurate exemplification of the moral ideal and hence as a particularly effective spur to moral excellence."[116] Regardless of the historical veracity of anything Jesus said, did, or was, the true import of Jesus' morality is the image of morality that he excites in persons. Kant is responding to the Enlightenment need for certainty that no amount of historical integrity can provide due to the lack of credibility of any historical source. Enlightenment rationality can never achieve the kind of certainty necessary for knowledge from historical investigation. This is detrimental to a faith founded upon a particular historical figure to which no direct access is available.[117] Kant therefore minimized the historical person of Jesus in favor of the rational, which was accessible universally and, so Kant thought, unambiguously. Clearly the problem with Kant's Christology is its failure to affirm Nicaea. Barron categorizes Kant among the Nestorians because he clearly constructs Jesus as "God-bearer," a position that was declared anathema at Ephesus in 431.[118] His Christology fails to adequately proclaim Christ as ontologically one with God.

Another Enlightenment reaction to the need for certitude has been the project of a historical-critical "quest for the historical Jesus." The only significant difference here is the philosophical reliability of historical investigation. Historical critics argued that Jesus' teaching and morality could be discovered from the Gospel accounts. Multiple pictures of Jesus have resulted from this project with little consensus. The common trait which most of these positions share is a philosophically modernistic materialism. Miracles and the supernatural are exchanged for Enlightenment certitude, and dogmatic theology is dispensed with in favor of Harnack's Hellenization thesis.[119]

Barron looks favorably upon these historical critics because they have provided a service to the church, which has devoured Kantian religion of morality and Schleiermacher's neo-pietism with it. Historical critics have reminded theologians that unmitigated speculation must be resisted in favor of biblically-informed Christology. Christianity must resist the

---

116. Barron, *Priority of Christ*, 26.

117. Ibid., 27.

118. Ibid., 33–34.

119. Ibid., 36–47.

temptation to become a generic philosophy.[120] However, much of the program of historical criticism is deeply problematic because it dismisses the church's tradition of biblical interpretation and reflection. The way forward, then, includes considerable investigation into the person of Jesus of Nazareth without assuming philosophical materialism and antidogmatism. By attending to the historical account of Jesus as a guiding principle, theology avoids excess speculation in a way analogous to the limitation placed on figural readings by the literal (or "plain-sense") reading of Scripture in patristic four-fold interpretation.[121] However, generations of theological investigation have yielded considerable dogmatic fruit. Without the ecumenical council's decrees guiding theological conclusions, modern exegesis is tempted to repeat the errors of the past.

I would suggest a framework for proper consideration of the historical person of Jesus by means of a dialogue with the proposals of Wolfhart Pannenberg. After determining the role of the historical Jesus in determining dogma, I will then attempt to apply this principle to making claims about ethics. Pannenberg's methodology must be both appreciated and critiqued, but he provides a helpful conversation partner going forward.

Pannenberg takes historical concerns quite seriously, though he too has methodological problems. Pannenberg presumes a methodological antidogmatism. And Pannenberg seems to succumb to a clear heresy that is certainly adoptionist and likely Pelagian as well.[122] Adherence to the church's dogma would avoid these heresies and the theological consequences that come with them. These concerns are not insignificant, but they may be set aside for the moment to observe what can be learned from his use of history.

Pannenberg claims that Christology must be *"pursued* 'from below.'" Pannenberg's choice of words is unfortunate because they remind the reader of the Ebionite heresy, but Pannenberg is suggesting a research trajectory for theologians, not the trajectory for the incarnation of the Word. Pannenburg's own conclusions may be adoptionist, but this is not a necessary conclusion of his methodology. What Pannenberg means by a Christology pursued "from below" is that dogmatic Christological conclusions must begin with an investigation of the historical Jesus. He outlines a history of Christological methodology "from above," which extends from Ignatius and the Apologists, through the "Alexandrians," and up to Karl Barth.[123] Three key characteristics of this strand are rejected. First, Christology should not

---

120. Ibid., 42.

121. Ayres, "Patristic and Medieval Theologies of Scripture," 14–17.

122. See, for example, Pannenberg, *Jesus, God and Man*, 350–51.

123. Ibid., 33–35.

presuppose the divinity of Jesus because presenting reasons for concluding Jesus is the Christ is the most important task. Second, Christology "from above" rarely considers the relationships between Jesus of Nazareth, the Judaism of his time, and the Old Testament with their proper significance. Third, persons cannot stand outside of the world of experience "in order to follow the way of God's Son into the world."[124] The historical Jesus is the only point of authentic investigation because the incarnation is otherwise beyond our imagination.

Pannenberg's points are well-taken, though I suggest his account misses the point. The theologians which Pannenberg critiques presume the work of an earlier generation of theologians which concluded that Jesus is the Christ from historical investigation and then went on to investigate the metaphysical consequences of such a claim. By the time of Ignatius, the church's proclamation regarding the divinity of Christ had become quite clear. This claim was contrasted against both Gnostic and Roman imperial paganisms' "incarnations." Even by the second century, the church proclaimed Jesus as Christ based on historical conclusions, but this proclamation demanded further explanation because of the infiltration of heretical claims (especially Gnostic claims) similar to the ones made by Christians.[125]

Therefore Christology must simultaneously proceed along two paths that are logically sequential. First, because of the historical testimony surrounding the life of Jesus of Nazareth, Christology must determine the relationship between Jesus and the God of Israel. There is no need to presume objectivity in this endeavor. As I have suggested repeatedly, objective investigation is an oft-repeated myth of the Enlightenment. Rather, the theologian investigates the historical testimony of Jesus from the position of one who has submitted her life to Jesus Christ. The second path of Christological investigation concerns the philosophical dilemma(s) that the mystery of the incarnation brings to the fore. Neither of these paths may be neglected in dogmatic theology or evangelistic and apologetic witness.

The former path is the one with which Pannenberg concerns himself, primarily for its obviously apologetic purposes. For Pannenberg, as for the first century Christians, the defining historical event that leads one to necessarily conclude that Jesus is the Son of God is his resurrection from the dead. While this miracle is problematic for modern materialism, it is as historically verifiable as most other historical events by academic standards. N. T. Wright's recent eight-hundred-page volume, *The Resurrection*

---

124. Ibid., 35.

125. Grillmeier, *Christ in Christian Tradition, Volume One*, 85–105; Behr, *Way to Nicaea*, 83–86.

of the Son of God, shows that the historical claim has academic credence.[126] Wright and Pannenberg agree on at least one critical point: in the first century Jewish milieu, the resurrection of the one who claimed to be the Son of Man could mean nothing other than the consummation of the world as God intended it to be. The end times had arrived in the present. Evaluation of Jewish apocalyptic material and a survey of ancient beliefs about the body and resurrection reveal that the apostles' claim of his resurrection could only mean that he had been raised to life into a transformed body.

The proclamation of Jesus' resurrection to the first century Jew must have meant that the hoped for future had begun in Jesus. This evaluation provides three relevant realms of investigation into the historical work of God in Jesus Christ. Playing freely with popular culture's ethical question "What would Jesus do?" I suggest that at least three similar questions can and should be asked.

What did Jesus do? This is the question of the historical work of Jesus of Nazareth and particularly his teaching. This question is most closely related to the office of prophet that is classically attributed to Jesus. Jesus came critiquing the Jewish community with which he considered himself to be in full continuity. Jesus cannot be separated from the Jewish prophetic tradition of calling the people of God to repentance for their neglecting proper worship of God, commitment to the poor and sick, and their covenantal commitment to peace and justice. This prophetic call was not therefore to a set of ethical laws and prohibitions, but to a way of being. Taking on this way of being, the Christian *ethos* is the process of becoming like Jesus. Simply doing the things Jesus did is not to take on Jesus' *ethos* as the living prophet. Rather, one must be transformed into a new way of being that is in conformity with Christ's image.

Similarly, the Christian must also ask *"What is Jesus doing?"* This is a question about the priestly office of Jesus, a task and office which has been extended to the whole church in the words of Peter: "[You,] like living stones, are being built into a spiritual house to be a holy priesthood, offering spiritual sacrifices acceptable to God through Jesus Christ . . . You are a chosen people, a royal priesthood, a holy nation, a people belonging to God . . . *Live such good lives among the pagans that, though they accuse you of doing wrong, they may see your good deeds and glorify God on the day he visits us"* (1 Pet 2:5–12, NIV, emphasis mine). The purpose of the priesthood is that of mediator between God and people. Of course, in the words of the author of Hebrews, Jesus is the Great High Priest. But the task of showing the world what God is like is not only for Jesus Christ, but the whole church. The

126. N. T. Wright, *Resurrection of the Son of God.*

answer to the question "*What is Jesus doing?*" in every age must be answered by a discussion of what the body of Christ, the church, is doing.

Christ's office as King is most closely related to the question of "*What will Jesus do?*" To speak about anything as good, it is necessary to determine for what purpose it exists. Likewise, determining in what sense the Christian ethics is good ethics, one must know what is the good end that serves as a canon of conformity. Jesus is returning as Lord of the entire universe, as the Apocalypse of John describes, and indeed already occupies that place in heaven since the ascension. The answer to the question "*What will Jesus do?*" is found in the message of the imminent Kingdom and the consummation of all things under Jesus' Lordship.

Though I divide these offices and the questions associated with them here for pedagogical and illustrative purposes, a clear demarcation of the office of King into the distant future is inappropriate, not only because the Kingdom has come "already," but also because the office of King has extended back at least since Jesus' ascension and could arguably be extended to the reign of David. Likewise, Jesus' prophetic ministry in the past is inherited by him from Israel's prophets and extends to the church's contemporary ministry. Of course, Jesus' ministry as priest does not stop when the kingdom comes in final glory. Rather, I liken these offices as proper to particular parts of Jesus' ministry, though extending beyond them. Augustine explains the inseparable operations of the Trinity by saying, "The Son indeed and not the Father was born of the Virgin Mary; but this very birth of the Son, not of the Father, was the work of the Father and the Son. The Father indeed suffered not, but the Son, yet the suffering of the Son was the work of the Father and the Son."[127] In classical Trinitarian theology, the persons each maintain particular actions, but the work is attributed to the Trinity. The whole Trinity sends forth the Son in particular to do the work of the whole Trinity. If the persons of the Trinity cannot be discerned to have separable operations, then neither can offices be made clearly separate with the one person of Jesus.

What Did Jesus Do?

The Christian must ask this question, not only to understand the person Jesus was, being the truest *imago Dei*,[128] but also who the Christian is to be.

---

127. Augustine, *Sermon* 52.8.

128. Though *imago dei* is properly applied to persons made in God's image, Jesus is the image of God in the stronger sense that we saw above in the interpretation of Hebrews.

Jesus' character must become the character of the Christian. To simply repeat the actions of Jesus is misplaced because Jesus' historical particularity limits the usefulness of his recorded actions. It becomes impossible, for example, to know how Jesus would participate in democracy in America by surveying his participation in government and politics in first century Palestine under Roman monarchy. There is no useful equivalency. Rather, the goal of the Christian ethics in this mode is to understand the character of the person of Jesus through his actions and teaching. What stance did he take towards particular kinds of immorality? How did he regard society? With which matters of moral import was he most concerned? By understanding how Jesus responded to a particular historical situation, the Christian begins to understand something of the divine *ethos*. To take on this divine *ethos*, which Paul called being "transformed by the renewing of your mind," enables one to test what God's good and pleasing will is (Romans 12:1–2). This is why seminaries and churches appropriately use the term "spiritual formation" to describe the process of discipleship. One cannot simply change their behaviors to be like those of Jesus, but must have their character changed to be like his character. How does one go from a story about a first century Palestinian Jew to a Christian *ethos* in twenty-first century Western culture? Understanding the role of the Gospel's narrative about Jesus can be drawn from an analogy to character performance in dramatic theory.[129]

Kevin Vanhoozer surveys the techniques of method acting developed by actor and director Constantin Stanislavski, and applies these techniques to the process of spiritual formation. Rather than teaching symbolic actions that represent particular emotions, such as dancing or particular styles of diction, Stanislavski taught actors to imagine themselves within the persona of the person they were portraying. The emotions and inward experience of the actor was then portrayed because they were actually being experienced on stage. The actor strives to imagine how they would respond in the situation of the character that they are portraying. Stanislavski would encourage his actors to do extensive research into their character and even invent details that were not given about the character. This gave them the fullest conception of the character possible and formed them in the person they were meant to portray.[130]

Vanhoozer relates this to how Scripture and the church's doctrine should be used as a script that causes the Christian to perceive the role that they are called to play. Because Scripture is the authoritative source for the

129. For more on the *analogia dramatis* and similar concepts, see Vanhoozer, *Drama of Doctrine*; Wells, *Improvisation*; and N. T. Wright, *New Testament and the People of God*, 140–43.

130. Vanhoozer, *Drama of Doctrine*, 369–74.

character at a previous historical point, the actor is then called to improvise the actions that the character would perform in this situation. The performance must be believable as consistent with the character portrayed. Two dangers must be avoided. The actor must avoid pre-planning the action before actual performance. This manipulates the situation and the other actors by usurping control of the performance. The danger to a performance of the Christian *ethos* is that each new situation will demand the embodiment of a whole host of Christians who improvise an appropriate response. Because no one Christian's response can be taken as authoritative for the priesthood of all believers, each individual must contribute to the performance without wresting control of it according to a preplanned idea of the Christian ethical response.[131]

A second concern when improvising is the temptation to be original. Improvisation is not to be confused with ad-libbing. Random action is out of harmony with the other performers and is inconsistent with the previous actions of the character performed. Vanhoozer adds that an improv actor, like the jazz musician, is responsible to the idea of the piece. The import for Christian ethics brings us directly back to the role of Scripture, which is the authoritative source for performance of the Christian *ethos*. A Christian therefore cannot "ad-lib" on Christian ethics because of the authoritative source of true *imago Dei*, Jesus. "Ad-libbing is the theatrical equivalent of heresy, where one person stubbornly insists on going his own way instead of playing the game."[132] In improvisation, therefore, memory takes a central role in performance. Christian ethicists, like improvisers, are like a person walking backwards, who sees where he has been and not where he is going.[133] The Christian ethicist must therefore look backward and ask "*What was Jesus doing?*" in order to understand how to perform the Christian *ethos* in contemporary improvisation.

What Is Jesus Doing?

Scripture calls the church the "body of Christ." Luke makes it clear that the reason the church can be named such is because of her relationship with the Holy Spirit. The same Spirit which came upon Jesus at his baptism (Luke 3:22) came upon the church at Pentecost (Acts 2:1–4). This pneumatological rendering of the church makes it possible to claim that the church is the "body of Christ"; this designation implies that Jesus' work is the work done

131. Ibid., 337.

132. Ibid., 338.

133. Ibid., 339.

by the Holy Spirit through the church. As Stanley Hauerwas has said, "there can be no separation of christology from ecclesiology, that is, Jesus from the church."[134] The work the church is called to is primarily the task of the priesthood, a calling affirmed by the biblical injunction for the church to be a "royal priesthood and a holy nation." James William McClendon points out that this was already the biblical injunction towards Israel: "The Sinai covenant did not authorize a kingdom *with* priests (what nation did not have such?) but a kingdom *of* priests, one in which by God's commission *all* were holy" (emphasis in original).[135] As Peter said, this priesthood's primary task is to live in such a way that others "may see your good deeds and glorify God" (1 Pet 2:12). The question *"What is Jesus doing?"* is primarily a question about the mission of the church, and therefore is primarily a question about a community's ethic.

Stanley Grenz argues that this aspect of the Christian ethic accords well with many postmodern construals of ethics. Many contemporary ethicists favor a virtue theory of ethics that derives a concept of the good from a traditioned community's standards of ethics. The virtuous person is one who acts in accord with the standards of virtue of the community. Enlightenment ethics often preferred an anthropological construction that rendered the individual as an empty vessel that *did* good or bad things.[136] Foundational to virtue ethics is the idea that ethical judgments are constituted within a particular community. Grenz insists that Christians have always known this, insofar as they self-identify in baptism and gathering for worship and thanksgiving.[137]

The fundamental guidance for this community arises from the biblical narrative; Christians are indeed a "people of the book." The community's historiography is centered within this particular telling of its narrative, which reveals the community's current place in the narrative. The church is the community empowered by the Spirit to do Christ's work in the world between Christ's ascension and his return. Christ's work is the work of the priest, doing good works so that others may glorify God. By observing the priestly work of the historical Christ in the biblical narrative, the church learns to feed, heal, and forgive. By observing the priestly work of the body of Christ, the church, the world learns to feed, heal, and forgive.

By performing these tasks, her unique claim to community with God and neighbor is displayed for the world as the image of God, which is the

---

134. Hauerwas, *Community of Character*, 37.

135. McClendon, *Witness*, 360.

136. Grenz, *Moral Quest*, 209–10.

137. Ibid., 231–32.

essence of the priestly task. While other communitarian ethics may claim to have equal standing with the Christian one, only the church pursues ethics after the true *imago Dei*. This claim is logically circular, but all presuppositional conceptions of rationality are such. The coherence of the whole Christian conception of rationality reveals its truthfulness. The Christian's apologetic argument consists of a reaffirmation of Christian doctrine's truthfulness.

Jesus is not physically present in contemporary society. But the body of Christ, the church, is actively participating in ministry in business, medicine, military and public service. Each of these ministries requires a Christian interpretation of the ethical life. In this sense, the question of "*What is Jesus doing?*" is bound to the question of what is the worldwide catholic church doing. For all of her failures throughout history, the church has been doing the work of Christ since her constitution by the Holy Spirit at Pentecost. The priestly ministry of Christ is the service of the church to the world.

What Will Jesus Do?

The creation ethics described above was clear to designate between what the world is and into what it will be transformed. This final question concerns the *telos* of creation, which can only properly be discerned from the resurrection and ascension of Christ as two distinct moments of the central event of Christ's life, the former is the backward-looking restoration of all that God intended humanity to be, the latter being the forward-looking movement of Jesus towards the right hand of the Father "from whence he will come to judge the living and the dead." The creed's affirmation of the ascension of Christ is closely tied to his future return as King and Lord to judge the nations.

Certain strands of Christianity have rightly stressed the radical nature of the love and forgiveness of Christ, and yet have failed to equally affirm the judgment seat that Jesus occupies and will exercise. Anyone whose name is not written in the book of life will be judged according to their deeds and will suffer punishment at the Great White Throne judgment (Rev 20:11–15). Those who have followed the way of Jesus will enjoy eternity in the peaceful presence of the Almighty.[138]

This rhetoric is particularly problematic for enlightened thinkers. God is love, grace and mercy. Many think this means he cannot therefore be full of wrath; the two are considered mutually exclusive. However, as

138. For a vivid explication of the biblical evidence, see Menzies and Horton, *Bible Doctrines*, 243–52.

Miroslav Volf has written, "A 'nice' God is a figment of the liberal imagination, a projection onto the sky of the inability to give up cherished illusions about goodness, freedom, and the rationality of social actors."[139] Volf is not critiquing goodness and freedom, but their realization among sinful persons. The "liberals" of whom Volf speaks imagine a God who goes on patiently waiting and trying to draw evildoers into God's loving embrace. This is the God of Scripture, but the obverse of God's love and patience is his vengeance on evil. Both "moderns" and "postmoderns" have critiqued this image of God as one that supposedly promotes religious violence.

Kant and his Enlightenment contemporaries were convinced that a full developed society would be free from violence as universal and autonomous reason controlled irrational violence. People's societal interdependence and the concentration of power in the state would reduce violence until non-existent.[140] Not only did human persons freed from religious impediments not reason their way to a peaceful coexistence, but since Kant, some of the greatest evils have been perpetrated on the largest scale. Volf suggests that the state's monopoly on power and societal control make grand atrocities such as the Holocaust possible. The state argues it is providing a service by creating a better state and is thus justified in its use of violence.[141] Neither can the other brand of enlightened peace-making, inter-religious dialogue, deliver promised peace. Not all wars, after all, are religious wars.[142] Each of these modern approaches assumed that the cause of violence was religion and its predisposition towards exclusion and judgment.

But does not Christianity promote such a religious violence, particularly in its vision of God's judgment as a tool of justice? If this is so, then violence is at the very heart of Christianity, and modernity was correct in excluding religious dialogue. Volf has shown that Christian conceptions of judgment are necessary if peace is a possibility. Not only did Jesus accept violence on the cross without returning violence, but he struggled against violence (albeit non-violently) throughout his life. The modern/postmodern critique of Christian violence is overturned by a theology of the cross. Moreover, the theology of Revelation is also among the Christian canon. Here Jesus returns to violently judge the nations. His judgment is final. "Why must God say the unrelenting 'no' to a world of injustice, deception, and violence in such a violent way?" asks Volf, and answers: Because the fantasy of nonviolence's persuasive power is a myth of the "civilized" West.

139. Volf, *Exclusion and Embrace*, 298.

140. Ibid., 279–80.

141. Ibid., 281.

142. Ibid., 286.

The theology of Revelation reflects the realization that nothing will change persons who are determined to be "beasts."[143] If God were to continue to wait patiently while violence persists, then God would be evil's collaborator. But violence is not the last word. God will destroy violence so that peace will have the last and unending word.

Whatever theology and ethics spring forth from the question *"What will Jesus do?"* God's judgment upon evil and the vindication of the persecuted must be the final word. In the intermediate period, the role of persons exercising temporal judgment is debatable. Volf argues that no retaliation or violence can be legitimated by religious arguments, though he concedes that nonviolence may be impossible in a fallen world of violence.[144] Oliver O'Donovan argues that God's final judgment does not preclude human's exercising penultimate judgment.[145] But no Christian account of the good that attempts to draw on the question *"What will Jesus do?"* can claim final judgment as the task of one who is not God, nor can such an account arrive at a kingdom of peace without the violent judgment of God preceding it.

CONCLUSION

This chapter has covered a great deal of ground—beginning with the ontology of D. Stephen Long and working through the account of aesthetics and ethics that make judgments about the truthfulness of the Christian narrative possible. The consistent thread that runs through this chapter is an ontological grounding for the transcendental predicates of being that is discernible by the observers of Christian faith and life and known most fully by participation in it. This is not to say that persons will not need to be taught to see the good, the beautiful, and the true. How they will be taught to do so will be the subject of the final chapter. But I have shown that each of these transcendentals is grounded in a stable and trustworthy ontological reality– the very being of God.

The first implication of postliberal theological reasoning for a postconservative apologetic is the need to appeal to both ethics and apologetics in the argument for Christian faith. Long provided a more thoroughgoing metaphysics than the one explicated by Lindbeck. The implication of adopting such metaphysics is the imperative to appeal to truth, goodness, and beauty that can be observed by all persons. Therefore a theological ethics and a theological aesthetics are their own apologetic. None of these

143. Ibid., 299–301.
144. Ibid., 305–6.
145. O'Donovan, *Ways of Judgment*.

transcendentals will have the logic of a formal argument. I will argue in the next chapter that this is no less applicable to truth than is the case for beauty and goodness. We need not be concerned about the lack of formal argument. As we will see, justification of religious truth claims is nevertheless possible.

3

Rational Justification in a Postliberal Mode

INTRODUCTION

As STATED IN CHAPTER 1, Lindbeck himself claims that postliberalism is bound to be skeptical about "apologetics and foundations." A "foundational" apologetics that "stands at the center of theology" is obviously a form of correlational apologetics. This project, however, is more concerned with the kind of foundations that are the aim of conservative apologetics. These too are a concern for Lindbeck, but not in such a way that he elaborates his criticism. Rather, he suggests that postliberal theology must exclude apologetics "that is systematically prior and controlling in the fashion of post-Cartesian natural theology." Presumably this is the "foundational or natural theology of the modern type" that he contrasts with Aquinas' "probable arguments."[1]

If Lindbeck is simply suggesting that apologetics cannot in the contemporary age appeal to a deductive argument from beliefs that are justified without reference to other beliefs (called "basic beliefs"), then he did not suggest anything beyond what most contemporary apologists accept. This is not to say that there are no classical apologists that do argue in this way.[2] But those that argue such are now the exception rather than the rule. In the first section of the chapter I will outline two common apologetic methods that also reject the classical foundationalism that Lindbeck is excluding. I will attempt to show in this section that rejecting classical foundationalism

1. Lindbeck, *Nature of Doctrine*, 115.

2. Geisler, *Christian Apologetics*; Sproul, Gerstner, and Lindsey, *Classical Apologetics*.

does not actually hinder the apologetic enterprise as Lindbeck seemed to think it would. This section will conclude by identifying Lindbeck's proposal as a particular kind of apologetic enterprise, that of the "cumulative case" method.

In the second section of this chapter, I will discuss whether competing narratives can be rationally compared, and will outline the criteria that may be used in making judgments between competing narratives according to the cumulative case notions of apologetics. This should provide relatively clear direction for the postliberal apologists as well as dispel the often-repeated notion that *ad hoc* apologetics turns out to be something less than apologetics after all.

COMMON APOLOGETIC METHODS THAT REJECT "POST-CARTESIAN NATURAL THEOLOGY"

Two common approaches to apologetics share the postliberal critique of foundationalism and the apologetics that springs from it. Before discussing these in depth, it helps to say that there is also a third approach that will not be considered. The presuppositionalist apologetics closely associated with Cornelius Van Til and John Frame also critiques classical foundationalism and proceeds with apologetics unabated.[3] For our purposes it will be enough to say that presuppositionalism is a more extreme and less philosophically sophisticated version of Reformed epistemology.[4] I will begin with the Reformed critique of foundationalism before I treat cumulative case apologetics, of which postliberal apologetics is but a particular case.

The Reformed Epistemologists' Critique of Classical Foundationalism

Philosopher/theologians Nicholas Wolterstorff and Alvin Plantinga edited a volume in 1983, *Faith and Rationality: Reason and Belief in God*, which

---

3. Van Til, *Christian Apologetics*; Van Til, *Defense of the Faith*; Frame, *Apologetics to the Glory of God*; Frame, *Cornelius Van Til*.

4. It would actually be more historically accurate to say that Reformed epistemology is a less extreme version of presuppositionalism. But neither of these construals is completely accurate. The two methods are really cousins, with Calvin and Dutch Calvinists such as Abraham Kuyper as common ancestors, than they are offspring of one another. But the conclusions of presuppositionalism, do not add anything to what I say about Reformed epistemology.

started a movement among Christian philosophers of religion.[5] This movement maintains an orthodox Reformed epistemology while taking the postmodern condition seriously. The Reformed epistemologists claim that some of the insights of postmodern thought are central ideas of the Reformed tradition. "For example, postmoderns typically reject classical foundationalism, which has also been rejected by such doughty spokespersons for Christian belief as Abraham Kuyper, William Alston, and Nicholas Wolterstorff and, for that matter, in anticipatory fashion by Augustine, Aquinas, Calvin, and [Jonathan] Edwards."[6] Of course, these theologians do not consider themselves to be submitting to postmodern objections; indeed, they reject much of postmodernity. Instead, they argue that classical foundationalism is itself problematic for a Christian (Reformed) epistemology. What they mean by classical foundationalism can be considered synonymous with what Lindbeck called "post-Cartesian natural theology," as will be described below.

Foundationalism is (according to the Reformed epistemologists) the assertion that all justifiable beliefs are held in one of two ways; they are either *immediate* or *rational*. An immediate belief is one that is not held on the basis of other beliefs. A rational belief is one that is supported by some other belief as its primary evidence. As an explanation of this distinction, Plantinga often employs arithmetic as illustration.

Consider a simple arithmetic truth, such as $2 + 1 = 3$, and compare it with one like $24 \times 24 = 576$. I know each of these propositions, and I know the second but not the first on the basis of computation, which is a kind of inference. So I have immediate knowledge of the first, but not the second.[7]

Foundationalists recognize that some kinds of truth can be "proven," but only by means of employing other truths that are immediate for us. For example, the proposition 24×24 is dependent (for most people who do not know this truth immediately) upon our immediate knowledge of propositions such as $4 \times 4 = 16$, $4 \times 2 = 8$, $2 \times 2 = 4$, $1 + 8 = 9$, etc., and follows by rational means to the conclusion, 576. While the simpler equations are *immediate* to most of us, the more complex equation can be justifiably known *rationally*. Limiting what can be known to this two-fold classification of justifiable knowledge is what Plantinga identifies as foundationalism.

Plantinga himself admits that he is a kind of foundationalist,[8] but he distinguishes his view from *classical foundationalism*. Classical foun-

---

5. Plantinga and Wolterstorff, eds., *Faith and Rationality*.

6. Plantinga, *Warranted Christian Belief*, 423.

7. Plantinga, "Reason and Belief in God," 57.

8. Plantinga, *Warranted Christian Belief*, 343–44. Wolterstorff actually claims that

dationalism only admits a few kinds of propositions into the category of *immediate* knowledge. *Self-evident* propositions are those which someone simply sees to be true, such as our earlier proposition, 2 + 1 = 3. Additionally, propositions about one's own consciousness about which one cannot be mistaken are considered *incorrigible*. Wolterstorff and Plantinga often use the example of feeling dizzy.[9] I simply feel dizzy without need for further explanation or proof. For the classical foundationalist, no other propositions may be known immediately. One might describe other kinds of immediate propositions as beliefs. But these are the only kinds of propositions that can achieve the certainty of knowledge. Plantinga suggests a third category that may indeed be a derivative of incorrigibility. Plantinga argues that foundationalists before the dawn of modern skepticism were willing to grant that those propositions that were *evident to the senses* were properly basic. Premodern foundationalists could accept the proposition "I see a tree." Modern foundationalists rejected this premodern confidence in sense perception. Cartesian skepticism doubted even the senses, knowing that the seeming appearance of a tree may indeed be a hallucination or some other failure of the senses. They therefore concluded that this proposition must be made into an irrefutable proposition: "I am being appeared to tree-ly." Even if there is no tree in fact there, it is irrefutable that I apparently see a tree. The latter proposition is incorrigible for me. Whether one is skeptical of the senses and must therefore reduce those propositions evident to the senses to incorrigible propositions, or if one generally accepts the function of the senses as reliable, Plantinga argues that both of these epistemological construals can properly be called *classical foundationalism*.[10] The key element being that any proposition that cannot meet the standard of certainty of foundationalism is a belief (i.e. not knowledge).

In these earlier stages of foundationalism, one might very well believe a proposition that did not meet the criteria for knowledge, but one must believe the proposition on faith. For Aquinas, a proposition that is previously believed can achieve the status of knowledge, which he calls *scientia*, by a rigorous rational investigation of the evidence. Reasoning and evidence can serve to validate beliefs, but beliefs can stand on the basis of revelation alone, and do so for most people who do not have the time, intelligence, or training to investigate their beliefs. "The fact is that Aquinas is an evidentialist with respect to *scientia*, scientific knowledge. But it doesn't [sic] follow

---

foundationalism itself is no longer tenable. "Our future theories of theorizing will have to be nonfoundationalist ones" (Wolterstorff, *Reason within the Bounds of Religion*, 57).

9. Wolterstorff, "Introduction," 3.

10. Plantinga, "Reason and Belief in God," 57–59.

that he thought a person could properly accept belief in God, say, only if he had (or there are) good theistic arguments. On the contrary, Aquinas thought it perfectly sensible and reasonable to accept this belief on faith."[11] Anselm's ontological argument seems to follow a similar line of thinking. For medieval theologians, some things can be believed on faith, but understanding and knowledge of what is believed gave one more confidence and, more importantly, makes the one who knows more devoted to God. But this rationalism and evidentialism is of a different character than that of the modern foundationalists.

Wolterstorff argues that the *evidentialist challenge to theism* grows out of the modern version of classical foundationalism and its more skeptical impulse. The first to issue this challenge is John Locke. To explain what Locke means by his evidentialist challenge, it is necessary to understand his intellectual context. Locke proposes a radically different criterion for validating Christian belief, but he does not do so to invalidate Christian belief. Like Plantinga, Wolterstorff shows that the earlier project of natural theology is concerned with showing what was already believed on faith to be rationally grounded. This is stated most explicitly in Anselm's *Proslogion*: "For I do not seek to understand so that I may believe, but I believe so that I may understand."[12] This provides the context for Anselm's ontological argument, which is presumably the epitome of "proving" God from natural theology. In a sense, medieval theologians do regard rational argument as a kind of proof, because the argument enables beliefs to be placed within the category of knowledge. In layman's terms, they can be proven. Beliefs are valid for the medieval theologians without providing proofs; they are valid by faith and trust in revelation. Proofs validate justification of belief such that what is believed can now be known. This conception of knowledge is thus dependent upon earlier categories that divide beliefs and knowledge into different complementary categories. In the pre-Enlightenment construal, beliefs can legitimately be believed without being justified as knowledge: this is called faith. "No one in their milieu was claiming that it was permissible to believe that God existed only if one did so on the basis of adequate evidence, and with a firmness not exceeding the strength of the evidence."[13] Locke's proposal, the challenge that one should only believe what can be believed on the basis of evidence, is an innovation and his contribution to the foundationalist epistemology within the Christian tradition.

11. Plantinga, *Warranted Christian Belief*, 82 n. 17.

12. Anselm, "Proslogion," 1.

13. Wolterstorff, "Can Belief in God Be Rational?" 141.

Locke obviously thinks that Christianity can meet this evidentialist challenge; his is not an extreme skepticism. In fact, one might argue that even Locke does not intend to take the position that Barth identified as epistemological atheism: that is, Locke does not intend to imagine himself an atheist for the purposes of argument. Wolterstorff explains that the evidentialist challenge originates with Locke as an intrafaith dialogue with British enthusiasts whom he considered to be irrational and dangerous to authentic Christian faith. Plantinga references notes in the margin of James Tyrell's personal copy of Locke's *An Essay Concerning Human Understanding*. Tyrell was presumably one of the five or six friends present at the discussion that Locke mentions in his prologue as the impetus for his writing the *Essay*. Tyrell's marginal notes indicate that the discussion was about "the principles of morality and revealed religion."[14] This reveals that Locke's *Essay* is written, at least in part, to discern between the enthusiasts and authentic Christianity. This concern for the enthusiasts makes sense of Locke's accusations that the dangerous divisions in religions, especially his own Christian religion, are "in good measure" due to the opposition of faith and reason.[15] He thinks that faith without validation by reason can lead persons in irreconcilable and strange opinions, such as the enthusiasts' claim to have access to and experience of private revelation. Locke proposes the evidentialist challenge as a way of discerning between authentic Christian faith and the irrational errors of the enthusiasts. Evidentialism was originally a mechanism to navigate competing Christian claims, not an apologetic challenge to prove Christian belief to those outside of it on their own terms. Wolterstorff briefly explains that Locke would have done better to show the enthusiasts adequate reasons for the falsehood of their beliefs, rather than demanding reasons from them that justify their belief.[16] This helps explain the role of rational argument and apologetics for Wolterstorff. Instead of showing the enthusiasts why they are irrational, Locke proposes that the enthusiasts must provide evidence for why their beliefs are justifiable and furthermore suggests that they should not believe anything with more conviction than the evidence demands. Locke then goes on to argue for his version of the Christian faith according to the same criteria. Thus, Locke must presume the falsity of his beliefs until they meet the evidentialist criteria of belief. Here is where Locke falls prey to Barth's concern with epistemological atheism: he must argue as if he is something other than a Christian theist, although presuming that his reasoning will lead him back

---

14. Plantinga, *Warranted Christian Belief*, 72.

15. Locke, *Essay Concerning Human Understanding* IV.xviii.11.

16. Wolterstorff, "Can Belief in God Be Rational?" 177–78.

to orthodox Christianity. Accusing Locke of epistemological atheism, however, is premature. Delineating Locke's criteria for governing assent is first necessary.

Like any other classical foundationalist, Locke thinks that one can only be certain of those propositions that are self-evident, incorrigible or can be demonstrated from other self-evident or incorrigible propositions.[17] Furthermore, when it comes to these things that one "knows," one cannot govern assent. Not admitting these foundational propositions amounts to a rational defect. Only the most thoroughgoing skeptics will even consider them. But a vast majority of what a person thinks is not knowledge of this kind. Much of what is believed is, according to Locke, opinion. Regarding opinion, persons should (and can) govern assent to propositions based on the degree of certainty which reason can give. Regarding revealed truth (such as the Christian doctrines of atonement and incarnation), one need not be certain of the probability of the proposition, but certain that the proposition is a proper interpretation of that which was truly revealed. Whatever God has revealed will certainly be true.[18] But reason must judge whether God has truly revealed a proposition. How does one know that a supposed revelation from God is not simply the rambling of a deranged lunatic or a cruel joke? Certainty and belief may only be granted to the degree to which the revelation can be trusted as truly coming from God. Other kinds of knowledge and certainty are likewise governed by reason, but these are not nearly as important for the purpose of apologetics as are Locke's proposals regarding revelation. And, if Wolterstorff and Plantinga are right about Locke's concern with the enthusiasts, the degree of certainty one can place in revelation was Locke's most pressing concern.

Besides his evidentialist and foundationalist assumptions, Plantinga argues that one final assumption makes up the Enlightenment package inherited by modern thinkers. Locke argues that God created persons with rational minds, and therefore a person *ought* to govern their assent based on their reason. God's creating persons with reason makes them ethically responsible to follow their reason regarding all to which they give assent. This is Locke's deontologism.[19]

Of course, later atheists, following this tripartite criterion, have concluded that Christianity is therefore false.[20] Some academic apologists have also accepted Locke's deontological and foundationalist evidentialism and

17. See Plantinga's summary in *Warranted Christian Belief*, 75–77.

18. Locke, *Essay Concerning Human Understanding* IV.xviii.10.

19. Ibid., IV.xvii.24; cf. Plantinga, *Warranted Christian Belief*, 85–88.

20. For example Russell, *Why I am Not a Christian*; Flew, *Presumption of Atheism*.

argued that Christianity meets the criteria of rational acceptability.[21] Ironically, Plantinga identifies Basil Mitchell as an evidentialist of this same kind, but without explicating Mitchell's work.[22] Mitchell is the only apologist to whom the postliberals refer. The following section will show how Mitchell's work is acceptable as a criterion for truth for postliberals, especially because the postliberals are antagonistic towards evidentialist apologetics. For now, it is enough to say that some academic theologians and philosophers have confidently used Locke's criteria to try to justify orthodox Christianity. Much of popular contemporary apologetics cannot help but follow this epistemological conception, especially because of the inerrantist reading of the Bible that lies behind these popular works. For these inerrantists, it becomes necessary to show that the Bible is God's revelation in much the same way as Locke proposes, and with a similar confidence that they share with him regarding the Bible's ability to withstand the challenge. These popular apologists are direct descendants of the late nineteenth and early twentieth century Princeton theologians, following B. B. Warfield and Charles Hodge. While the Princeton theologians exchange Cartesian doubt for the common sense realism of Thomas Reid, they accept the notion that evidence must lead back to an affirmation of Christian belief. Reid's confidence in sense perceptions and mental operations means these evidentialists granted a high degree of objectivity to knowledge. Because persons generally trust their senses and mental operations in everyday life, it is not surprising that popular apologetics has followed this common-sense evidentialism. The additional confidence that God, who created the world, would not make a world which did not correspond with the truth of the Bible leads evangelical apologists to conclude that science and objective rational beliefs will eventually lead to Christianity. In fact, B. B. Warfield had a significant high-profile controversy with Reformed epistemologist Abraham Kuyper in regards to knowledge. Warfield was also a Reformed theologian, but he was perplexed by Kuyper's notion that the regenerate mind functioned in a wholly different way than the unregenerate. His common-sense realism is predicated on the notion that minds all generally function in the same way. Thus, the Christian apologist should be able to show the non-Christian the error of their intellectual ways and lead them to Christian faith by manner of a strong argument based on the evidence.[23] Though much of Plantinga's work is concerned with and indebted to Thomas Reid, much of the

21. See Abraham, *Introduction to the Philosophy of Religion*.

22. Plantinga, *Warranted Christian Belief*, 90.

23. Marsden, "Collapse of American Evangelical Academia," 252–54. See also Mascord, *Alvin Plantinga and Christian Apologetics*, 16–18.

work of Plantinga and Wolterstorff is also concerned with the shift from natural theology to evidentialist apologetics that is outlined above. Reid is the transitional figure that makes the popular works of apologists such as Josh McDowell and Norman Geisler possible. The argument we are tracing, the Reformed epistemologists' critique of evidentialist apologetics and its similarity to postliberal concerns with apologetics, does not necessitate tracing the genealogy from Locke through Reid to Warfield and Hodge and finally to popular evangelical apologists such as McDowell. The Reformed epistemologists critique Locke at the base of the evidentialist epistemology, thereby making these later evidentialists irrelevant for the discussion. Plantinga argues that the evidentialists' assumptions, that which he calls the *classical package* of foundationalism, evidentialism, and deontologism, are presupposed by post-Enlightenment philosophy and are rarely even questioned. He admits that in his early work *God and Other Minds* he assumes Locke's version of evidentialism without question.[24] He had already begun to question the presuppositions of evidentialism by 1983, when *Faith and Rationality* was published. Much of his work, and that of the other Reformed epistemologists writing in the same vein, has been to show that evidentialism itself rest on philosophical presuppositions which are not self-evident or defensible. Here the Reformed epistemologists are much more thorough than the postliberals, and anticipate the postliberals' concerns with apologetics. Nevertheless, as we will see, they do not assume that there is no method left for apologetics, as some postliberals do.

Plantinga's two-fold critique of the position is relatively brief. The most problematic critique to Locke's position is Plantinga's self-referential critique. To be counted as knowledge according to its own criteria, Lockean evidentialism would have to be self-evident, incorrigible, or evident to the senses. While the system might seem to have some self-evidential support, self-evident propositions are those that we immediately see to be true and which no one who understands them may deny. A whole host of persons, including many postmodern philosophical academics, have rejected Locke's form of evidentialism, and we dare not say that the whole host of them is rationally defective. Evidentialism is not about one's mental state, and therefore cannot be incorrigible. Finally, a concept of knowledge and rationality is not an object perceptible by the senses, and therefore cannot be evident to the senses. If evidentialism is not of these immediate kinds of knowledge, then it must rationally follow from immediate truths. Plantinga says little more than that he knows of no such argument that attempts to rationally argue for Lockean evidentialism from immediate beliefs. Therefore, if this

24. Plantinga, *Warranted Christian Belief*, 81.

construal cannot meet its own criteria for being counted as knowledge, then it may very well be true, but it certainly cannot be considered justifiable.[25] That is, Lockean evidentialism, if it is true, must also be based on a presupposition that cannot be defended on its own criteria. Plantinga admits that other forms of evidentialism may very well hold together, but this Enlightenment form and its skepticism will not hold sway. Furthermore, Plantinga mentions a second, less disparaging critique, that of Reid against Hume and other skeptics: most of our beliefs are simply not formed in the way that Hume and other skeptics claim. Most people do not apply such a high standard of rationality to everyday beliefs, and yet count them as knowledge to the degree that they make life-dependent decisions upon them. These people are not generally considered morally or rationally deficient.[26]

Similarly, the postliberal critique of apologetics is predicated on the argument that whole systems of theological rationale (and every other kind of rationale) presuppose a language game that actually forms the criteria by which that way of reasoning may proceed. The Reformed epistemologists have leveled this claim against the evidentialists, though without the hermeneutic and linguistic flavor of postliberals. Plantinga and Wolterstorff have expounded the presuppositions of Lockean evidentialism to show that Locke assumes criteria for what counts as knowledge that are based on Enlightenment skepticism. Furthermore, this criterion cannot withstand a self-referential critique. It simply is not possible to argue that one should only believe that which can be believed upon evidence, for there is no evidence for evidentialism as Locke has explained it.

At some points of argument in both Plantinga and Wolterstorff, it becomes clear that they are suggesting a kind of circularity not unlike what the postliberals are suggesting. Plantinga calls this epistemic circularity, and claims that William Alston has shown that all of our belief-forming practices are socially established and necessarily circular. While Plantinga rarely thinks anything is "proven," he thinks Alston "gets as close to establishing this conclusion as philosophers ever get to establishing any important conclusion."[27] Essentially, the argument is that any argument for the reliability of a belief-forming faculty is dependent upon that faculty for the truth of one of its premises. For example, even the most basic of belief-forming faculties, arithmetic intuition, can only be shown to be reliable by using arithmetic intuition. While people generally trust their belief-forming

---

25. Ibid., 94–95; cf. Plantinga, "Reason and Belief in God," 61–63.

26. Plantinga, *Warranted Christian Belief*, 97–99; cf. Plantinga, "Reason and Belief in God," 59–61.

27. Plantinga, *Warranted Christian Belief*, 119.

faculties, they have no evidence that any of their faculties are reliable, except insofar as the faculties seem to be reliable and generally do not lead them astray, as far as they can tell. This seems very close to the circularity that postliberals argue is implicit in narrative knowledge. In fact, Alston and postliberals both get their circularity arguments from their Wittgensteinian heritage.[28] Though Plantinga rarely uses more than passing (and often derogatory) reference to Wittgenstein, he accepts many of Alston's conclusions and admits that Alston is dependent on Wittgenstein. This would seem to bring his academic genealogy quite close to the postliberals. Though it would be imprudent to stress the similarities between Plantinga and the postliberals, they both insist on a certain epistemic circularity in our belief forming practices.

Postliberals suggest that one may only judge Christian truth claims from inside the language game formed by the Christian narrative. Reformed epistemologists, especially Plantinga, claim that Christian truth claims are only warranted (or justified) if what Christians claim about reasoning is true. One would not be able to make the claims that Plantinga makes without first admitting some of Plantinga's core theological commitments. Plantinga does not think these are merely theological language games, of course. He is not claiming that his proposal is true if persons presuppose the truth of his argument. He is claiming his proposal is true if Christian doctrine is true, and false if Christian doctrine is false. He is not here primarily concerned with the evidential requirement which Locke proposes, though he does seem to think what should be admitted as evidence should be broadened.[29] Neither is he attacking Locke's foundationalism, as Plantinga considers himself to be a kind of foundationalist. Rather, he attacks the deontological element in Locke's tripartite construal. Plantinga insists that there are relevant epistemic duties, but not those Locke and evidentialists suggest (in particular, the duty that a person should believe only to the degree the evidence demands).

Put simply, Plantinga proposes that all persons are born with the capacity for innate (immediate) knowledge of God in response to those sorts of experiences that stimulate the working of the sense of the divine. This *sensus divinitatis*, as Calvin calls it, does not function automatically. Therefore, not every person will elicit a response that God exists when placed within the proper context. It is a capacity, much like the capacity for other kinds of knowledge perception, which must mature in a persona child who

---

28. Ibid., 118. Cf. Alston, "Doxastic Practice Approach to Epistemology"; Alston, *Reliability of Sense Perception.*

29. Ibid., 102–3.

has not matured enough to "see" that $2 + 1 = 3$ still has that capacity; the child just has yet to mature. Likewise, all persons can perceive God given the proper belief-in-God-producing circumstances.[30] People are created with a sense of the divine; this sense is part of the *imago Dei* as classical Christian doctrine has understood it. Therefore, when a person experiences the extravagant worship of committed believers or looks up at the vast beauty of the night sky, the sense of the divine within them functions to draw them to the conclusion that God is among God's people and created the whole world for God's own glory. Of course, sometimes this faculty does not operate properly because the conditions are not right for it to do so. Just as sense perception may not function as it was intended due to circumstances that are not conducive for it, the sense of the divine may also fail to function properly. Plantinga explains that some conditions inhibit other senses in an analogous way. A dark room or a dense fog can prohibit someone from seeing properly. Eyes are not designed to function in those environments. Sin creates an environment that prohibits the proper function of the sense of the divine. Furthermore, the sense of the divine has actually been damaged by the effects of sin as well. Not only does sin damage the sense of the divine's original ability to perceive God in worship and the beauty of creation, but sin also creates a resistance to the proper conclusions to which the sense of the divine lead. Therefore, even when the sense of the divine functions properly and leads persons to the conclusion that God exists and is leading them towards redemption in Jesus Christ, they yet resist that conclusion and even desire for it to be untrue. Even when persons are drawn towards God in the midst of worship, the sin nature causes them to desire being somewhere else, or reminds them of the great challenges of the Christian life such that they want little to do with it.[31] "We see through a glass darkly" is more than just a metaphor. Like sight, the divine sense can also be incapacitated or hindered by a cognitive environment that is not conducive to it, and sin has darkened that capacity. Plantinga explains that the effects of sin are twofold. The *affective* effect causes us to love things and self before God. The *cognitive* effect of sin is blindness (or at least dullness) to the perception of God.[32]

Redemption and regeneration goes a long way to restoring the sense of the divine, but God goes even further than simple restoration of this original sense. The internal instigation of the Holy Spirit enables the believer to see with clarity not available with the sense of the divine alone. Following Calvin, Plantinga insists that the normal mode of believing consists of some

30. Ibid., 170–75.
31. Ibid., 203–17.
32. Ibid., 280.

encounter with a proclamation of the Gospel (through preaching, reading Scripture, personal testimony, etc.), whereby the Holy Spirit illumines a person to respond to the Gospel supernaturally. This idea, too, is classical Christian doctrine. What Plantinga helps us understand is how this, if it is true, is a justified belief. Belief formed by a miraculous (and Plantinga insists that it is indeed miraculous) act of God is rationally justified belief. That is, it is the proper and justified response for a person to believe in God when this miracle occurs in them. But one cannot investigate whether this miracle of Holy Spirit instigation has occurred except by experience and testimony.

If this construal of truth is true, if persons are naturally drawn towards God by the sense of the divine in which they were created and the internal instigation of the Holy Spirit, then it should not be surprising that a great number of believers do not govern assent by evidential skepticism at all, but by an insistence in spite of challenges that God does indeed exist and loves his own creation. If this theological proposal is true, then persons are justified in believing in God without evidential proof. If Plantinga and Christians are wrong about the sense of the divine, then indeed some other capacity leads persons to faith in God when in these circumstances. Christian despisers suggest that belief in God was actually some inborn overactive anxiety in humanity's primal ancestors, which caused them to be more suspicious of predators than they ought. They imagined something "trying to get them" behind every bush, which later led to humans believing in a God and spirits which they cannot see. This irrational fear was a positive selective trait because the anxiety it created made its possessors more difficult prey.[33] The sense of the divine is not the only explanation for Christian belief formation. Plantinga admits that if Christian belief is false, then the sense that Christians have that God exists is without justification.

Of course, Christian belief in God could still be true even if there is no sense of the divine which orients persons towards God. In fact, this is exactly how Locke suggested that reason was supposed to function. God gave persons the ability to reason so that they could be properly oriented towards God. Plantinga would not argue with Locke that reasoning, properly oriented, would lead towards God, but Plantinga argues that reasoning and argument will leave one far short of justifiably believing in God. He critiques the logic of Richard Swinburne[34] to argue that even where various conclusions about God are probable, they nevertheless fall far short of certainty when taken together. Plantinga argues that belief founded on this

33. Keller, *Reason for God,* 135–39.
34. Swinburne, *Existence of God.*

kind of calculation-based reasoning process would be of a very feeble kind. When Plantinga argues in this way towards the doctrine of the Incarnation as revealed in Scripture, the most generous certainty estimates he can imagine only grant a 35 percent chance that Jesus was God incarnate with the probability calculus. Plantinga admits that assigning real numbers to any of these estimates is impossible, and the argument could be made in a different way with a different number of steps. But to argue against the details of Plantinga's argument would miss his point. He is explaining that belief founded upon an evidential argument will necessarily be unstable belief because some doubt is introduced into each proposition of the argument. Besides the uncertainty introduced by the weakness of the probability calculus, belief would wane with each new discovery against Christianity.[35] Anyone who has been a Christian for very long knows that Christian belief is not grounded in this way or shakable in this way. While some Christians may have periods of crisis of faith, even thinking post-Enlightenment Christians dismiss a great amount of the evidence against Christianity with confidence beyond what the evidence for Christianity would allow. This fact alone does not explain how Christians can be justified in that belief, however.

It is impossible to test the validity of the belief-forming mechanism without appealing to the belief-forming mechanism, which Christians will always affirm and non-believers will always deny. The epistemic circularity explicated by Alston and followed by Plantinga comes back into view. A person who sees the truth of God's existence via the redeemed sense of the divine within her and the instigation of the Holy Spirit that summons her cannot explain the truth of her experience except by appealing to her experience of being illumined to and seeing the truth of God's existence. She just does believe that she has seen truly. And, if Plantinga's Christian thesis is correct, she is justified in believing how she does.

All of the above exegetical work has brought us to one central conclusion: Reformed epistemologists are saying something very much like what postliberals have said about the way logic and reasoning function. Reformed epistemologists use their analytic philosophy to deconstruct Enlightenment epistemology, especially the seminal evidentialism of John Locke. They conclude that this construal is no longer tenable in the Western mind because of the introduction of skepticism that is far more reaching than even Descartes or Locke could muster. To some degree, Western thinkers must admit the localized epistemology to which every discourse is limited. Justification of Christian belief is dependent upon acceptance of Christian doctrinal claims, especially the sense of the divine and the internal instigation of the

35. Plantinga, *Warranted Christian Belief*, 272–80.

Holy Spirit. If persons really are enabled to properly know God via these belief-forming processes, then Christians are justified in their belief. If these Christian doctrines are not true, then Christians are not justified in their belief. However, justification of these two processes is dependent in some way on the reliability of the processes. As Alston argued and Plantinga repeated, all belief-forming practices follow a similar epistemic circularity, and Christianity should not be criticized by criteria beyond what other belief-forming practices are.

Postliberals argue that all religious systems consist of language games which are narrative-dependent and which cannot be judged based on the criteria of another narrative's rationality think the Reformed epistemologists and postliberals are naming the same incommensurability, albeit with language grounded in different philosophical discourses. My purpose here is not to name those differences, but to recognize that both groups of thinkers are naming the same problem that arises from postmodern epistemology. Both groups, the Reformed epistemologists to a greater degree than the postliberals, claim that Christian doctrine insisted on this epistemology before the dawn of postmodern thought. My purpose here is also not to argue that the Reformed epistemologists and postliberals are saying *exactly* the same thing. It seems clear to me that the Reformed epistemologists are properly within the first approach to theology in Lindbeck's typology. Propositional theories of truth are still primary for Plantinga and Wolterstorff, but I do not think it is irrelevant that Plantinga often speaks of a proposition as just one element within a larger Christian worldview and narrative. "For the Christian doesn't [sic] accept just *theism*; she also accepts the rest of the Christian story, including fall (along with corruption of the image of God), redemption, regeneration, and the consequent repair and restoration of that image."[36] In spite of this emphasis, I have no doubt that postliberals would be uncomfortable being identified with Plantinga's (modified) foundationalism. At the same time, Plantinga explicitly says that postliberals do not have a strong enough notion of truth to satisfy his Calvinist orthodoxy.

> Christians, on this account, don't [sic] merely find their identity
> in the Christian story, or live in it or out of it; they *believe* it,
> take the story to be the sober truth . . . In this way, the model
> [that Plantinga has proposed] (apparently) differs from the
> postmodern Yale theology of Hans Frei and George Lindbeck,
> which emphasizes the role of the Bible in the Christian life but
> is a bit coy as to whether its apparent teachings—creation, sin,
> incarnation, atonement, Christ's resurrection—are to be taken

36. Ibid., 283.

as actually *true*. This standoffishness about truth is perhaps the 'postliberal' element in Yale theology; according to the present model, however, it is also unnecessary. The model is designed to show that straightforward, downright, out-and-out *belief* in the great things of the gospel can have epistemic virtues we are considering.[37]

Plantinga finds the postliberal resistance to claims about "truth" problematic. He does not say enough to interpret whether he actually understands the postliberal notion of truth well. Lindbeck admittedly misconstrues truth and correspondence, as we saw above, and this is likely the root of Plantinga's concern. It may also be the case that his position as a theologian of Lindbeck's first kind may prohibit him from understanding Lindbeck's proposal here. This project will not reconcile those differences, but I think the issue with which Plantinga is concerned is precisely the relevant one if postliberal construals are to be appropriated for evangelical apologetics. A "postconservative" approach might be necessary to satisfy theologians such as Plantinga, who are dissatisfied with the postliberals' evasiveness on the issue of truth.

In spite of these stated differences, the two groups of theologians share a similarity that would seem to prohibit interreligious or apologetic dialogue. Persons with different epistemological presuppositions appear to have incommensurable rational differences. In spite of this shared assumption, the Reformed epistemologists do not neglect apologetic discourse as the postliberals seem to do with their "ad hoc apologetic" proposal. In fact, Plantinga and other Reformed epistemologists have spent a good deal of their careers writing apologetic arguments.

Cumulative Case Apologists' Critique of Modern Reasoning

The cumulative case apologists are not nearly so thoroughgoing in their critique of the post-Cartesian position. The two most significant proponents of the cumulative case method are Richard Swinburne and Basil Mitchell. Though their individual approaches vary significantly, they are both more prone to positively state their own position than engage in the detailed deconstruction of the opponent's position characteristic of the Reformed epistemologists. Both of them also assume that the procedure of the sciences is the rational standard that a proposal for arguing religious paradigms will need to meet, and so their critique focuses less on the philosophical candidates for rational standards such as classical foundationalism, logical

37. Ibid., 247.

positivism, and so on.[38] They both suggest that the way the sciences interpret data and propose potential paradigms is *no more certain* than the way
that metaphysical approaches to interpreting data and proposing potential
paradigms proceeds. Mitchell justifies the comparison to the natural sciences by simply stating that our contemporary era is one which has un-
necessarily restricted reasoning to only this type of reasoning, and that this
is not the first candidate that philosophy has put forward for this magisterial
role. He suggests that, "The history of philosophy could be said to be the
story of successive attempts to limit the concept of reason to some preferred
type of reasoning, thus dismissing as beyond the scope of reason properly
so-called any thinking that did not conform to the required definition."[39]
While Swinburne focuses his analogy of religious reasoning to scientific
reasoning, Mitchell also argues that reasoning in exegesis, history, law, and
everyday matters such as judgments about the intentions of another person
proceed this way. In each of these cases of complex judgments, rather than
demonstrating a proof for a belief, persons proceed by an inductive argument that Mitchell calls a cumulative case argument. Since both of them
think that this way of reasoning is a good way of reasoning, they do not
explicitly critique and undermine this way of thinking. Rather, they proceed
by showing that the way of reasoning in these other disciplines is reliable
and that religious reasoning is of this same sort. Their proposal will be explained below with the analogy to sciences and the deconstruction of the
notion of the sciences' superiority highlighted throughout.

Mitchell thinks that the failure of positivism, and the justification of
scientific reasoning that it provided, opens up excellent opportunities for
Christian apologetics in the academy. If metaphysics and theology cannot
be dismissed without argument, then theology can be considered, along
with materialism and other worldviews, as a rational enterprise. This was
not so when positivism held an uncritical superior position. It also has returned the apologetic discourse back to the same sorts of discussions that
everyday persons have long used to debate Christianity, such as evidence
for the resurrection, the cosmological argument, and so on, rather than the
esoteric philosophical arguments that were limited to epistemology and
hermeneutics.[40] He is not optimistic that this opportunity is as ripe among

38. Mitchell does state briefly that the reasoning of the natural sciences is based on
positivism, but he never actually deconstructs positivism as a worldview. He states that
positivism fails the self-referential critique. That is, scientific explanation itself cannot
be accounted for on positivist reasoning, and instead relies upon the kind of cumulative
case reasoning that he is proposing. Mitchell, *How to Play Theological Ping Pong*, 27.

39. Ibid., 200.

40. Ibid., 27.

laypersons and general culture, however, not only because of the naïve scientism that is still present in everyday conversation, but also because of the inability of theologians to once again engage the topics that are most pressing. Liberal theologians have been deficient in metaphysical reasoning, and conservative ones have too long neglected real engagement with the most pressing modern and cultural questions.[41]

Neither Mitchell nor Swinburne is devoid of critique of those religious arguments proposed to be proofs. In the book that lays out his cumulative case method, *The Justification of Religious Belief*, Mitchell is largely dependent upon the well-developed critiques of others to show that he too is skeptical of providing a proof for Christian belief. Plantinga was content to critique only classical foundationalism as it was presented in the modern period, which seems to me to be the precise concern of Lindbeck regarding "post-Cartesian natural theology." But the swath of Mitchell's criticism will be much broader, even if far less detailed.

Mitchell repeats the essentially Kantian critique of the ontological argument that existence is not a perfection of being. He traces this in its multitude of varieties, including the arguments that *"necessary* existence is not a perfection of being" and "existence is not a predicate of being." Mitchell thinks that this will not be a problem for Christians, because the Christian doctrine of God is such that all creation is dependent upon God but that God is not dependent upon creation. The notion that God necessarily exists by definition of what we mean by "god" does not actually make him dependent upon creation or the definition, however; Mitchell missteps here. But I take it that he makes this argument for two reasons. First, he is trying to show that Christian philosophical reasoning is dependent upon theological reasoning, and not *vice versa*. Second, and maybe more importantly, this argument is a rhetorical device to move to his discussion to the cosmological argument, as God's independence and creation's dependence are central ideas for that argument. This is important for his later argument for a cumulative case because he is already beginning to show their interdependence.[42]

The criticisms of the cosmological argument that Mitchell cites are a bit more varied, but two are central. Mitchell's first criticism is that, where the cosmological argument suggests that the existence of the universe *must* be explained, the atheist would simply reply that, if this is so, then God too must be explained; or, the atheist might suggest that if God need not be explained ("I am") then neither must the universe be explained. Put simply, the atheist can deny either of the two central ideas on which the cosmological

41. Ibid., 33–41.

42. Mitchell, *Justification of Religious Belief*, 21–24.

argument depends, either by insisting that "creation" is not dependent upon anything or by insisting that God is dependent upon something.

Mitchell's second criticism is another repetition of Kant, in this case that there is an equivocation on the notion of causation. Anthony Flew follows Kant in saying that causation is a concept that applies only to the natural world itself. To use language that describes the natural world to describe God is to take that language out of the context in which it is intelligible. Mitchell's solution here as before is to restate the traditional notion that causation in this case is not as in science but rather an act of pure creativity. Again, this does not actually make a convincing argument that Christian doctrine is true, but simply reveals the degree to which both positions make claims that are not subject to proof.[43]

Mitchell begins his assessment of the teleological argument by recognizing the degree to which this argument has changed with the conclusions of modern science. The theory of natural selection has rendered earlier versions obsolete, but has opened up other possibilities of arguing from the order of the universe. It is often argued that a random universe does not have the capacity to create an ordered world such that it could produce sentient and even rational beings. But Mitchell argues that this designation is too simplistic because it does not specify the degree to which things would need to be ordered to create such a universe. Is not the existence of atoms and particles a kind of order? The gathering up of mass into planets and stars is another kind of order. Without some order there would be no cosmos at all, but surely the teleological argument is not for just any kind of order, but the kind that can produce just the sort of universe that we actually have. But this exact kind of ordering is not entailed in any theological claim. While Mitchell thinks the cosmological argument is fruitful in a certain sense, it simply is not a deductive argument. And it cannot be a strong inductive argument, because we do not have experience of multiple universes to know if only this way of ordering is capable of producing life.[44]

In addition to these three natural theology arguments, Mitchell also shows that the somewhat weaker argument from religious experience, while counting as evidence, simply cannot be taken as proof of anything like what religious persons claim to be God.[45] There are too many other alternative explanations that cannot be ruled out with certainty. He ends the chapter with an evaluation of arguments from revelation. While he think these arguments too have weight, they cannot be taken as proof because they are de-

43. Ibid., 24–27.
44. Mitchell, *Justification of Religious Belief*, 26–30.
45. Ibid., 30–32.

pendent upon historical arguments to validate the claim to revelation, and these historical arguments are undergoing constant revision. Even if biblical scholars could settle on the evidence in support of the Bible as revelation, the most significant argument for the truth of the Christian narrative is dependent upon the miracles and especially the resurrection of Jesus. Because science tests only repeatable phenomena, miracle is not a valid category for testing or proof. The most the historian can say is that something happened that is beyond explanation.

As I have said above, Mitchell does not think that any of these objections to the above arguments are conclusive, and that each can be met to varying degrees. The question for Mitchell is not whether any of the arguments are convincing, but whether they constitute a proof. But in each of these cases, he goes one step further to argue that none of these arguments alone can render Christian doctrine even probable.

The reasons why they cannot be used to render Christian doctrine probable is different in each case, however. He seems to argue that the nature of the ontological argument is such that it is either a deductive argument or is no argument at all, so probability is not applicable. If the cosmological argument is reduced to an argument for the probability of God's existence, then it provides no criteria for judging between its claims and any other because it is not, strictly speaking, a scientific hypothesis. Since there is only one universe, there is no basis for inductive reasoning. He quotes John Hick, who claims that "the cosmological argument presents us with the options: the universe as brute fact or as divine creation; it does not provide any ground for preferring one to the other."[46] The limit of having experienced only one universe also makes it impossible to assign probability to the teleological argument, even if it still has some force as an argument for probability. The fact that persons can only have their own religious experience and cannot compare it with that of others also limits the ability to assign a probability to this argument. So that, "In this connection, too, as with the arguments of natural theology, no satisfactory solution is to be found by relaxing the stringency of the claim and substituting probability for proof."[47] This is the key mark of distinction between Mitchell and Richard Swinburne. While Swinburne puts considerable stock in the probability of each of the various arguments in the fashion of analytical philosophy, Mitchell avoids this method altogether and opts for a more intuitive approach to judging between competing paradigms, as we will see below.

46. Ibid., 25.
47. Ibid., 31.

Swinburne is a formidable cumulative case apologist with a significant body of work. While Basil Mitchell writes briefly in refute of proof for the existence of God, Swinburne is very subtle in his critique of foundationalism, such that many scholars would still consider him a foundationalist.[48] That is, Swinburne would seem to suggest that Christian belief is justified if and only if the cumulative case for belief is at least probable. His entire case rests primarily on the trustworthiness of inductive arguments.

CUMULATIVE CASE APOLOGETIC METHOD

This section will survey the cumulative case apologetic method of Richard Swinburne and Basil Mitchell. Most other proponents follow the somewhat different lines of argument of one of these two. While their conclusions are very similar, their differences do matter for the case that I am arguing. Swinburne's is what might be called an "inductive cumulative case argument." Mitchell's might be called a "cumulative case by judgment."[49] William Abraham calls the former "hard rationalism" and the latter "soft rationalism."[50] While either of these terms might sound pejorative given differing perspectives, these are not wholly improper. While Mitchell is the one that brought this method to the fore of contemporary apologetics, I will treat Swinburne first.[51]

Richard Swinburne

Swinburne explains that most arguments made especially in the sciences are not valid deductive arguments, but are generally agreed to be inductive arguments. Deductive arguments are valid or invalid, but inductive arguments are relatively good or relatively bad. He further distinguishes between what he calls P-inductive arguments and C-inductive arguments. P-inductive arguments are good when the premises of the argument make the conclusion

---

48. Phillips, *Faith after Foundationalism*, 4.

49. Paul Draper calls Mitchell's an "emerging" cumulative case, though I think his name and description are not what Mitchell describes. In Draper's explanation, the paradigm that explains the world "emerges" upon evaluation of the evidence. In the case of Mitchell and Lindbeck, the paradigm already exists in an articulated theology of a community. Furthermore, because he continues to discuss the probability of individual arguments as we will see with Swinburne, his explanation is quite far from the character of Mitchell's. Draper, "Cumulative Cases."

50. Abraham, *Introduction to the Philosophy of Religion*, 98–129.

51. Hebblethwaite, "Basil Mitchell," 264.

probable. C-inductive arguments are good when they confirm the conclusion or increase the likelihood that the conclusion is true. So Swinburne suggests that a single P-inductive argument for the existence of God will be the sum of an entire series of C-inductive arguments. Swinburne insists that if all of the arguments for God are taken together and calculated according to the complex probability calculus of Bayes' theorem, then the result of this formula will be greater than a probability of .5, and reasonable persons should therefore believe in the existence of God. So Swinburne's method, then, is to make many of the same arguments made by classical apologists or those that might be considered "post-Cartesian natural theologians," but Swinburne does not think that any one of their arguments is a conclusive P-inductive argument alone. Rather, each of them is a C-inductive argument that increases the probability of the overarching P-inductive argument and cumulatively can be taken to make probable the existence of God. Swinburne himself recognizes that it is impossible to assign an individual probability for each of the individual arguments.[52] But just as we saw with Mitchell, Swinburne does not think that arguments for the probability of religious claims are unique in this aspect. He claims that competing scientific theories face a similar problem in assigning actual probability figures, and yet scientists decide every day which of several competing theories is most probable.[53] To add further complexity, when calculated with rather modest probabilities for each of the component arguments, Swinburne claims that every argument except the argument from religious experience would equal roughly .5. It is the argument from religious experience that puts the calculation finally over .5 and leads him to conclude that the inductive argument for the existence of God is indeed probable.[54] I say that this adds complexity to his argument because it is the argument from religious experience that is most vulnerable to claims of incredulity. Swinburne does argue in his later book, *The Resurrection of God Incarnate*, that the argument for and from the resurrection of Jesus is a very strong argument that would raise this probability over .5 by a significant amount.[55]

But a more significant problem with this kind of calculation is that we need something far higher than a probability of .5 before we can believe something or call it knowledge. In Plantinga's critique of Swinburne at this

52. Swinburne, *Existence of God*, 341.

53. I think this actually is a further challenge to the usefulness of the Swinburne's probability calculus. If these actual probabilities are impossible to assign in any debate of this kind, then what purpose would they serve except to cloud the real judgments that need to be made? Ibid., 329–33.

54. Ibid., 341.

55. Swinburne, *Resurrection of God Incarnate*.

point, he uses the example of a weighted coin. If we know that a coin is weighted, but do not know precisely how much it is weighted, then we know that the probability of its result is between .5 and 1. We cannot be sure that the result of flipping that coin will come out as we hope, even if the favorable probability may be enough to convince the gambler to bet on it. In spite of the likelihood that the coin flip will be as we hope, this is still not near the certainty of believing that it will do so.[56] I take Plantinga to be correct here. Even if it is slightly more likely that Christianity is true than if it is not true, this is not enough certainty that I would stake my life upon it, especially if the costs of doing so were very high.

What is even more concerning than the problem that Plantinga highlighted is the problem of alternatives. Usually when each of the individual arguments for the existence of God is made, there are only two alternatives considered. Either God exists, or God does not exist. Swinburne did well to define what he means by God.[57] But in the pluralistic modern world, we are not judging between just two conceptions of the world, one with and another without the kind of God that Christianity proposes. We are actually comparing an infinite number of worldviews, each with its own argument for probability. And it would appear that the relative strength of any one of those alternative arguments would weaken the probability of the argument for Christianity. Only the consideration of the probability of a few of the world's religions would likely be necessary to decrease the probability of the Christian argument enough to make believing it untenable. So the tendency in Swinburne's proposal is to understate the evidence against his proposal or to understate the probability of alternative proposals' interpretation of that evidence.[58] The result is a method that does little more than create an illusion of a kind of certainty with inadequate means of comparing competing claims to the evidence. So what would seem to be gained by Swinburne's probability calculus is of little value. And the weakness of Swinburne's proposal, comparing competing claims, will be the strength of Basil Mitchell's.

The importance of discussing Swinburne in this context is to show a very important rebuttal to the conclusions of the postliberal construal of the apologetic task. Swinburne is one of the widely known contemporary academic apologists, and his basic structure of apologetics and conclusions about the task of apologetics have very close affinities with that of Lindbeck. As Lindbeck had suggested, a religious way of being may be viewed as a

---

56. Plantinga, *Warranted Christian Belief*, 273–75.

57. For one instance of description that appears in multiple places, see Swinburne, *Existence of God*, 7–8.

58. Draper, "Cumulative Cases."

"single giant proposition."[59] This is what Swinburne has taught us to do. Any one of the formerly separate arguments for something like Christian doctrine are to be taken as C-inductive arguments, arguments that increase the likelihood that Christian doctrine is true, and together they make up a single P-inductive argument for Christian doctrine. This single argument is the "giant proposition" of the Christian doctrine and way of life that must be considered.

Even more important for our discussion, Swinburne is an apologist that has actually engaged the everyday apologetic tasks of making the case for the truth of the Christian case. In addition to his argument for method,[60] he has made individual arguments for the cosmological argument, the teleological argument, moral argument, arguments from religious experience,[61] and an argument for and from the resurrection of Jesus[62] and miracles. He has defended attacks against Christian doctrine in the form of the freedom of the mind and soul[63] and the truth of Christian Scripture.[64] And he has written extensively in refute of the argument from evil.[65] This massive body of work shows that to take natural theology less systematically than was done in post-Cartesian arguments and to take apologetics as a cumulative argument does not prevent the task from being less important or achievable. In spite of his providing justification for it, Basil Mitchell never provided the actual apologetic arguments that Swinburne did as his successor at Oxford. Even if on the whole we must reject the probability arguments made by Swinburne as misguided, the trajectory of Swinburne's work is consistent with how apologetics would need to proceed in a postliberal mode. Undoubtedly a truly postliberal apologetic will need to take on a more narrative structure than Swinburne's as well. His is still predominately a propositionalist proposal.

Basil Mitchell

In my previous discussion of Mitchell, I explained that he called into question not only the proof of various arguments for the existence of God,

59. Lindbeck, Nature of Doctrine, 37.
60. Swinburne, Coherence of Theism; Swinburne, Existence of God.
61. Swinburne, Existence of God; Swinburne, Is There a God?
62. Swinburne, Resurrection of God Incarnate; Swinburne, Was Jesus God?
63. Swinburne, Mind, Brain, and Free Will.
64. Swinburne, Revelation.
65. Swinburne, Existence of God, 236–72; Swinburne, Providence and the Problem of Evil.

but even the more relaxed standard of their probability. I know of no instance in which Mitchell addressed Swinburne's proposals on increasing probability,[66] but I think his conclusion would be the same. He begins his explanation of the "nature of cumulative case" by explaining thus:

> Among the reasons, both philosophical and theological, for denying that there can be a rational case for Christianity, the most influential has been the assumption that any argument, to be rational, must conform to the requirements of proof or strict probability. The contention of the present chapter will be that the assumption in question is false. In it I shall endeavor to show that in fields other than theology we commonly, and justifiably, make use of arguments other than those of proof or strict probability; and that, typically, theological arguments are of this kind.[67]

Both the "post-Cartesian natural theology" that Lindbeck eschewed and its typical alternative, fideism, often share the assumption that all real arguments will be formal arguments.[68] This is an odd assumption, since most arguments do not proceed this way. Mitchell suggests that the nature of theological argument is like those that we make in the fields of science, law, history, and exegesis every day. Rather than summarizing, I will quote his parable at length.

> Two explorers find a hole in the ground, little more, perhaps, than a slight depression. One of them says, 'There is something funny about that hole; it doesn't look natural to me.' The other of them says, 'It's just an ordinary hole, and can be explained in a hundred and one different ways.' Shortly afterwards they come upon a number of smaller holes in the same area as the first. The first explorer thinks they must be related to it: indeed he fancies that they have the same sort of oddness about them. The other pooh-poohs the idea. He sees nothing in any way remarkable about the holes—anything could have caused them, they are probably just natural depressions. Later, to their surprise, they find in a neighbouring cave a papyrus containing fragments of the plan of a building. 'Ah,' says the first explorer, 'now I see what was odd about those holes; the big one was made to take the centre post of a wooden building, the smaller ones took the other posts.'

---

66. Mitchell was ending his career and writing as Swinburne was beginning his.

67. Mitchell, *Justification of Religious Belief*, 39.

68. Abraham, "Cumulative Case Arguments for Christian Theism," 19.

'All right,' says the other, 'we can soon test your theory. Let us take the fragments of your plan and piece them together on the site. If they fit, well and good, but they probably won't.' So they take them to the site. The first explorer says he can see how the plan fits the site, and arranges the fragments accordingly, with what might be the centre of the roof over the largest hole. Then he sketches his reconstruction out on paper and shows it to his companion. 'This is all very well,' says the latter, 'but you haven't accounted for all the holes or all the features shown in the fragments. The way the remainder fit is purely coincidental.' The first explorer replies that he doesn't claim to know precisely what the original building was like, or how all the details fitted in. Moreover he thinks he can explain why some of the features mentioned in the plan should be missing in what remains on the site. If his impression of the character of the complete building is right, then these would be the first to be stolen or to disintegrate.

'But,' says the other, 'the facts as we have them are compatible with a number of quite different interpretations. Each of them taken by itself can be explained away without much difficulty. And as for the fragmentary plan in the papyrus, of which you make such extensive use, it could well be an imaginative construction with no reference to the real world at all.'[69]

For Mitchell, the parable explains the ways that we account for small pieces of "evidence" that would otherwise be inconsequential if taken alone. To proceed with the logic of the parable, few persons would conclude from the existence of a single odd hole in the ground that it is the former site of building. There are too many other possible explanations for the existence of the hole. And Mitchell thinks that this is what happens in the instance of a "Cartesian strategy of 'dividing the question.'"[70] Just as no reasonable person may assume that a hole in the ground can be taken as justifying evidence that a building once stood in that place, no reasonable person will find a single aspect of evidence such as, for example, the complexity explained by the cosmological argument, as justification for belief in God. Rather, this bit of evidence only makes sense in the context of the entire set of evidence and the various proposals for explaining the facts that have been observed.

So the procedure for this method of argument begins by explicating an overarching theological vision, a worldview, which aims to incorporate as much of the relevant phenomenon and as comprehensive in scope as possible. The argument more closely resembles a dialog between two or

69. Mitchell, *Justification of Religious Belief*, 43–44.
70. Ibid., 45.

more competing visions than a formal argument. The apologist slowly accumulates a more detailed and nuanced vision that accounts for each detail found to be important. Murphy and McClendon argue that all reasoning in postmodernity is of this more holistic type. Mitchell and Lindbeck are following a trend in postmodern thinking toward a more holistic pragmatism that asks two primary questions to justify knowledge. "The first is about individual beliefs and whether they fit properly into the network. The second arises from recognition that the network could be adjusted in numerous ways to maintain consistency— in fact entirely different networks can be imagined."[71] Both of these questions are consistent with the kind of inquiry suggested by Mitchell's analogy.

St. Augustine understood the need for a holistic conception of the biblical narrative when he suggested in *On Catechizing* that the task of catechesis requires laying out, with as much detail as a hearer will bear, the entirety of the Gospel narrative:

> But what we ought to do is, to give a comprehensive statement of all things, summarily and generally, so that certain of the more wonderful facts may be selected which are listened to with superior gratification, and which have been ranked so remarkably among the exact turning-points [of the history]; that, instead of exhibiting them to view only in their wrappings, if we may so speak, and then instantly snatching them from our sight, we ought to dwell on them for a certain space, and thus, as it were, unfold them and open them out to vision, and present them to the minds of the hearers as things to be examined and admired.[72]

For Augustine, this could be done in the short form of the last two pages of *Catechizing*, or may take the form of the five hundred or so pages of the last half of *The City of God*, both of which follow nearly identical outlines. This process of explicating the whole narrative of Scripture provides the context upon which any particular detail may be set within the theological vision. This entire vision is necessary because the meaning and importance of any part of the vision is often dependent upon other aspects of the vision, just as a stool is not a stool without all three of its legs.

---

71. Murphy and McClendon, "Distinguishing Modern and Postmodern Theologies," 200. They also mention Thomas Kuhn specifically in this context, to whom I will turn below.

72. Augustine, *On Catechizing* 3.5.

To show the subtle ways that facts can change the meaning and interpretation of other facts, another, more familiar parable is helpful. Let us imagine a set of imaginary facts:

A. There was a bank robbery.

B. John and Robert are two suspects with similar physical appearances.

C. John has been previously convicted of bank robbery.

D. John was known to be in the area of the bank at the time of the robbery.

E. John's fingerprints were found at the scene of the robbery.

F. Robert has no history of criminal wrongdoing.

G. Witnesses have identified Robert as the bank robber.

H. No physical evidence found at the bank can be linked to Robert.

If a person were to observe any one of these facts, there would be nothing convincing to convict either of these suspects of robbery. John's history, whereabouts, and his fingerprints are far from significant to the case individually. Only G can be counted as evidence for Robert's guilt, but B provides an easy alternative explanation. Certainly the arguments that are made in either case would be inconclusive, but it is just as likely that proponents of both persons' guilt could be found, and each side would imagine their case to be a rational explanation. However, if just a few more pieces of evidence are taken into account, it becomes much easier to sort out the case with a higher degree of confidence.

I. John is a customer of the bank.

J. John works at the factory down the street from the bank and was known to be working at the time of the robbery.

K. Robert was found to have money known to come from the bank in his possession.

L. Robert owns a gun similar to the one identified by witnesses.

M. Robert cannot account for his whereabouts at the time of the robbery.

As in most cases of this sort, there may still be advocates for Robert's innocence. These are even more likely to come from those who know Robert personally and believe him to be an honest and upright person. But the combination of G, K, L, and M would likely convince most reasonable persons that Robert is guilty of the robbery. In contrast, J almost singlehandedly clears John, and I would contribute to an alternative account for the most damning piece of evidence against John (E). While this new evidence may still not be enough to convince a jury "beyond a reasonable doubt" of

Robert's guilt, most reasonable people would conclude that John is almost certainly innocent and Robert is the best explanation as the guilty party. This is the kind of "argument" that is made in cases of law every day, and is generally considered reliable and reasonable.[73] It is most certainly not a deductive argument. It is a broadly inductive argument, but not a formal or linear one. Some pieces of evidence do seem to point toward one suspect or the other, but they do not straightforwardly make the case on their own. One would even struggle to call these premises at all, but would better be called evidence. Even those pieces that most count against John (C, D, and E) are not convincing on their own. But taken together, they make a relatively strong case against him. And in an even more difficult judgment, the most damning piece of evidence against Robert, G, could actually be used in conjunction with B to make a somewhat weak case for John's guilt if no other evidence were found against Robert. The difficulty of explaining how and why we make these judgments is due to the lack of a linear explanation, but we nonetheless think them reliable and reasonable.

Mitchell explains that most decisions between competing theories or explanations use this sort of logic, both in everyday life and in the academic disciplines. One of the strengths of this cumulative case proposal is that it is capable of investigating and even requires a more nuanced paradigm than the very generic formulations of "god" that typically are exhibited in natural theology.[74] Swinburne's is an example of attempting to explain "God" by a definition relatively close to the traditional Christian notion. And he has gone on to argue quite traditional Christian doctrine on his proposal, not the least of these being the deity of Jesus. Mitchell's proposal, without the need to reduce evidence to the oversimplified syllogisms of formal logic, requires the articulation of a detailed and nuanced interpretive paradigm such as is typical in most academic arguments and other arguments of substance. As an example, the proposed solutions to the classical synoptic problem with the Gospels are not decided upon generic arguments, but about very specific arguments about the composition, community, and authorship of the various texts. To reduce these arguments to syllogisms would distort

---

73. For an explanation of the similarities of cumulative case arguments and legal reasoning, see R. G. Wright, "Cumulative Case Legal Arguments and the Justification of Academic Affirmative Action," 1–41. Wright explains that legal arguments are divided between those that are argued directly and those that are argued from circumstantial evidence and identifies that latter as a cumulative case argument. But he also acknowledges that the difference is a matter of degree, because all legal arguments require some inference. Kuhn was also criticized for the division described below for too much distance between "normal science" and that of a paradigm crisis. While these kinds of distinctions are largely heuristic, they are nevertheless helpful.

74. Abraham, "Cumulative Case," 23.

the arguments themselves. The informality of Mitchell's approach better accounts for how these arguments proceed. The advantage for the apologist is the ability to argue for not just a generic "existence of god" but the whole-bodied Christian Gospel, and even the nuance of his or her own Pentecostal Gospel, Lutheran Gospel, and so on.[75] These very specific proposals are what will be argued, just as in other forms of discourse.

The three disciplines that serve as examples for him are that of critical exegesis of a text, interpretation of history, and decisions between various scientific theories. The points that he makes in each of these examples are overlapping; I will focus on the example of shifting scientific paradigms, since it provides the most thoroughgoing analogy and is the example that most intrigued Lindbeck.[76]

Thomas Kuhn's *The Structure of Scientific Revolutions* delineated two different stages of scientific research. The first of these he called *normal science*, which is the basic fact gathering and research that most scientists do for most of their careers. They operate within a given paradigm that sets the parameters for what is considered important scientific questions and answers. Each subsequent discovery may modify the paradigm within certain parameters, and in fact this is the reason that such normal science is done. Kuhn calls this a "mopping up" operation after an interpretive paradigm is discovered.[77] Scientific paradigms are adopted because they answer a few acute problems, but their discovery always entails leaving far more questions unanswered than are answered. The paradigm then gives direction for further experimentation and limits what is counted as real science by the questions it asks and answers.

Though Mitchell never makes this analogy explicitly, this process of normal science is roughly equivalent to the kind of doctrinal formulation and articulation that is the normal work of theology. Professional theologians, thoughtful lay persons, and denominational boards and structures all go about this work on a regular basis as they attempt to articulate what is generally accepted theology and doctrine in light of contemporary challenges. Theology is sometimes changed subtly in the process, but typically only within certain parameters. While I will not pursue the question here, there may be more to learn about the ways that this process of normal science illuminates the kind of cultural-linguistic framework for ecumenical

---

75. Though a particular argument for Christianity or any other alternative is required for the argument, Mitchell sketches his method such to accommodate "some degree, but not too great a degree, of flexibility." See Mitchell, *Justification of Religious Belief*, 3–4.

76. Lindbeck, *Nature of Doctrine*, 116–17.

77. Kuhn, *Structure of Scientific Revolutions*, 24.

dialogue that Lindbeck was after. Kuhn also is concerned with the ways that the paradigm supplies "rules" which govern legitimate exploration.[78]

Each of these subtle changes in the paradigm is brought about by anomalies for which the paradigm does not fully account. As scientists investigate these anomalies, the theory is refined by incremental changes until the anomalies actually become the expected.[79] It is only when the body of researchers proves unable to modify the prevailing paradigm to account for anomalies that the paradigm comes under crisis and potentially becomes subject to revolution. And it is only against the backdrop of a tested paradigm and researchers that understand well what is to be expected from the paradigm that anomalies can emerge. Without that kind of precise understanding of the paradigm, the anomaly appears to just be another question that the paradigm has not yet answered. But the well-developed paradigm functions to reveal the acute problems that bring about a crisis in the paradigm itself.[80]

This is part of what makes the work of normal science so valuable. Without the precision and understanding even of a paradigm that proves inadequate, anomalies cannot be discovered. This has a clear parallel in the theological questions that we are now investigating. Those who are uninitiated into a rigorous study of theology, and especially a particular paradigm for understanding theology, will be unable to articulate appropriate responses to troubling "anomalies" in the paradigm's interpretation of the world, even when these can in fact be discovered. Furthermore, it is only those that understand the paradigm well that will be able to articulate when it is in crisis. This will be the problem that will be taken up in chapter 4 and illuminates the troubling conclusion of Lindbeck at the end of *The Nature of Doctrine* when he suggests that a much more thoroughgoing catechesis will be necessary for evangelism and conversion to be possible, a catechesis that he ultimately thinks difficult or impossible in the current state of the church.[81]

In the process of scientific revolution, the crisis caused by the emerging consensus of unaccounted-for anomaly is the impetus for research and proposal of a new interpretive paradigm.[82] But even when there is

78. Ibid., 39–42.

79. Ibid., 52–53.

80. Ibid., 64–65.

81. Lindbeck, *Nature of Doctrine*, 118–20.

82. This is actually only one instance of a number of paths to revolution that Kuhn explains. These paths would make an interesting study and parallel into the psychology of religious conversion as well. Often, perceptions are changed not because there is a perceived need for a new paradigm, but because another scientist that discovers a better

some consensus that a new paradigm is needed, the old paradigm is never rejected until a new one has proven to take its place, and then only after considerable resistance. Once a scientist or a community of scientists finally give themselves over to the new paradigm, it changes their entire perception of what was previously considered science. Kuhn uses the language of the famous duck-rabbit to illustrate this shift in "gestalt switch."[83] But unlike the one who is observing the duck-rabbit, the scientific community simply does not have access to the new paradigm such that it can be taught how to observe the problem differently. This is available only after a new paradigm is discovered. And after this new gestalt is observed, the scientist does not have two optional ways of viewing science as does the observer of the duck-rabbit. That is, the scientist cannot choose to go back and use the previous paradigm as if it is simply another way of observing the phenomenon. Rather, the scientist will always refer to the way that they used to imagine the world, now seeing their previous worldview as a mistake.[84]

There simply is no way to compare the conclusions of the two positions either. In fact, many of the previous experiments will now need to be done again, with scientists using different criteria and controlling for different variables. The previous way of viewing the world simply is no longer adequate for making sense of the data, and the new paradigm potentially is capable of doing so, though this will still need to be proven by way of normal science.

The process of gestalt switch is not straightforward, and often proponents of two (or more) theories will coexist for some time, often in direct or indirect conflict with one another. This is due in part to a lack of complete understanding of the new paradigm, precisely because it is yet incomplete. Not unlike MacIntyre's acquisition of a "second first language," the scientist of the old paradigm is unable to see the intricacies of the new paradigm. In the case of MacIntyre's illustration, this is because of immaturity in understanding the new "language." In the case of a new scientific paradigm, the immaturity is due to the fully developed paradigm not yet being available. This will only be developed after much work of normal science. So these two competing paradigms will go on operating in their separate "schools" until the new paradigm is able to account for the problems it illumines adequately.

---

paradigm works very diligently to convince his or colleagues that the new paradigm is more adequate at explaining anomalies. You might say that the scientist who discovers this new paradigm becomes a herald of the good news, something of an evangelist.

83. Kuhn, *Structure of Scientific Revolutions*, 111f. Cf. Mitchell, *Justification of Religious Belief*, 65.

84. Kuhn, *Structure of Scientific Revolutions*, 114–16. Cf. Mitchell, *Justification of Religious Belief*, 65.

The comparison to the apologetic enterprise and the process of gestalt shift necessary for a religious conversion should at this point be obvious. If a person can be shown via detailed theological analysis that a worldview is inadequate to account for the facts of the world as they are observed, then the anomalies with the worldview will shift a person into a crisis of faith. As alluded to above, actual narratives of conversion are not that straightforward. But the logic of this shift holds nonetheless. As a person, either after having been shown the anomalies or after having discovered them on his or her own, realizes that the anomalies cannot be accounted for, there is an opportunity for a new paradigm to answer the questions left by the old paradigm. Especially as the person newly considers the alternative paradigm, he or she will not yet understand all of the ways that this paradigm answers other anomalies or accounts for other observed facts. But given adequate time and understanding, they can experience the gestalt shift that accompanies accepting a new worldview. Mitchell argues that this period of transition and upheaval that is present in the periods of paradigm change in the sciences is always present in the humanities. There is never the kind of consensus that is often present in the sciences, and therefore the field is always in a state of multiple competing paradigms.[85]

One of the key reasons that Mitchell finds Kuhn compelling at this point is Kuhn's insistence that there simply is no proof that resolves the tension between these paradigms. Rather, those scientists that best understand both paradigms are able to make judgments about which paradigm best fits the observed facts and makes sense of those facts.[86] Their relative mastery of one theory or another makes them best qualified to make this judgment.[87] More appropriately, Kuhn thinks the decisions between competing scientific paradigms will best be done by a community of scientists. "[T]ake a *group* of the ablest available people with the most appropriate motivation; train them in some science and in the specialties relevant to the choice at hand; imbue them with the value system, the ideology, current in their discipline . . . and finally, *let them make the choice*."[88] Perhaps the

85. Mitchell, *Justification of Religious Belief*, 90–91.

86. Kuhn, *Structure of Scientific Revolutions*, 52–53. As Kuhn suggests, there are no "brute facts," and the distinction between fact and theory is an artificial one. They are observations made within the confines of the paradigm. These are not without merit and need not be subject to skepticism, but are limited by the same paradigm that helped illuminate them.

87. Kuhn is quite skeptical about whether those of the old paradigm will be convinced by anything short of a conversion of their scientific vision.

88. Kuhn, "Reflections on My Critics," 237–38. This was incorrectly cited by Mitchell as a quote from *Structure of Scientific Revolutions* (Mitchell, *Justification of Religious Belief*, 77).

most significant challenges to the analogy to science emerge at this point. First, there is no equivalent body to this team of scientists that could make decisions about religious worldviews, because the religious worldview is so much farther wide-ranging than the scientific one.[89] The analogy would better fit the process of a team of persons deciding between just two competing worldviews. Mitchell imagines a conversation between Christianity and atheism. We might similarly imagine a comparison within Christianity itself, or between Reformed Christianity and Tibetan Buddhism. The potential paradigms competing for attention are infinitely more diverse than this, and the "experts" of one paradigm would have little expertise in the workings of another paradigm. This is where the analogy to science is of less value. The scientists judging between two competing scientific paradigms would share similar training and assumptions about other areas not related to the paradigm difference.

The second challenge to the analogy to science emerges from the historical lack of consensus among religious scholars. Even if we were to imagine that, for instance, the great academic community of religious scholars would be comparable in this case, the lack of any consensus would lend little confidence in whatever judgments they might make. The assumption that any one individual person must make a personal judgment about his or her own world-view without even the benefit of the consensus among the scholars complicates the matter further. Even presupposing that laypersons are epistemically justified in making decisions about the position they will hold on the basis of authority;[90] there is still a significant difficulty in knowing which authority to place one's trust. It does not follow, however, that the logic of this reasoning process is of a radically different kind than scientific judgments. Rather, the plurality of religious paradigms and complexity of the competing theological visions only complicate this by a matter of degree. It is still a reasonable and rational process, even if a difficult one.

Because ultimately the acceptance of a paradigm comes down to a choice, Mitchell emphasizes that Kuhn is not arguing for irrationalism. These choices are rational ones, but they are not subject to formal argument or proof. Rather they are choices based on the ability of one paradigm or another to account for the facts that are most pressing. The massive scope of this kind of judgment is likely the reason that a group of well-trained persons is best able to make such a choice. The variety of details and required

89. Mitchell, "Faith and Reason," 131–44; Thomas, "Cumulative Arguments for Religious Belief," 37–47.

90. Mitchell affirms the justification in making decisions based on authority, in religion and other fields. Mitchell, "Faith and Reason: A False Antithesis?"

expertise is too great for one person. But a team of rightly trained persons will together make a judgment as to the reliability of the paradigm.

What will count as "facts" is dependent upon the paradigm itself. But Mitchell argues that comparison and conversation is nevertheless possible as to what constitutes the criteria for judgment, even if members of both parties will never give up arguing for those facts that will inevitably lead to the adoption of their own conclusion. Between two opposing positions, Mitchell says that rational judgment is yet possible.

> [The opposing sides of the debate] will not make progress so long as they fail to recognize that different presuppositions are involved; but there seems no good reason to deny that rational choice is possible between presuppositions, for they can be judged by their capacity to make sense of all the relevant evidence. There is an essential role for trained judgment in all these rational activities, not least when a choice has to be made between conceptual systems.[91]

The criteria upon which these judgments will be made must, as Mitchell rightly suggests, be neutral, such that those of competing paradigms can agree on at least these criteria. Kuhn calls these criteria "values," and gives a list similar to that of cumulative case apologists: consistency, coherence, simplicity, elegance, explanatory power, and fertility. While Mitchell insists that there are some significant differences between religion and science, there are enough similarities to show that other realms in which judgment between paradigms is necessary, persons do in fact make rational judgments between those paradigms.[92]

Just as I have done throughout this chapter, Mitchell's primary mode of justifying the method that he proposes is to show that this just is how persons make rational judgments, and that these judgments are in fact rational. There is nothing unique about religious judgments in this regard. Furthermore, Mitchell shows that there is significant precedent within theology as well. As we have already seen with Swinburne and Mitchell, Cardinal Newman also sought to show that the cumulative case mode of reasoning is the way judgments are made in other disciplines, especially history, religion, and morality.[93] Mitchell summarizes Newman's thought with a reconstruction that could easily be taken as his own method.

---

91. Mitchell, *Justification of Religious Belief*, 91.

92. Ibid. Mitchell thinks that the most significant difference between science and religion is that science has more clearly defined criteria as to what constitutes actual scientific inquiry and research. Religion and other humanities have no such criteria.

93. Mitchell, "Newman as a Philosopher," 226.

1. Much of our reasoning is tacit and informal. It cannot be expressed in syllogistic form (for Newman the only form available to logic) but involves the continuous exercise of personal judgment operating upon a range of disparate considerations. "It is the cumulation of probabilities, independent of each other, arising out of the nature and circumstances of the particular case which is under review; probabilities too fine to avail separately, too subtle and circuitous to be convertible to syllogisms, too numerous and various for such conversion, even were they convertible."

2. Most arguments upon matters of any substance are cumulative in form. They involve taking account of a range of considerations, none of which alone suffices to generate the required conclusion, but which together converge upon it. Newman has no difficulty in providing illustration of this informal and cumulative process of reasoning from everyday life:

   "Let a person only call to mind the clear impression he has about matters of every day's occurrence, that this man is bent on a certain object, or that that man was displeased, or another suspicious; or that one is happy, and another unhappy; and how much depends in such impressions on manner, voice, accent, words offered, silence instead of words, and all the many subtle symptoms which are felt by the mind, but cannot be contemplated; and let him consider how poor an account he is able to give of his impression, if he avows it, and is called upon to justify it. This, indeed, is meant by what is called moral proof, in opposition to legal."

3. There is no bar to the possibility of arguments of this type achieving certainty. The various considerations to which appeal is made may cooperate so effectively as to put a particular conclusion beyond reasonable doubt.[94]

Mitchell's reconstruction of Cardinal Newman's apologetic reasoning is particularly interesting, because the article was written so late in Mitchell's life and seems to display even more confidence that the cumulative case mode of justification could produce a high level of rational certainty. It is not the case for Mitchell or Newman that these cumulative case arguments "should be accepted only as a last resort after formal arguments of a more rigorous kind have been found inappropriate."[95] The argument for these men is that an attempt to turn a complex argument into syllogisms both

94. Ibid., 227.
95. Abraham, "Cumulative Case Arguments for Christian Theism," 30.

oversimplifies and distorts the argument. A better argument will include all of the complexities of a cumulative case.

POSTLIBERAL THEOLOGY AS AN APOLOGETIC METHOD: CONCLUSIONS THUS FAR

Lindbeck only imagined apologetics of two kinds: correlational theology and proof from natural theology. He rightly recognized that a postliberal theology could follow neither of these paths. Instead, Lindbeck identified postliberal theology with a philosophy of religion he found compelling, one that entails its own thinking about justification: cumulative case apologetics. The detailing of this method of reasoning through the works of Mitchell and Kuhn has revealed very little more than what we had learned from the description of Lindbeck above. Though it was appropriate for Lindbeck to distance himself from these other kinds of apologetics, the ways in which the term "ad hoc apologetics" has been bantered about as a mostly pejorative term is unwarranted. The question still remains as to how postliberal theology does affect the task of defending the truth of Christian faith. Bringing together several themes from what has been argued so far should bring some clarity.

The version of postliberal reasoning and religious justification outlined by Lindbeck is identifiable as a relatively well-established method of apologetics that is typically called cumulative case. Cumulative case apologetics does not proceed by formal logic, but it is a rational process with straightforward criteria. The fact that this is not a formal logic process does not invalidate the method, as it is the same process used in such important and rational matters as legal judgment and judgments between scientific paradigms, which are both considered reliable reasonable processes. Therefore, Lindbeck's criticism of "post-Cartesian natural theology" does not set him apart from acceptable apologetic practice and reasoning. Most modern apologetic methods do not consist of the classical foundationalism of this type.

While the mode of rational justification of Lindbeck's postliberal proposal falls neatly under the category of cumulative case apologetics, the narrative and intratextual element of the cultural-linguistic type does make it a unique species of this larger genus. The overarching theological vision of the Christian religion will not emerge through the process of formulating the apologetic argument as was sometimes thought in classical apologetics or natural theology. Apologetics will not start with a somewhat barren notion of God and build toward a distinctly Christian theology. And it will not assume that a distinctly Christian theology will "emerge" through the process of investigation.[96] The postliberal apologetic will begin with the theological vision entailed in the biblical narrative, and proceed in a Barthian fashion by articulating and re-articulating the multiple ways that this theological vision makes sense of our experience of the world in a much better way than alternative visions. To use John Milbank's terminology, the apologist must "out-narrate" alternative theological or atheological visions.[97]

Despite all of the criticism to the contrary, Lindbeck does articulate a notion of truth that is not less than a correspondence notion of truth. Lindbeck calls correspondence "ontological truth," and does not diminish its necessity. Rather, he adds additional prerequisite criteria related to understanding religious utterances within a cultural-linguistic matrix. He refers to these preconditions by the unfortunate term, "intrasystematic truth," but Lindbeck has explained that this is his way of adding the intratextual conditions by which truth claims are made intelligible. The result is the necessity of all theological language being dependent upon a cultural-linguistic matrix from which it cannot be extracted. Apologetics therefore should not appeal to neutral rationality, but must highlight the traditioned nature of all reasoning, including that of the apologist's interlocutor. The challenge that this adds to the apologetic task is related to incommensurability of competing narratives. MacIntyre's notion of learning a "second first language" enables us to understand the ways in which this challenge can be overcome. Apologists that accept the postliberal theological construal will be bound to acquire a much deeper understanding of the tradition(s) of their interlocutors. They will also need to invite their interlocutor into a kind of preliminary catechesis so that the interlocutor can evaluate Christianity on its own terms.

As Lindbeck suggested in *The Nature of Doctrine*, apologetics in a dechristianized culture will require nothing less than the formation of community, with all the attendant practices required to sustain it. This will be no easy task. This community will need to be so immersed in the narrative and practices of the Christian vision that it will be able to sustain living this vision as a witness for the world. This community of practice will also

96. This is the approach of Geivett, another cumulative case apologist. Without evaluating the merits of this approach to apologetics, the differences from an intratextual approach are significant. "One begins with a very general phenomenon, such as the existence of a temporally finite universe, and infers the existence of a non-natural reality as the best explanation of this phenomenon. Further investigation into particular features of this spatiotemporal world subsequently yields an increasingly precise conception of the non-natural reality causally responsible for the space-time world." Geivett, *Evil and the Evidence for God*, 92–93.

97. Milbank, *Theology and Social Theory*, 330–33.

be the best place for non-Christian apologetic interlocutors to experience the paradigmatic Christian vision. Those who are serious about engagement with the Christian vision will have no better opportunity. The formation of this community will be the subject of chapter 4.

4

Worship, Apologetics,
and the Need for Catechesis

INTRODUCTION

APOLOGETICS IN A POSTLIBERAL mode is much more dependent upon the formation of Christians and on the formation of apologetic interlocutors, such that both groups can "see" the world with a Christian vision. For the non-Christian, this will only be in a preliminary way. They nevertheless must recognize that understanding is dependent upon the necessity of a Christian way of seeing. The Christian is dependent upon formation in a more thoroughgoing sense. The Christian's contribution to the apologetic task is not only to "see" in a Christian way, but also to embody the Gospel which Christians proclaim in evangelical witness.

The preceding three chapters have focused largely on how the faith must be articulated to make sense of this way of seeing for the non-Christian. The subject of this chapter is the actual method and processes for formation of the Christian and the church that are necessary for apologetics. Lindbeck's direction for apologetics registered only a brief mention near the end of his already short book. Catechesis is to be preferred to apologetic "translation." Lindbeck's reference to catechesis includes a two-fold notion of learning both Christian beliefs and Christian practices. Ways of thinking and ways of acting are bound up together in a "form of life" that precedes the ability to intelligently and responsibly evaluate the truthfulness of the Christian faith or to profess the faith.

In previous chapters, I agreed with the substance of Lindbeck's conclusion regarding theological reasoning. Rational justification is possible but is dependent upon reasoning that is not foundational. But I dissented from Lindbeck's pessimism about this conclusion. I argued that this way of justifying beliefs has an established method and tradition in the Christian faith and need not be considered inferior. Similarly, I agree with the substance of Lindbeck's conclusion that apologetics in a postliberal mode will be primarily about catechesis. But I am not as pessimistic as he about the prospects for this task. Lindbeck wrote that the dechristianization of Western culture limited the effectiveness of Christian socialization of previous generations that would have provided the catechesis necessary. For Lindbeck, it is no longer possible for persons to absorb a genuinely Christian form of life from surrounding culture. He considers a genuine conversion by catechesis to be impossible because so many persons still imagine themselves to be vaguely Christian, even if their lives and beliefs do not resemble a traditional Christian form of life. Confrontation with a genuinely Christian form of life is not jarring enough to nominal Christians to elicit further exploration and commitment. Even when a person submits himself or herself to catechesis, Lindbeck thinks that the life of the congregation to which they submit themselves will not sufficiently embody the way of life to which they are called.[1] Without a community of formation capable of witnessing to a genuine form of life, neither can persons be formed into this way of life.

While I share Lindbeck's conclusions on these matters, I do not share his pessimism at this point either. In part, this may be due to the success of a number of renewal movements that have arisen since Lindbeck's writing. Ekklesia Project and the movements often referred to under the headings of "the New Monasticism" and "the missional church" are the ones that are most clearly connected to postliberal thinkers. While each of these have some different emphases, they all share a commitment to deeper and more thoughtful practices of formation as the primary way to become more effective and faithful in evangelism and witness. Instances of congregations that took this kind of formation seriously, resulting in a vibrant Christian witness, are easy enough to discover. I suppose that one might argue that this is true because the "continuing dechristianization" of America has proceeded for another twenty-five years since Lindbeck wrote *The Nature of Doctrine*. He argued that this would provide new opportunities for a new catechesis. Whatever the reason, I do not think we need to be discouraged about the prospects of a genuinely apologetic witness arising from congregations that are committed to deep formation.

1. This paragraph is a summary of Lindbeck, *Nature of Doctrine*, 118–20. See also Lindbeck's assessment of the lack of spiritual formation upon the training of clergy, "Spiritual Formation and Theological Education," 285–302.

This final chapter is therefore intended to be a roadmap for how this kind of formation can be employed with attention to apologetic witness. I will show that apologetics of this variety must pay attention to doctrine and practice without sacrificing the former for the sake of a rhetorical emphasis on the latter. I will also explore four specific aspects of the apologetic witness that arise from each of the four major segments of the most quintessential Christian practice: Christian public worship. The fourfold order of *gathering, proclamation, response,* and *sending* will symbolize four contributions to apologetic methodology that arise from postliberal theology.[2]

The *gathering* orders our way of life by inviting us out of the plurality of our family and working vocations and into our common vocation as the Christian community. Apologetics in the postliberal mode must also invite an interlocutor to consider his or her own way of life as one among many. It invites those outside of the Christian way to consider a new way of seeing, whether in a preliminary or committed way, for it is only from a new way of seeing that evaluation of the Christian way of life is possible. Likewise, the serious apologist may also have to enter the conceptual world of his or her interlocutor for the dialogue to reach sufficient depth.

The reading and *proclamation* of Scripture in worship informs Christian apologetic and must also be informed by the narrative emphasis of postliberalism. While other segments of worship will focus on the practices of formation, proclamation is the aspect of worship most clearly aimed at the formation of a Christian way of thinking. The postliberal emphasis on narrative must be reflected in congregational preaching. I will explain how the narrative of Scripture must be employed in preaching to form worshippers into the Christian way of thinking.

Response is the place where our affections are most acutely formed. While in one sense all of worship is the prior response to God's call to discipleship, the response to the proclamation is paradigmatic for the whole life of responding to God's call. The archetypal response to the Word is the call to dine at the Eucharist. In the modern church, there is a plethora of alternative responses used in the liturgies of churches, some of which are quite appropriate as formation into the Christian way. I will explore how all of these various responses help shape the affections of worshippers in the way of Christ.

---

2. Other liturgical scholars divide the liturgy somewhat differently. For instance, Stanley Hauerwas and Samuel Wells are two postliberals who divide the Eucharistic and non-Eucharistic (or better, pre-Eucharistic) aspects of *response* (Hauerwas and Wells, *Blackwell Companion to Christian Ethics*). I follow Constance Cherry and others who identify a fourfold order. See Cherry, *Worship Architect*.

Sending orients worship toward the church's mission to make disciples of all nations. As has already been argued above, the church's apologetic witness is in large part dependent upon her ability to proclaim and enact the goodness of God. I will argue that working toward the justice that is proclaimed by the Christian narrative is integral and prerequisite for evangelism, to which the church is called. While this is true in every age, this is particularly true in the twenty-first-century, in which the church has increasingly lost the reputation as the world's strongest advocate for justice.

GATHERING

Beginning with the etymological implications of the English word "worship," Philip Kenneson claims that every human action "ascribes worth," and the ways that people gather is but one of these.[3] It is readily acknowledged that gathering is expressive of shared understanding and values ("You and I both like the Colts, therefore we both go to their games"; also, "I value our meeting together more because I invited you to dinner for steak, rather than meeting for a quick service burger"). Kenneson also claims that gathering together is formative, by shaping participants' moral and imaginative framework by the narratives implicit in gathering.[4]

Worship is expressive of the innermost commitments of participants. The very fact that participants gather with this community, rather than participate in the multitude of other callings and recreations to which they might respond on a given Sunday, is enough to mark them out as a peculiar people.[5] Smith claims that this entails a bit of scandal because as we go to worship we go past many who will choose not to respond to God's call to worship. They will choose to golf, garden, or recover from an evening of indulgence.[6] But God's peculiar people will respond to God's call to gather for worship, sometimes walking past neighbors and family to do so. Alexander Schmemann says it this way:

> The journey begins when Christians leave their homes and beds. They leave, indeed, their life in this present and concrete world, and whether they have to drive fifteen miles or walk a few

---

3. This is a correlative to James K. A. Smith's point that worship is that thing that is most human. That which is most human is also most likely to be distorted. Romantic love is another example here. Though it is part of God's design, perversions are plentiful. Smith, *Desiring the Kingdom*, 159–66.

4. Kennesson, "Gathering," 53–54.

5. Smith, *Desiring the Kingdom*, 159–60.

6. Ibid., 161.

blocks, a sacramental act is already taking place, an act that is the very condition of everything else that is to happen. For they are now on their way to *constitute the Church*, or to be more exact, to be transformed into the Church of God. They have been individuals, some white, some black, some poor, some rich, they have been the "natural" world and a natural community. And now they have been called to "come together in one place," to bring their lives, their very "world" with them and to be more than what they were: a *new* community with a new life.[7]

This act of gathering is a response to the prior act of God revealing himself in Jesus Christ as worthy of worship. "Rightly understood, therefore, the gathering of the *ekklesia* is not simply a prerequisite to worship, but is already itself an act of worship."[8] By the very fact that these people have gathered with this community and not some other, they have ascribed worth to the God who is the object of its worship. As many apologists contend, apologetics is to some extent "a dialogue between the believer and the unbeliever in the heart of the Christian himself."[9] Though the faithfulness of the Christian presupposes a commitment to worshipping God implicit in gathering, the expression of this commitment is also a willing subjection to the formation that this gathering institutes. As E. Byron Anderson writes, "Socially and psychologically, the sharing of meaning enacted and constructed in the course of ritual identifies a person with (or outside of) a community even as it grounds that person's sense of self."[10] Admittedly some that gather each Sunday do so with a bit of hesitancy, as at least some of them would rather join their friends on the golf course or their family in the garden. Even when the call to worship is answered begrudgingly, "our response in gathering is already a sign of God's redemption and regeneration at work."[11]

The expression of commitments implicit in the gathering necessarily reinforces and further forms those commitments. As Kenneson writes,

> Because human beings are social creatures, when they gather together they inevitably presuppose and reinforce much about the shape, meaning, and purpose of the world that they understand themselves to inhabit. Indeed, all human gatherings are a kind of worship to the extent that they presuppose and reinforce certain ascriptions of worth. For this reason, human gatherings

7. Schmemann, *For the Life of the World*, 27.

8. Kenneson, "Gathering," 60.

9. Dulles, *History of Apologetics*, xvi.

10. Anderson, *Worship and Christian Identity*, 64.

11. Smith, *Desiring the Kingdom*, 161.

are inevitably formative, not least because such gatherings construct an imaginative landscape (a 'world') within which all future action and reflection upon it will take place.[12]

So this gathering forms these stories more deeply in the Christian, who is then able to more deeply articulate various implications and connections of varying aspects of the story.   Persons always receive these imaginative frameworks from the narratives that are implicit and explicit in the practices in which they engage. For instance, these can be explicit in the "talking heads" on network news that communicate a vision of reality, the problems that must be overcome, and the solutions to those problems through constant and deeply partisan "reporting." At other times the narrative employed is implicit, though not necessarily subtle.

Many postliberals have taken aim at consumer capitalism and marketing as the most ubiquitous counter-narrative to Christianity in contemporary culture.[13] It is a prime example of the practices that employ an implicit narrative, in part because the employment of that narrative is so well documented in marketing literature.[14] Christians, like every other modern person, participate in the practices associated with this counter-narrative alongside their Christian practices. No one is isolated such that they participate in only one narrative and its constitutive practices. Therefore, the Christian that has awakened early on Sunday to submit themselves to the formative practices of the church may very well end their day watching a Disney movie with their children. This may lead to a trip to McDonald's or the mall for the carefully marketed toys that accompany that movie. The entire process of marketing and consumption is designed to give persons an imaginative framework based on a different narrative. You might imagine this to be a consumerist "Roman's Road" or "Four Spiritual Laws."[15]

All the images that cross our television screens and meet us at every intersection, the images of beautiful people smiling and enjoying friends, are not meant to give the viewer the same feelings of joy and "the good life" that they project. Those images are meant to display a life that the viewer does not have, and maybe no one has. It is a fabricated life, a kind of pornography that projects an image that cannot be realized.

12. Kenneson, "Gathering," 55.

13. Cavanaugh, *Being Consumed*; Pahl, *Shopping Malls and Other Sacred Places*; Kenneson, *Life on the Vine.*

14. See Schmitt, *Experiential Marketing*; Linn, *Consuming Kids*; Dretzin and Goodman, *Persuaders.* For helpful direction on resisting the marketing influence in youth ministry see Berard, Penner, and Bartlett, *Consuming Youth.*

15. The analogy of marketing as capitalist evangelism comes from Smith, *Desiring the Kingdom*, 95, 102–3.

The liturgies of the mall and the market inscribe in us a sense that something is wrong with us, that something's broken, by holding up for us the ideals of which we fall short. On the one hand, those ideals draw on the power of authentic human desires for friendship, joy, love, and play. On the other hand, they also tend to implant and exaggerate less laudable ideals, focusing on particular conceptions of external beauty that are culturally relative and often impossible to achieve, being the products of digital manipulation; a supposedly ideal body type that can only be achieved in ways that are artificial and/or unhealthy; superficial fixations on image and the perceptions of others; and the celebration of a kind of irresponsibility masking itself as a "carefree" attitude but that is blind to questions of justice. In addition, such images are meant to impress upon us a deep sense of lack, thereby engendering a powerful sense of *need* that would otherwise be absent (as when a child begs a parent, "I *need* a PS3!").[16]

The "original sin" that must be resolved in the market's narrative is a "falling short" of ideal perceptions. Marketing presents the unholy icons of the consumerist saints in these images of the ideal type. Like holy icons, the images are not intended to be realistic, but are instead intended to represent an ideal type to which we are to aspire.

Like Christian faith, the market too calls persons to gather. The mall serves as the market's sanctuary. While the church's gathering was to join together in a community for the sake of a shared way of life and mission, this gathering is inherently competitive. The individual shopper chooses stores that portray the image that they most want to adopt. This initiates them into a kind of "community" with others that shop at this store. The beautiful people that shop at this store are imagined to be the community to which one belongs. But the community quickly turns to competition as each person compares themselves with the others. The icons in the advertising serve as the ideal type to which each is compared. She who looks most like the ad wins.[17] Even the gathering together reinforces the narrative, because everyone "loses" at least some of those competitions with their fellow shoppers to be like the icon. While the market promotes itself as a way to exercise freedom and individuality, it actually forms us to be much like one another. If someone wants to make a truly counter-cultural choice, they feel the need to justify themselves to others. As Kenneson writes, whether someone purchases a Honda or a Chevy will not be questioned. But if some-

16. Ibid., 97.
17. Ibid., 98.

one decides to forsake owning an individual car to ride a bike or bus, she is likely to explain this choice away. She will say that she is saving money or trying to get more exercise. This response assumes that the image of every person driving their own car is indeed the goal to be achieved. But she is very unlikely to challenge the system by suggesting that individual choices about travel are causing foreign wars over oil and unnecessary greenhouse gas emissions.[18] She has learned that the market has set the standard to which she will be compared.

Also like the Christian narrative, the market's narrative proposes a resolution to the brokenness that it portrays. Purchasing this good or partaking of that service will make the consumer like those happy and beautiful people in the advertisement. This is so blatant that at times it is not even necessary to feature the product in the advertisement. If a desirable image is portrayed, then the product or brand can swoop in at the last moment to be associated with the image. In marketing the new airline Song (a name in no way associated with air travel, but one associated with lots of personal and public narratives), Delta Air Lines spent one third of their initial marketing budget on commercials that did not mention flying, airplanes, low cost, or unique services at all. They instead portrayed the kind of woman that would be using their service. They told a story. Nothing more was needed.[19] John Kavanaugh explains it this way:

> Friendship, intimacy, love, pride, happiness, and joy are actually the *objects* we buy and consume, much more so than the tubes, liquor bottles, Cadillacs, and Buicks that promise them and bear their names. And since none of these deepest human hopes can be fulfilled in any product, the mere consumption of them is never enough; "more" of the product, or a "new improved" product, is the only relief offered to our human longings.[20]

Smith explains that shopping promises to relieve affliction in two ways. Shopping itself becomes "retail therapy," as the process of shopping and purchasing enchants its participants with possibilities. Hours are spent roaming aisles for just the right item, or even "bargain hunting" to find the item at just the right price. The store is beautiful, and the shopper is the center of attention for the staff that waits upon them. Additionally, "retail therapy" results in the acquisition of goods that have been sold on the promise of

18. Kenneson, *Life on the Vine*, 69–70.

19. This airline did fail, so maybe this is not a great example. Their story and this statistic about their budget are featured in the PBS Frontline documentary, *The Persuaders*.

20. Kavanaugh, *Following Christ in a Consumer Society*, 34.

beauty, joy, and friendship. Our *needs* are met with the goods that promise to fulfill those needs.

Notice that the purchasing of goods alone is not capable of producing the narrative that motivates the purchase. I would suggest that proper formation in the Christian (or some other) narrative is capable of redescribing the act of purchasing and consumption into a quite different practice that accords with the Christian way. To do so will require nothing less than the clash of these two narratives and the revelation that one of them is indeed more true, beautiful and good. Only then will persons be willing to make intentional choices that will redescribe the act of purchasing into another narrative. As I have acknowledged, Western Christians will always have at least these two narratives competing for their attention. The one that tells the most compelling and truthful story will win the heart of the believer.

Part of the apologetic process will be the description and deconstruction of these competing narratives. In the case of the market narrative, this only requires the revelation that these goods never actually satisfy their intended ends. The new car does not have new friends included. And the new jeans do not actually make anyone thinner or more toned. They failed to meet their promises.[21] In fact, the advertising itself intentionally makes the product obsolete so that another has to be purchased in this season's style. This market narrative is not beautiful, good, or true.[22]

Though the purchasing of goods alone does not produce the narrative or form participants in it, no one is *just* purchasing goods. Everyone views the ubiquitous advertising and is attended by charismatic clerks and salespersons. According to Kenneson, how deeply a gathering is able to form its participants are dependent upon at least five factors. Frequency, the stability of the participant group, the scope of the vision entailed, the intensity of the social interaction, and willingness of those gathered to be a part of the vision are all important factors.[23] The intentions of both the individual participants and the governing community still seem to be the most significant factors. Returning to the shopping example, a Christian may very well subvert the consumerist narrative by inserting a prayer of discernment into their purchasing liturgy. One such prayer was printed on small key tags to be prayed before each purchase:

---

21. Smith, *Desiring the Kingdom*, 99–100.

22. Though I did not mention it, Smith shows that the effects of consumption and waste are not "good" because there are costs and injustices that cannot be seen on this side of the world. Overuse of natural resources and exploitive labor are required to produce these goods. Smith, *Desiring the Kingdom*, 101.

23. Kenneson, "Gathering," 57.

> *Lord, help me to be grateful for what I have, to remember that I*
> *don't need most of what I want, and that joy is found in simplicity*
> *and generosity.*[24]

Whether such a practice can subvert the entirety of the formative effects is doubtful. But this practice can revolutionize the consumption practices of those who enter with intentionality and works to resist the market narratives that surround it. If we do not intentionally subvert such practices, then an unconscious participation still has the effect of formation. "Whether we intentionally choose to participate in a practice, or unintentionally just find ourselves immersed in it over time, the result is the same: the dispositions become inscribed into our unconscious so that we 'automatically' respond the way we've [sic] been conditioned."[25] Nevertheless, to intentionally engage in purchasing goods *embedded in another kind of practice* changes the kind of formation altogether.

Thus far I have primarily focused on the ways in which gathering can form participants as a kind of apologetic that enables the participant to make sense of the world in a narrative way. As we have seen, one need not intend to be formed by one's practices. No one would choose the marketing narrative that leaves them with lower self-esteem and smaller bank accounts. The "pairing" of the practices associated with purchasing and consuming and the narrative that accompanies them creates dispositions that are unconscious. This "automaticity" creates a universe and paired dispositions that operate independent of our choosing the narrative. "All of the ingredients for automation might be present without our consciously or intentionally *choosing* to be shaped in this way."[26] The intention to be formed by the practice does increase the likelihood and the magnitude of the formation, however.

The Christian that gathers for the purpose of becoming a more faithful follower of Jesus will be more dramatically formed by the call and response of the liturgy than one that does not. Kenneson's point about the intentionality of the participant raises questions about whether a person that is only "participating" in the liturgy as an aspect of an apologetic discourse can genuinely be formed by it. That is, my earlier suggestion about how two competing paradigms can properly be evaluated requires that each paradigm must be approached from the inside. This can be done in part through

---

24. Hamilton, *Enough*. Ironically, the book, stewardship program, and key tags were all slickly marketed and took part in the consumerist narrative that they worked to undermine.

25. Smith, *Desiring the Kingdom*, 81.

26. Ibid., 81.

the description and redescription of one's own position to one's interlocutor. But it will likely require, likely at some advanced stage of dialogue, participation in those practices most paradigmatic of the other's view of the world. Worship is not the only or maybe even the best place that persons will witness the Christian way, but it is the paradigmatic place. In worship, the Christian way is put on display most explicitly for an apologetic interlocutor to observe in its barest nakedness.

In a dechristianized and increasingly secular culture, the "adherents" of competing paradigms will often not be committed to their way of seeing in a way that would prohibit participation in Christian practices, in part because those competing narratives are often not explicitly religious. Returning to the market narrative, persons that would have strong allegiance to the story of redemption that the market proposes would be rare. This does not suggest that the formative forces at work are not strong and comprehensive. Rather, even those most formed by this narrative will not have such strong loyalty to it that they will not sometimes participate in practices that challenge it. For example, it is not unusual for me to meet college students that will purchase some "fair trade" goods and be thankful for the opportunity to contribute to a counter-narrative of production and consumption. But only a few students actually remake their other consumption practices to do so. Many are content to purchase goods that challenge the system and others that perpetuate it without recognizing the dissonance between these practices. Similarly, persons formed by the market narrative are unlikely to object to participation in Christian worship on the grounds that it challenges their commitment to capitalism. Welcoming persons formed by narratives that they do not intentionally choose to participate in is unlikely to produce immediate dissonance. But some persons are committed to counter-narratives to which they are deeply loyal, and the dissonance between those narratives and full participation in Christian liturgy will be obvious to them. In these cases, we must forge a path that does not violate the conscience of either person in the apologetic dialogue if there is to be any progress. Denominational resources are widely available that give suggestions for creating rituals that are hospitable to persons of various religious commitments. Some guidelines for giving and receiving hospitality in the process of an interfaith apologetic dialogue can be adapted from these.[27]

As I argue above, the way toward resolving concerns about the rational incommensurability of various positions is best understood with MacIntyre's notion of learning a "second first language." The Christian way of

---

27. I highly recommend the Presbyterian Church's (U.S.A.) *Respectful Presence*. I also have a set of best practices in Gibbs, "Preserving Integrity," 34–41.

talking and thinking may at first seem mundane and familiar, especially for those living in a formerly Christian culture such as Western civilization. But continued evaluation of the depth of the grammar of Christian theology reveals that the grammar of authentic Christian faith belies the familiarity of the surface grammar. The primary place where Christian and interlocutor will learn to properly use the Christian grammar is Christian worship, where the language, formative practices, and dispositions of the Christian way are most carefully kept.

While it is initially a presumptive notion that a person must first gather in Christian worship to be enabled to evaluate it, postliberals insist that there is no neutral translation of this idiom. Therefore all apologetic discourse must take place within an idiom. Bryan Stone rightly argues that evangelism must remain non-violent in its form and content. Inviting persons to participate or even to just observe the Christian way is not violent in itself. He rightfully suggests that, "Christian apologetics must refuse to consider believers as either barbarian or irrational."[28] This recognition of the dignity and humanity of one's interlocutor is enacted in part by recognition that he or she has the reasoning and fortitude to reject the Christian way and narrative if they do not find it compelling. We need not worry that our invitation to "taste and see that the Lord is good" is coercive if we can respect that our interlocutor is free to reject this way of life if it is not found to be compelling. There have been times in the church's history (and it doubtless happens in our era) that persons have not been free to reject the Christian way because of political, social, or physical violence or their threat. If we keep our witness free of the threat of violent coercion, then we are also free to witness to the Christian way while recognizing the dignity of our interlocutor to reject this way.

If MacIntyre and the postliberals are correct, then there is no other way than the acquisition of this other language. The Christian apologetic will require the acquisition of this language by its own adherents and in a preliminary way by its interlocutors. Similarly, the Christian apologist must also attempt to evaluate the way of seeing of the other and acquire proficiency in that way of seeing. And here we are faced with the most difficult aspect of this language acquisition. Some religious practices are strictly forbidden for those who are not themselves committed to the faith. The most obvious example that I have in mind is the prohibition to participate in the Eucharist.

While there is a certain sense that this prohibition prevents persons from fully participating in a ritual that is central to the Christian conception

---

28. Stone, *Evangelism after Christendom*, 12.

of reality, to be prevented from partaking is itself formative and an atypical kind of participation. Because of my multiple ecumenical associations, participation in Catholic Mass is a somewhat regular occurrence for me. I cannot receive the Eucharist in this context, and therefore cannot participate in what other participants consider the highest aspect of worship. I have made it a point to always go forward and receive a priestly blessing, with my arms crossed over my chest. As I have reflected on this practice, I realize that I am being formed into a mixed continuity and discontinuity with the Catholic Church. While I worship with her, I am not part of her. I find that this reflection further shapes my relationships with Roman Catholic friends and colleagues. I have learned well that I am often a welcomed guest, but there is a distance between us that is not entirely overcome. Those who participate in Christian worship but who are barred from full participation by the Christian community's commitments or their own commitments, religious or otherwise, are also being formed into the Christian way of thinking *by the occasion of non-participation*. For an uncommitted person to participate in the fullness of Christian worship would actually be a distortion of the kind of commitment and allegiance required to be a part of the worshipping community. While partial participation or even a simple observation has its apologetic limitations, it is nonetheless necessary for a proper understanding of the Christian way. Similarly, Christian non-participation in the non-Christian religious rituals of a committed interlocutor produces a similar kind of understanding. While this may seem like a difficult obstacle to overcome, we find that thoughtful non-participation is itself a formative level of participation and catechesis. We should not overlook the patristic practice of *disciplina arcani* and its prohibition for catechumens to be present for the Eucharist. Long after fears of the rituals being discovered by persecutors were gone, the church kept this as an essential aspect of the formation of catechumens.

The result of this exploration is twofold. First, the gathering of the congregation is itself a formative practice. In gathering, participants submit themselves to formation that can enable them to see the world more completely in a Christian way. The paradigmatic vision that is displayed and enacted in worship reshapes their own vision such that they can better articulate and embody the way of Christ. Second, gathering with the church offers the most elaborate insight into the Christian way for apologetic interlocutors. If a person really wants to see Christianity from the inside, as postliberals insist that they must, then worship is the paradigmatic place to do that. It is also the place where the narrative will be most explicitly and comprehensively articulated, which is the aim of proclamation.

PROCLAMATION

The practice of *proclamation* of the Word of God requires both the reading of Scripture and the preaching of the good news for the gathered people. Imaging this aspect of worship with regards to apologetic is likely the most natural given all that has been written thus far. According to the apologetic that I have sketched, the aim of preaching will be to proclaim the Christian narrative in such a way that worshippers and those who gather with them might see that the Christian vision of the world is the most truthful and compelling vision of the world. As I will argue below, preaching should excite the affections of the gathered community. The beauty of this story should make the hearer desire to be part of it. The goodness of this God and these people should entice a hearer to worship him and join them. The ways in which this story accounts for the challenges and beauties of life with poignancy and accuracy should convince the believer that this story is the truthful one. Preaching is always aimed at the articulate proclamation of the Christian narrative, and always calls for a response to submit to and be formed by this narrative. This articulation is the most quintessential apologetic moment in the life of the church, and the call to respond to proclamation is the essence of what it means for an apologetic interlocutor to embrace a new vision of the world. Precisely because preaching is the place where the Christian narrative is the most naturally apologetic, the most serious questions for preaching and apologetics concern how the church might preach differently in light of this postliberal proposal.[29]

Several of the emphases of postliberal thought have implications for preaching that must be elaborated here. These unique contributions to preaching are not specifically attuned to the task of apologetics. As has been insisted on by many postliberals, theology and the life of the church should not be beholden to apologetics. Apologetics is just one aspect of theology done rightly. The same is true of preaching. Apologetics will not determine the form or content of postliberal preaching. But when preaching is done well, the apologetic task will nevertheless be accomplished.

Charles Campbell's book, *Preaching Jesus*, is the closest to understanding how the cultural-linguistic theory of religion should revolutionize the aim of preaching. He explains,

> Preaching models the use of Christian language and thereby plays a role in nurturing believers in that language usage.

---

29. Mark Ellingsen claims that Brevard Childs, Frei, and Lindbeck have never articulated the implications of postliberal hermeneutics for preaching. I have no evidence to the contrary. Ellingsen, *Integrity of Biblical Narrative*, 15.

> Sermons become a means through which the Christian com-
> munity enters more deeply into its own distinctive speech, so
> that Christian ideas, beliefs, and experience become possible.
> Preaching seeks to create a universe of discourse and put the
> community in the middle of that world—instructing the hearers
> in the use of the language by showing them how to use it.[30]

Just as worship as a whole is the paradigmatic way of being for Christians, so
proclamation is the paradigmatic way of Christian speaking (and preaching
is an element of proclamation). The best way to understand how Christians
will learn to think and speak as Christians will be to contrast postliberal
"narrative preaching" with the "narrative preaching" typically referred to by
those of experiential-expressivist theologies.

Campbell analyzes five different homileticians known for "narrative
preaching" that he identifies as closely tied to experiential-expressivist theology. In summary, Campbell claims that their method is flawed primarily because, in their method, the category of narrative is primary. Each of
these narrative preachers gives primacy to narrative for different reasons
and in different ways, most of them pragmatic. Stories are what captures the
hearer's imagination and so therefore preachers should variously use stories
to illustrate, use stories to remain relevant to contemporary audience, or
pattern their sermon with the formal structure of a story. For Eugene Lowry,
narrative (which he distinguishes from story) is the primary category for
sermons because preaching is done in time and not revealed all at once like
a painting.[31] Whichever prescription is given, Campbell explains that each
of the practitioners of this New Homiletic ultimately end up taking the human experience as primary and subordinate the biblical narrative.[32]

---

30. Campbell, *Preaching Jesus*, 234. Campbell explains that this prescription is a
paraphrase of Hans Frei's summary of the work of Karl Barth. Cf. Frei, "Afterword," 100.

31. Lowry, *Homiletical Beat*.

32. Campbell, *Preaching Jesus*, 147–66. Campbell claims that only one (Edmund
Steimle) of these narrative homileticians even considers the specifics of the biblical narrative, and his is a highly reductionistic account of good versus evil (Campbell, *Preaching Jesus*, 168). Campbell thinks that Eugene Lowry also falls victim to this failure,
but insists that Lowry is most interesting at this point. Because Lowry wants to allow
the Gospel to raise the "problem" and provide the "solution," his approach will be the
most closely tied to biblical narrative. Like the narrative of the Bible, It could be said
that Lowry's approach follows the genre of ancient comedy, as the problem is always
overturned by the surprising appearance of Gospel truth. Richard Eslinger provides
a sympathetic summary of Lowry's approach in Eslinger, "Tracking the Homiletical
Plot," 69–86. For a good introduction to Lowry's thought in more recent development,
including attention to William Placher's theology, see Lowry, *Sermon*.

While Hans Frei has not been discussed explicitly, it is undeniable that Frei's hermeneutic proposals and his story of the loss of biblical narrative are central to what later came to be called postliberalism. Frei's entire project in hermeneutics was intended to show that modern biblical hermeneutics had allowed a particular kind of hermeneutics, the historical-critical, to dominate the biblical text in the interest of apologetics.[33] The Bible that once served as foundational narrative(s) was taken as either historical in the modern sense (sociological study of religion, fundamentalist apologetics, etc.) or as ancient wisdom literature (Marcus Borg, Jesus Seminar, etc.).According to Frei, neither of these approaches are faithful to the long-standing role of Scripture as a narrative that gives the church community identity as the people of God.[34] At the center of this proposal was his suggestion that Scripture has for most of Christian history been read as a "realistic narrative." As Campbell rightly argues, Frei did not defend the centrality of narrative because he thought narrative was important. Frei originally borrowed this notion from the notion of "realistic narrative" that was popular in late-nineteenth century literary theory. Frei issued caution about the appropriateness of this analogy, because to utilize this concept is just to bring one more foreign paradigm from outside the text. By the time of his death, Frei showed some reluctance that a school of "narrative theology" had gained influence under his name because of the ways that this hermeneutical framework from outside the text—extratextual—has been given authority over the text.[35] Neither should preaching defend narrative on this ground.[36] Frei argues that the only defensible reason to prioritize narrative is that a specific set of texts that happen to be narrative are primary within Christian tradition and within the Scripture itself.[37] Other

33. When Frei speaks of apologetics, he always has two things in mind. First, Frei is thinking of the theology of correlation that I have already discussed extensively in Lindbeck. Second, Frei is also concerned with an evidentialist apologetic for the historicity of the bible (see Frei, *Identity of Jesus Christ*, xi–xii). He does not seem to address whether and how the truth of Christianity should be defended. In fact, he sometimes seems a little more concerned with defending the truthfulness of Christianity than either Barth or Lindbeck. See for example his "qualified sympathy" for those that push Lindbeck on questions of truthfulness in Frei, "Epilogue," 278–79.

34. Frei, *Eclipse of Biblical Narrative*, 105–54.

35. Frei, "'Literal Reading' of Biblical Narrative in Christian Tradition," 66. Cf. Eslinger, *Narrative and Imagination*, 24; Placher, "Modest Response," 197–98. Vanhoozer has also critiqued Frei on this point. See Vanhhozer, *Biblical Narrative in the Philosophy of Paul Ricoeur*, 174.

36. Kevin Vanhoozer is right to note that not all Scripture is narrative and to treat it all as such does not do justice to the texts. Vanhoozer, *Drama of Doctrine*, 29.

37. Frei, "Literal Reading," 72; Eslinger, *Narrative and Imagination*, 24; Campbell, *Preaching Jesus*, 190.

kinds of "narrative preaching" begin with the reality of the human listener and attempt to apply the Scripture to that reality. A postliberal "narrative preaching" requires starting with the story of Scripture and redescribing the whole world into the text. Precisely because it is preaching, and not only the reading of Scripture, the sermon is not a simple repetition of the biblical story. Rather the sermon situates the contemporary story within the reading of Scripture.

Imagine a contemporary sermon that addresses an atrocity that is very recent at the time of this writing. On April 15, 2013, two young Russian-American Muslims detonated two improvised explosives near the crowded finish line of the Boston Marathon. Three people were killed and hundreds were injured in a senseless act of violence on American streets. How might a preacher respond to this national tragedy? The liberal "problem-solution" method, whether narrative or some other preaching style, might suggest that Christians are to respond like Jesus would respond.

> "Jesus taught that his followers should turn the other cheek and love their enemies. Therefore we should try to love these violent terrorists and refuse vengeance. Loving our friends is easy, but Jesus teaches that we should radically love our enemies as well."

This would not be opposed to the Christian way and would include some elements of it. But it does not actually account for the fullness of the Christian belief about violence and evil. Jesus becomes nothing more than a moral hero and teacher.

Postliberal narrative preaching would invest this story with the grammar of Christian faith that makes a Christian response to violence possible.

> "The two brothers who set this bomb have succumbed to the same disease of sin that every person has given themselves to. Just like every other person, God created these men good. But sin has ruled their hearts. When they do violence, we should not be surprised, for we too have done violence even to those we love dearly. Jesus is not only a moral hero that shows us a better way, but he has initiated a Kingdom that will one day rule over these violent men. Judgment in that Kingdom will not belong to us, but to God alone. God will eventually set the world to rights and has begun that work in Jesus and through his Church. So the Church now has a call to love these men because loving

enemies witnesses to a coming Kingdom whereby all are in right relationship to God and one another."[38]

Proclaiming the story in this way does not only tell believers how they are to respond to atrocity. It also helps them to situate this particular current event within the larger framework of Christian narrative theology. It does not just explain how to respond to this situation, but models what it means to be and think the Christian way.[39]

For preachers to be able to speak this way without simply reciting Scripture again requires that they too be immersed in the narrative. Campbell employs an often-used analogy to the way that jazz musicians learn to improvise. Jazz improvisation is not like composing an entirely new piece of music. The musician improvises upon a theme that is already established by the piece within a set of established musical structures that maintain the theme while allowing freedom for the musician. Musicians learn to play pieces within the jazz tradition by imitating exemplary pieces. By imitating the best of the tradition, they learn how to keep the tradition and take it in new directions for new pieces.[40]

N. T. Wright draws on an analogy of an unfinished play to illustrate this point in a way that more closely ties to the church's performance of Scripture. Wright asks us to imagine discovering a previously unknown script by an otherwise famous playwright. However, the script that is discovered is incomplete, with only part of the final act having been completed. How could someone perform a play in which only the first four acts and the beginning of the final act have been written? Experienced actors and theater experts who know the author's work well could read the unfinished script and study its internal cohesiveness. After forming judgments about

38. The comparatively longer length of this text from the one above is not due to the above having less to say. Because I am suggesting the latter as a unique way to approach preaching, I assume that the outline of the former represents an argument that the reader's imagination can fill with details and rhetoric.

39. This may be one of the most obvious places where suggesting "the Christian way" will most obviously suggest a single way of being and speaking that does not exist. MacIntyre's analysis above that there only are specifically instantiated languages (English-as-in-the-time-of Shakespeare) and not general languages avoids this concern. Many different Christian traditions will speak differently about the Boston Marathon bombing. But for each of these traditions, I contend that this just is what it is to be Christian in that tradition. Methodists do not believe that Methodist thought and practice is the best Methodist way; they think it is the best Christian way. Even if a tradition wants to be identified more narrowly, this does not change the formal application of the method that I am suggesting.

40. Campbell, *Preaching Jesus*, 236. Eugene Lowry, who is himself an accomplished jazz pianist, has expanded on this metaphor extensively. See Lowry, *Homiletical Beat*.

the character of its actors and the hints at its ending contained within, the actors could compose an ending which would be fitting. Experts on the script and the author could give opinions as to whether the rendition was faithful. In this scenario, the actors begin to interpret themselves in light of the story that they have read. They take on the personalities of its characters and try to perform the lives of the characters of the script. They are guided by the script. Wright claims this is an appropriate metaphor for how the Bible is authoritative for the Christian community.[41] Christians use the Bible as a guide to forming their character by interpreting their own lives in light of the biblical story. Once formed in the character of the people of God, Christians then live out of that wisdom and character to participate in the drama of redemption. This is not a simple restatement of the previous script, but a creative and *faithful* reenactment within the contemporary context.[42]

Construing Scripture in this way follows somewhat naturally from perceiving the Bible principally as narrative.[43] In Wright's construal, the main themes of Scripture are developed in five "acts" which are self-evidently (1) creation, (2) fall, (3) the life of the people of God in the nation of Israel, (4) the redemptive Christ-event, and (5) the consummation of all things in the eschaton. This final *telos* of creation is only partially revealed in Scripture and begins with the life of the church in the New Testament. The church therefore lives between the authoritative telling of God's story found in Scripture and the reconciliation to God in the consummation.[44]

41. N. T. Wright, "How Can the Bible Be Authoritative?" 7–32.

42. N. T. Wright, *New Testament and the People of God*, 140–43. This analogy has already been used in regards to ethics in chapter 2.

43. N. T. Wright, *New Testament and the People of God*, 140–41. Notice I advisedly say that it follows somewhat naturally. Essentially Wright is attempting to construct a hermeneutic model which makes sense of the entire Bible as authoritative for the community. This canonical model (though Wright does not use this term) places primary interpretive authority on the whole of salvation history and in this sense takes the "authoritative interpretation" away from the human authors' particular view and places it somewhere in the midst of the texts as they form one muddled story of salvation history. This flows naturally precisely at the point of community formation and ethics. As will be shown below, the Bible as drama makes the community's ethical task clear.

44. Ron Allen exhibits a common misunderstanding that should be apparent from the ways that this accounts for Scripture. "The Bible does not voice one unified theological narrative or viewpoint, but contains diverse (and sometimes quite different) theological perspectives" (Allen, "Theology Undergirding Narrative Theology," 39). Cf. Allen, *Interpreting the Gospel*, 76–77. Allen thinks this creates problems for postliberals because they are not able to deal with difficult texts within the bible (polygamy, rape, killing, etc.). Placher shows that this is a mistaken conclusion. Placher, "Struggling with Scripture," 32–50. See also Placher, "Is the Bible True?" 924–28.

Grenz and Franke identify this approach to authority as consistent with the evangelical notion of biblical authority and the postconservative approach that they are commending.[45] This approach is an intratextual approach because its cues are taken from the biblical narrative. Read as a whole, the biblical canon is largely historical narrative punctuated at key historical points by supplementary material.[46] The canon ends by pointing towards the consummation. This construal alone would force non-narrative texts into a narrative construal. However, once the narrative construal is constructed from the reading of the canon as a whole, a more nuanced reading of non-narrative literature can be achieved.[47] The question that one must ask then is whether the narrative deserves primacy in the interpretive schema. I suggest that it does because of the aforementioned canonical structure and because the majority of the material is narrative. While this construal can be critiqued as to its comprehensiveness, its intratextuality is apparent. The biblical narrative itself is used to interpret the Bible.

This scheme also clarifies the task of the preacher and the theologian. Preacher and theologian alike are part of this group of "experts" that are to imagine how the characters and the plot of the biblical narrative are to be faithfully performed on the contemporary "stage." The preacher then provides guidance for the community's performance of the narrative by helping them situate themselves within it.[48] "As Alasdair MacIntyre notes, a tradition must actively engage with itself and the world or else die. This engagement is perhaps the fullest description of what goes on in a good sermon, most especially in the pews and subsequently in the lives of the hearers who also become doers of the Word."[49] Situating the stories of these people on this day within the over-arching biblical narrative is a difficult

45. Grenz and Franke, *Beyond Foundationalism*, 128.

46. Ellingsen would also argue that non-narrative texts are in some way supplemental to the narrative ones. "The most significant nonnarrative material seems to be concerned with questions about how the narratives should be interpreted or with elaborating on the narratives through praise" (Ellingsen, *Integrity of Biblical Narrative*, 22 and 29).

47. It is telling that this is precisely the how Augustine claimed that persons should be taught the Christian faith: telling the whole of salvation history with emphasis on the key moments. He says so explicitly in *On Catechizing the Uninstructed*. His apologetic *City of God* follows the same outline as *Catechizing* only much longer and less the outline is less explicit. Augustine thought that this narrative of salvation history was a key interpretive principle. I will say more on this below.

48. I think Campbell is right to suggest that postliberalism, more than other paradigms, also considers the preacher's character essential in the performance of the narrative, because the practicing of these virtues can only be from a thoroughly insider perspective. Campbell, *Preaching Jesus*, 219.

49. Pinches, "Proclaiming," 180.

task that takes wisdom and the mastery of the narrative. The act of preaching this way is itself an education in the intricacies of the narrative and how to improvise on the themes present there. Like the student that travels for a language immersion program, the congregation enters into this community of paradigmatic speech, exhibited in prayers, songs, Scripture, and preaching. They learn more than the vocabulary and grammar of the language in a technical sense. They learn how to use the language of faith by imitating its exemplary use.[50]

While Campbell is helpful to understand how the cultural linguistic framework revolutionizes the aims of preaching, he fails to see the implications of some other important aspects of postliberalism. He emphasizes the character of Jesus, which is the primary narrative of Christian preaching. While his emphasis upon the preaching of Jesus and his character seems an appropriate corrective to earlier narrative preaching, it fails to recognize that Jesus' life and ministry does not make sense in a dechristianized culture without the whole of the Christian narrative. Campbell rightly elevates typological and figural interpretation and preaching to connect the story of Israel through the "pivot" of the story of Jesus to the life of the church. This instinct is correct, but still falls short of setting Jesus within the full narrative context that only the full story of the Christian narrative provides. When discussing figural interpretation as the way in which precritical Christian interpreters connected Old and New Testaments, Frei emphasized the overarching story as the aim of these interpreters.[51] Frei claims that Augustine is an exemplar of this earlier mode of narrating Christian history:

> Long before a minor modern school of thought made the biblical "history of salvation" a special logical inquiry, Christian preachers and theological commentators, Augustine the most notable among them, had envisioned the real world as formed by the sequence told by the biblical stories. That temporal world covered the span of ages from creation to the final consummation to come, and included the governance both of man's natural environment and of that secondary environment which we often think of as provided for man by himself and call "history" or "culture."[52]

50. Campbell, *Preaching Jesus*, 237.

51. Frei, *Eclipse of Biblical Narrative*, 2–3. At this point I wonder if Campbell's extensive use of Frei's *Identity of Jesus Christ* does not lead him to lose sight of the necessity of the broader story.

52. Frei, *Eclipse of Biblical Narrative*, 1. Pasquarello also claims that Augustine was the prime example of a narrative preacher in the early church. Pasquarello, "Narrative Reading, Narrative Preaching," 177–93.

Augustine's sermons display this well and are readily available. But his theological treatises make explicit the narrative structure that is only implicit in his sermons.[53]

As I explained in chapter 3, Augustine outlines salvation history in both *City of God* and *On Catechizing* in the same way. He sets salvation history into seven ages: From Adam to Noah, from Noah to Abraham, from Abraham to David, from David to the Babylonian Exile, from the return of the exile to the incarnation, and the age of Christ and the church is the sixth age. The final age is the eternal City of God. He sets each of these ages into the framework of the seven days of creation. This makes great sense when considering that the sixth day is when the church is being formed in the mind of Christ, in the same way that God created humans in the likeness of God on the sixth day.[54] The seventh day of creation foreshadows the eternal city in its peace and rest.[55]

In *On Catechizing*, Augustine has the teaching of catechumens in mind. This is not specifically an occasion for preaching, a relevant fact given that Lindbeck emphasizes the ways in which catechesis is required in contemporary worship. It also serves as a window into how Augustine believes persons come to understand Christian faith. I quote him at length:

> The narration is full when each person is catechised in the first instance from what is written in the text, "In the beginning God created the heaven and the earth," on to the present times of the church. This does not imply, however, either that we ought to repeat by memory the entire Pentateuch, and the entire Books of Judges, and Kings, and Esdras, and the entire Gospel and Acts of the Apostles, if we have learned all these word for word; or that we should put all the matters which are contained in these volumes into our own words, and in that manner unfold and expound them as a whole. For neither does the time admit of that, nor does any necessity demand it. But what we ought to do is, to give a comprehensive statement of all things, summarily and generally, so that certain of the more wonderful facts may be selected which are listened to with superior gratification, and which have been ranked so remarkably among the exact

53. Ellingsen seems to have missed the narrative structure of the *City of God* even while citing it as an example of narrative preaching. Ellingsen, *Integrity of Biblical Narrative*, 48.

54. Augustine, *On Catechizing* 22.39.

55. My master's thesis analyzed the narrative elements and apologetic function of Augustine's preaching and especially his *City of God*. See Gibbs, "Performative Metanarrative and Postmodern Apologetics. Some of my treatment of him here is adapted from material from the thesis.

turning-points [of the history]; that, instead of exhibiting them to view only in their wrappings, if we may so speak, and then instantly snatching them from our sight, we ought to dwell on them for a certain space, and thus, as it were, unfold them and open them out to vision, and present them to the minds of the hearers as things to be examined and admired. But as for all other details, these should be passed over rapidly, and thus far introduced and woven into the narrative. The effect of pursuing this plan is, that the particular facts that we wish to see specially commended to attention obtain greater prominence in consequence of the others being made to yield to them.[56]

Augustine provides two sample narrations as exemplary instances of what he was instructing catechists to do. He suggested further that the catechist was to give as much and as full of an explanation as his or her hearer could receive with joy.[57] His shortest version of the narration was roughly two pages of a modern book. *On Catechizing* also includes a version that goes on for some fifteen pages or so. His longest version is roughly five hundred pages in the second half of *City of God*, all three of these following the same narrative outline.

I think Augustine provides a more exemplary framework for teaching the Christian vision of the world than does Campbell. Frei himself lifts up Augustine as a prime example of this kind of narrative preaching. In an age where catechesis is necessary even for some Christians, the entirety of the narrative must be on display for every sermon. Similarly, reading Scripture from the Old and New Testaments helps to hold this overarching narrative together. "There is at the heart of the liturgical use of Scripture a narrative understanding of the world that places human life in relationship to human life and the whole created order before the face of God."[58] As Augustine instructed above, this also does not mean that the entirety of the narrative will be given the same emphasis each time. It only means that the whole narrative will need to be in view.

Augustine had another rhetorical device that is particularly helpful for the postliberal emphasis upon practices. One of his main pedagogical tools in teaching salvation history was his mystagogical preaching. William Harmless, who has been an advocate of the Roman Catholic RCIA, explains the common methods used in mystagogy.[59] Mystagogy must hold

56. Augustine, *On Catechizing*, 3.5.

57. Ibid., 2.4.

58. Saliers, *Worship as Theology*, 173.

59. Harmless, *Augustine and the Catechumenate*, 69–78. See also Mazza, *Mystagogy*. Smith also recognizes mystagogical preaching as a valuable resource for teaching Christians to reflect upon worship. See Smith, *Imagining the Kingdom*, 187–88.

two concerns in tension if the liturgy is to tell the truth of the Christian narrative. First, the hearer must understand what is being done. If someone attends worship, either to worship or observe, and does not hear the institution narrative before the breaking of the bread, then the breaking of the bread remains unintelligible to them. In this way the institution narrative functions like mystagogy. The hearer is able to make connections between the ritual event and biblical narrative, imagery, and language. For some this imagery and language will be completely foreign. For others, cognitive and emotional connections are made among the varied elements of the order of worship. Those that watch the drama unfold over the course of liturgical year or season will begin to get the whole story through the words of Scripture and sermon, the actions of Eucharist and baptism, and the bodily actions of bowing, kneeling, and standing. But part of that unfolding narrative will be the words of the preacher acting as a narrator, giving the audience clues as to how the drama is unfolding.

The second concern is that the liturgical rites are, in the end, mysteries. This means that they should never be fully explained. As soon as they are explained fully, they have been explained improperly. The narration of mystagogy will constantly point at the mystery inherent to the liturgical acts. The mystagogue does not want to explain the mysteries in order to explain them away, but to open them for fuller participation. Harmless explains with an illustration: "Mystagogical catechesis is thus less an explanation and more an exploration; it is less an explication and more an evocation. It works like sonar: it plumbs the depths not to deny the depths, but rather to point out how deep they really are."[60] When this mystagogy takes place in the exposition of the sermon, or as part of the ritual act such as the institution narrative, it becomes a part of the performance of the liturgy that makes the rest of the liturgy intelligible.[61]

The liturgy will never be comprehended in its fullness, but meaning continues to increase for the participant over time. In fact, if Harmless's notion of mystagogy is adequate, then the more a participant understands the liturgy, the more mysterious it will be. The mystagogical sermon explains the liturgical en-actment, but it does not explain it away. Using Lindbeck's terminology, Reinhard Huetter claims that "catechetical theology thus always has a basic pragmatic-apologetic character; it is 'ad hoc' apologetics."[62]

60. Harmless, *Augustine and the Catechumenate*, 364–65.

61. Some discussion will come below in our discussion of Augustine's baptismal liturgy regarding the *disciplina arcani*. Some have come to the conclusion that the ritual must be experienced before explanation can come. I am of the opinion that it is preferable that mystagogy become an integral part of the liturgy itself. I think our look at Augustine's sermons below will provide a glimpse into my prescriptions.

62. Huetter, *Suffering Divine Things*, 51.

Augustine was so consistent with this mystagogical reading of Scripture that his congregation would often begin to cheer so loudly that they would interrupt his sermon when they would hear him refer to the Red Sea or other passages that had baptismal overtones.[63] This makes it clear that his congregations would not be able to think of these Scriptural passages without thinking of the sacraments and vice versa. The mystery of the sacraments and the biblical narrative had become bound to one another through Augustine's consistent mystagogy.

For Augustine and many of the fourth and fifth century churches, a strict *disciplina arcani* prohibited the unbaptized to be present at the Eucharist or to know the mysteries of the faith. This presents a problem for understanding the liturgy for the catechumens and Augustine recognized the problem. Harmless says, "On the one hand, [Augustine's] pedagogical instincts dictated that he turn and explain things to the catechumens; on the other, his respect for church tradition dictated that he not violate anything as venerable as the *disciplina arcani.*"[64] In these situations, Augustine would make allusions to the biblical narrative that he found in the sacraments without explicating fully. This likely had a great effect on the catechumens' learning the biblical narrative, because so little was known to them about the rites and the little that he told them was the sacrament's connection to the biblical story. He asked the catechumens, "You who have not come, why are you afraid of coming to the baptism of Christ, of passing through the Red Sea?"[65] In this case, nothing was told to the catechumens except the biblical narrative that Augustine associated with the sacrament. Later in their formation, Augustine explained this narrative connection in more detail.

As the catechumens entered their names for baptism, Augustine would "hand over" the Creed to them and give a series of sermons on the creed. He took the opportunity to discuss baptism more thoroughly on the phrase of the Creed, "I believe in the forgiveness of sins." His mystagogy was thoroughly narrative and biblical at this point. Rather than simply stating that baptism is the occasion for the forgiveness of sins, he developed a multi-layered allegory of baptism as an image of the Exodus account of crossing the Red Sea and the "washing" in the blood from Christ's side. Like the pursuing Egyptians, sin is drowned in the waters of baptism. Augustine's baptismal font apparently had some sort of red tile lining it, and he used this to draw the illusion to Christ's blood. In this case, the red font is

---

63. Harmless, *Augustine and the Catechumenate,* 171.

64. Ibid., 172.

65. Augustine, *Expositions of the Psalms* 80.8.

a symbol for both the Red Sea and the red blood of Christ.[66] The enactment of both of these events is collapsed into the moment of baptism. The catechumens would not have only learned the biblical narrative for its own sake, which is obviously one of Augustine's concerns in *On Catechizing*, but they would also have learned how to appropriate their story into the biblical story. Though the catechumens have sin in their lives, the sin is washed clean in the waters of baptism and the blood of Christ. The newly baptized is brought out of the captivity of sin by crossing the waters of the font. The individual's story is interpreted through the biblical stories.

This account shows how Augustine would have taught the biblical narrative through the liturgical act and taught the liturgical act through biblical mystagogy. Harmless points out that Augustine's mystagogy often makes use of extensive allegory from nature and daily tasks as well.[67] But it nearly always relies heavily on the Scriptural narrative. This is both a pedagogical and a rhetorical device. Augustine's training as a rhetorician makes him aptly aware of how people would remember what they were being taught and how the beauty of the allegory would bring them delight. Augustine does not have any need to rationally explain how the baptism would be efficacious for cleansing the baptized of sin. To be a Christian is to understand one's life through the biblical story, just as Augustine has exemplified for the catechumens.

I have outlined three ways that postliberal theology changes the role and method for preaching. The cultural-linguistic emphasis upon learning Christian grammar reveals the sermon to be a prime example of paradigmatic Christian speech. This speech, more than any other, will teach persons how to think and speak in a Christian way. The intertextual emphasis upon biblical narrative implores the preacher to make the sermon an opportunity for placing the contemporary situation within the overarching biblical narrative, and not only through instances of individual biblical stories. Therefore postliberal preaching will require illuminating the entire biblical narrative as the framework for each instance of preaching. The postliberal emphasis upon practices and the formation that they entail motivates preachers to use mystagogical preaching to illuminate the implications of the liturgical acts.

All of these elements are aimed at the conversion of the intellect and the affections of the worshipper. They call the listener to conversion. Every part of the proclamation, from the beginning of the first reading to the conclusion of the sermon, is aimed at the response of the worshipper. To that I now turn.

---

66. Augustine, *Sermon* 213.8. A similar theme is found in *Sermon* 223E.

67. Harmless, *Augustine and the Catechumenate,* 364–65.

RESPONSE

Just as preaching is the paradigmatic use of Christian speech, the call to response that follows preaching is the paradigmatic Christian disposition evoked by the Christian way. I argued in chapter 2 that in spite of apologetic's typical preoccupation with truth, the proper category with which to begin apologetics is that of beauty. I further argued that truth and beauty are "convertible."Therefore, when we appeal to the beauty of the Christian faith, we are also appealing to its truthfulness as both are ways of naming the conformity with God's own character. The most significant reason for this appeal to beauty was the necessity of conversion to this way of seeing. Beauty describes the "delight of the intellect" toward something, in this case the Christian vision of the world.

The response to the proclamation of the Word is the aspect of worship that most shapes the Christian's affections such that he or she loves God and God's vision for the world. Hence it is in worship that we learn to see the beauty of this Christian vision. Persons do not love the Christian vision of the world or anything else only because it is true. As we learned from Balthasar in chapter 2, the dutiful clattering of syllogisms does not captivate the imagination. The imagination is captivated by the aesthetic appeal of the Christian narrative articulated in preaching and narrated by the liturgy. It is in worship that we learn to take delight in the Christian vision of the world. And it is in worship that we are therefore motivated to respond to God's call to the hard task of discipleship. Put simply, it is in worship that we learn to love rightly. Augustine often defines sin as disordered love, so that rightly ordering love is nothing less than sanctification.

Eucharist is the quintessential response to the preaching of the Word, its *telos* being nothing less than the reordering of our love towards God.

> As we proceed further (from the reading and preaching of the Word) in the Eucharistic liturgy, the time has now come to offer to God the totality of our lives, of ourselves, of the world in which we live. This is the first meaning of our bringing to the altar the elements of our food. For we already know that food is life . . . We also know that to offer this food, this world, this life to God is the initial "eucharistic" function of man, his very fulfillment as man . . . We know that real life is "eucharist," a movement in which alone the meaning and the value of all that exists can be revealed and fulfilled.[68]

68. Schmemann, *Life of the World*, 34.

What may seem to unwitting "participants" to be simply the next act in the liturgy is actually its highest moment. In this movement the congregation is invited to give over their entire lives with the hope that they can be freed to love more rightly. It is this transformation and right ordering of loves that is the essential aim of Christian response.

Eucharist is the response to Word that enjoys the greatest catholicity. I will concur with a great many scholars that the Eucharistic liturgy is also the most proper act of response. As a Pentecostal theologian, I would be remiss if I did not defend the variety of responses that have been enacted by Christians in the last four hundred years, however. While some are rightfully critiqued, there are many that have elicited the call and response to Christian discipleship that is demanded by Christian worship. The Pentecostal altar call invites worshippers to join together as a community and pray for their brothers and sisters to receive the empowerment of the Spirit for mission. They also pray for one another to experience a foretaste of the kingdom and receive physical healing. I have argued elsewhere that the Pentecostal altar call properly orients the Pentecostal worshipper toward mission and eschatology.[69] I echo that assertion here. The Baptist call to baptism invites worshippers to answer the call to discipleship by joining the life of the church (like the Ethiopian eunuch). Prayers of confession, offerings, and the recitation of various creeds similarly are proper responses to the preaching of the Word that can stand apart from the Eucharist and not lose their liturgical and formational significance. While the Eucharist enjoys much of the attention due to its catholicity, all of these liturgies carry the potential to form Christians in proper response to the Word. These liturgies, as well as Eucharist, all have the potential to lose their narrative significance if not rightly celebrated,[70] but we do not judge a practice by its misuse. Churches where the Eucharist is no longer celebrated with frequency will find other faithful ways of shaping the affections of the congregation.[71] This is not to say that the form does not matter.[72] Not every response is a Christian one, no matter the words that are said in connection with it.

69. Gibbs, "Medicine is a Good Thing," 163–74.

70. Eslinger claims, but does not defend the claim, that there is a significant connection between the loss of a narrative structure to the prayer of Great Thanksgiving in the 7th–9th centuries and the great dissimilarity in Eucharistic theology in that time period: "The Eucharist involves a community of people who hear and respond to a narrative prayer and who see and receive the icons of bread and wine. Both are needed. The image interprets the narrative and the assembly, which now is revealed as the body. The narrative interprets the image so that what we taste and see is not just bread but the body of Christ." Eslinger, *Narrative and Imagination*, 87, 110 n. 130.

71. Cherry, *Worship Architect*, 97.

72. Smith, *Desiring the Kingdom*, 151–54; *Imagining the Kingdom*, 168ff.

Each of the faithful responses shares the aim of shaping the affections of the worshipper. Now delighted by the beauty of the Christian narrative and convicted of its truth, the worshipper is called to respond as preaching gives way to action. The body is called to stand, kneel, process, and eat. Even the words spoken, which have to this point been primarily declarative (praise, thanksgiving, etc.), take on a new illocutionary force: "I confess," "Peace be with you," and "This is my body." Reflection gives way to action. The appeal to the intellect (especially in preaching) has begun to work on the affections. The action of the body in a movement toward God will shape the worshipper's loves. The action (confessing, kneeling, and so on) is an active submission to the call that has been given in the proclamation.

It is fitting that "eucharist" would be central to shaping Christian action, because thanksgiving is a response to a prior act. In the Christian narrative, God acts first in Jesus Christ and the church gives thanks for God's prior action. It is fitting, then, that receiving the Eucharist requires a physical posture of reception. Worshippers cannot "take communion," but only receive it. And as they process toward the altar they must form this bodily posture of reception, stretching out their hands and welcoming the grace that accompanies bread. According to Cyril of Jerusalem, it is appropriate to "come not with your wrists extended, or your fingers spread; but make your left hand a throne for the right, as for that which is to receive a King. And having hollowed your palm, receive the Body of Christ, saying over it, *Amen.*"[73] *This posture of reception teaches worshippers in a primordial and bodily way that the proper disposition toward God is as willing recipient.*

Thus John Paul II highlighted the narrative construal of the whole Eucharist as a remembrance of the death and resurrection of Jesus, the Gift of the Father. Thanksgiving in this context is in response to God's gift of love. "Thus it is also a response that tries to repay that love immolated even to the death on the cross: it is our 'Eucharist,' that is to say, our giving Him thanks, our praise of Him for having redeemed us by His death and made us sharers in immortal life through His resurrection."[74] Therefore, when the worshipper receives this gift anew in the reception of the bread and wine, she is again welcomed into relationship with the one that gives abundantly. To be lavished with such a gift causes the receiver to love the one who gave anew as well.

> The Eucharist signifies this charity, and therefore recalls it, makes it present and at the same time brings it about. Every time that we consciously share in it, there opens in our souls a real

---

73. Cyril of Jerusalem, *Catechetical Lecture* 23, 21.

74. John Paul II, *Dominae Cenae*, sec. 3.

dimension of that unfathomable love that includes everything that God has done and continues to do for us human beings, as Christ says: "My Father goes on working, and so do I." Together with this unfathomable and free gift, which is charity revealed in its fullest degree in the saving sacrifice of the Son of God, the sacrifice of which the Eucharist is the indelible sign, there also springs up within us a lively response of love. We not only know love; we ourselves begin to love. We enter, so to speak, upon the path of love and along this path make progress. Thanks to the Eucharist, the love that springs up within us from the Eucharist develops in us, becomes deeper and grows stronger.[75]

John Paul II knows that the normal response to extravagant love is to return that love. To give thanks for God's charity invokes a return of that love. But this often does not happen radically, but incrementally as Eucharist is repeated weekly.

Most of the time worshippers do not recognize a significant change going on in their perception or affections. If the vision of the narrative is portrayed with vibrancy and clarity, the reaction may be no more than a casual compliment to the preacher or other worship leaders. The radical conversion experiences in the revivalist traditions are in many ways just a punctuated version of this gradual change. Those of us from these traditions have responded to many altar calls in our lifetime, sometimes understanding the change that happens there to be all encompassing and ever lasting. But upon reflection, many mature Christians will admit that it is the accumulation of these altar calls, each introducing a small change upon the life of the believer, whereby a person comes to live a sanctified life of love of God and neighbor. This process is materialized in the ongoing habitual response of walking to the altar, receiving the bread and the cup, and so on.

It is for this reason that the kind of bodily response in worship must be repeated. Even in those churches where Eucharist is not a weekly response to the Word, worship leadership is not to create new and innovative responses on every worship occasion.[76] The repetition is important for habituation. This should seem so obvious to us that it does not require an argument, though some have made the argument explicitly.[77] When a musician or athlete are learning the skills that make it possible for them to

75. John Paul II, *Dominae Cenae*, sec. 5.

76. They may cycle a small repertoire of such responses as suggested by Cherry, *The Worship Architect*, 104. In Pentecostal circles, it is not unusual to have an altar call every week in worship, though the subject of prayer at the altar may change from week to week.

77. Sittser, *Will of God as a Way of Life*, 63–68.

perform in a way that does not require conscious cognition, this is done by the constant repetition of a set of practices that embody the desired movement. When the pianist practices scales, he is not permitted to strike the notes in any way that he desires; rather, he must use particular fingerings and hand positions that enable him to master skills that are necessary for proficient piano playing. Similarly, the soccer player must not think about the mechanics of her leg movement, but must so embody the field and her own body that she simply acts without conscious cognition. We call this process habituation, and it is not only about the muscle memory of these particular skills. Habituation patterns the way the athlete inhabits the field. Only very rarely does an athlete step out of the playing field, though one may come within inches of doing so during every play. This familiarity with one's surroundings is not muscle memory, but orientation to one's environment that comes from inhabiting it often and repeatedly. Those who are not athletes experience something similar when they must navigate their home in the dark. Because we inhabit the space bodily, we can often find our watch on the table, avoid the ottoman that might trip us, and so on. Smith is right to acknowledge that Protestants typically are willing to accept this kind of habituation in every area except in worship. He claims that the Protestant "allergy to repetition" is partly due to associating repetition with spiritual insincerity and an effort to "earn" salvation.[78] The great tradition of monastic discipline and prayer should alert us that this allergy to repetition is misguided.

Recent advances in cognitive neuroscience and moral psychology confirm monastic wisdom. G. Michael Leffel explains that there are two different ways that moral reasoning are known to proceed. He refers to these as "cold cognition" and "hot cognition." Cold cognition involves the rational processing involved with moral reasoning. Hot cognition refers to the affective-processes that are initiated when persons act upon moral commitments. In this case, the rather pejorative "cold" is not unwarranted, because neuroscience has found that the affective processes always initiate moral action. Persons that respond with moral action process in the frontal and prefrontal area of the brain that is associated with emotion and affect. When presented with a moral problem that a person has decided not to act upon, they only activate the cold moral reasoning processes and the affective processes remain dormant. The cold reasoning processes, on the other hand, may or may not be activated by the one that acts morally.[79] Simply put, moral action must be initiated by emotion but not necessarily by reason.

78. Smith, *Imagining the Kingdom*, 181–82.
79. Leffel, "Who Cares?" 194.

The "moral emotions" necessary to activate the affective processes are closely associated but not the same as moral virtues. Moral emotions include such varied responses as anger, shame, compassion, and gratitude. "Moral emotions set in motion the implicit procedural enactment of a virtue (or vice) associated with an intuition, i.e., the execution of a behavioral script (schema) that specifies 'how to' act in this particular situation." And most importantly for our purposes, "The more frequently a virtue/vice has been activated, and the more recently it has been primed, the more accessible it is for use. Thus, while an affect-laden moral intuition initiates an action tendency to approach or avoid, and a moral emotion amplifies the strength of an intuition, a virtue and virtue complex shapes how the object in question is to be interacted with."[80] The moral emotion is required for a person to act morally. This affective response activates a "virtue complex" which governs the response. But this virtue complex is most available to a person if it has been used frequently and recently. Thus Leffel concludes that spiritual transformation centrally involves the automatization of moral affective capacities.[81]

Leffel explains that this automatization will necessarily come from repeated practices that invoke a neural "pairing" of action and affective engagement. Leffel speculates that future research may discover that different practices will help shape the affect than those that shape the virtue complex. I suspect that will be found to be true, but not in a dichotomous way, because often the shaping of these factors is due to different aspects of the same practice. We have argued that the narrative construal associated with a practice is the aspect that shapes the tradition specific virtues associated with the narrative vision. Not all practices communicate this narrative equally well.

For example, my earlier claim that Pentecostal altar calls shape the participants' eschatological vision leaves a great deal of the Christian narrative unaddressed. Pentecostal Christians are typically very eschatologically oriented for this reason, believing fervently that we are living in the last days. Those who practice in this way often fail to understand the ways in which the embodied aspect of healing prayer affirms the doctrine of creation and God's goodness. They also leave the close analogies between the patient suffering of healing prayer and the patient suffering of the prophetic literature largely unarticulated. Because this ritual lacks significant narrative construal, even those aspects of the ritual that could be narratively construed are left unarticulated. At the same time, even anecdotal evidence would show

80. Ibid., 193.
81. Ibid., 196.

that the Pentecostal altar call elicits more radical affective change than most any other Christian ritual, as evidenced by the continued growth of the Assemblies of God in dechristianized America. It remains the fastest growing orthodox Christian body as of this writing, and does so in an age when most Christian bodies are declining.[82] It has done so while maintaining theology that challenges most cultural norms. This happens primarily in the altar calls that elicit such dramatic affective conversion.

To compare this with the narrative construal of the Eucharist articulated above by John Paul II marks a stark contrast. The narrative is highlighted in a way that the virtues associated with this kind of response toward God and neighbor is clear. Much has been written to show the ways that Eucharist situates the worshipper in a meal that orients them within Jesus's relationship with the disciples, their relationship as this community for this time, and the coming eschatological Kingdom.[83] But it seems somewhat obvious that Eucharist does not ignite the radical conversion that is elicited by the Pentecostal altar call. This does not mean the affect is not transformed, as I have argued above that it is, just as the Pentecostal altar call does some work in narrative construal and thus formation of virtue. But Leffel's suggestion that some practices do more or less to form affect and also more or less in formation of the "virtue complex" is likely (though yet unverified according to Leffel).

Therefore the framework for moral action and moral reasoning suggested by Leffel would suggest that a variety of practices may be required to address two significant requirements for moral action. In both cases, the formation of affect and virtue, the frequent and recent repetition of the practices increased the likelihood that persons would act morally. Leffel cites research in social-cognitive psychology that suggests that those who reach certain levels of expertise, whether as athletes, auto mechanics, or in morality, are able to act more quickly and with less deliberation than novices. They are not only able to see the complexity of a given situation to a greater degree, but they act with a greater level of automaticity.[84]

Captain Sullenberger of US Airways Flight 1549 who ditched his commercial jet in the Hudson River is a prime example of this kind of excellence. American pilots are trained rigorously throughout their careers. While many rightfully call Sullenberger a hero, aviation experts say his quick and decisive action was the automatic result of years of such procedures. The

---

82. See numerous articles about this phenomena in *Charisma Magazine,* August 2013.

83. For example, see Wainwright, *Eucharist and Eschatology.*

84. Leffel, *Who Cares?* 187.

time from the engine failures to a successful ditching was less than three minutes. The decision not to go to one of two available airports was made in just seconds, which many experts agree was the correct choice. He and his co-pilot automatically attended to their separate duties that included attempts to restart the engines, communications with air traffic control, preparing the plane for ditch procedures and alerting the cabin crew to do the same, and carefully selecting a landing location that would avoid water traffic, prevent stalling the plane or the destruction of the fuselage, and make rescue from boats most likely. Maybe the most remarkable thing about the decisiveness and speed of the captain's decisions is the fact that he would have never made a landing even similar to this one in training. Simulators always practice these landings from much higher or much lower altitudes. The former is a true landing but without power. The latter is not a landing at all, but an effort to minimize the violence of crash. From three thousand feet, Sullenberger has just enough gliding time to do a ditch landing, but not enough to take the plane to an appropriate airport.[85] So he improvised based on the situations that he did know and did so with a level of speed and automaticity that only an expert could. Leffel argues that moral expertise functions in the same way. The practices associated enable an automatization of responses for the expert.

In the case of moral expertise, Leffel shows that, psychologically, there is an additional requirement that must be met before a person will act on what they "know." In this sense, spiritual expertise is likely not different than Leffel's discussion of moral decisions. The religious vision, like the moral vision, is comprised of tradition-specific virtues. These must be "activated" by the affect or they will not be engaged at all. The work of spiritual transformation is largely composed of shaping this affect; it determines what the worshipper loves. The paradigmatic location for this conversion of the affect is the response to the proclamation.

SENDING

Central to the Christian narrative is the notion that the hoped-for Kingdom of God has been initiated by Jesus in the church. The call for Christians is to serve as ambassadors of that Kingdom in the world. The narrative of Christian faith cannot be told in worship if worship does not end with a sending to go forth into the call that the narrative demands. The gathering together,

---

85. Newman, "How Sullenberger Really Saved US Airways Flight 1549"; St. John, "What Went Right.

or calling out, of the people of God must end with being sent, because mission is the proper response to the call of God.

I argued in chapter 2 that the question "What is Jesus doing?" is answered by inquiring into what the church is doing. The church is the *body* of Christ in the world. The gathering together with which this chapter began is the sacramental process by which this body is identified in the world. The sending is that moment where the body is then returned to the world to embody the narrative of God's redemption of the world. The body of Christ entering the world in mission is a prerequisite for all apologetics and is apologetic's public witness. Stone explains this way,

> The gospel the church offers the world is always public because it is, to put it bluntly, a body. The gospel is not a set of beliefs or doctrines that first need to be decoded and then reencoded so as to be intelligible in this or that context. The gospel is Christ himself; and Christ has a body. But bodies are public precisely because they are present. This is why it is so important that the church, which is Christ's body, be made holy in bodily ways through worship, habits, and service it has been given by God, for as the body of Christ it is a public sign of God's glory, not its own.[86]

The church cannot proclaim the Gospel of Jesus until it has lived the Gospel of Jesus. This does not mean that the church must live this vision perfectly; indeed the Christian story insists that these ambassadors of the Kingdom are not yet the consummation of the Kingdom. But it does mean that no apologetics and no evangelism have taken place without a public witness to the goodness of God.

I argued extensively in chapter 2 that the church's witness to the good, the church's ethics, is the most critical aspect of the Christian apologetic. Without the public witness of the Christian body living out her call, there is nothing to which apologetics arguments are able to point interlocutors as evidence of the vision that the church proclaims. I will not repeat those arguments here. It is enough to say that nothing is more universal than the Christian vision of the good life. Nothing is more beautiful than a community that has given their whole lives to come together for the sake of the world. In this limited way, faithfully living the Christian vision as the body of Christ is foundational to the church's witness and her apologetic.

Without retreating from this truth, it is not appropriate to insist that simply to do church well is our apologetic. Stone argues in an analogous way when he insists with William J. Abraham that "if everything is evangelism

---

86. Stone, *Evangelism after Christendom*, 211.

then nothing is evangelism."[87] Stone claims that it is not improper to claim that evangelism is an "intrinsic character of every Christian practice . . . so that all we say and do is a public witness, invitation, and offer of God's salvation to the world."[88] But the fact that evangelism is integral to all Christian practices should not negate the necessity of a more specific practice of evangelism. "Literally everything we do—indeed, the very existence of the church along with its distinctive social patterns and processes—may properly be construed as evangelism. On the other hand, we may also understand evangelism as a distinct, identifiable, socially established, cooperative, and intentional practice along the lines developed by MacIntyre."[89] Stone goes on to argue that evangelism is a distinct practice that involves the invitation to active Christian discipleship and formation proper to that discipleship. Therefore invitation, Christian service, baptism, catechesis, etc. are skills and practices that make up the more complex practice of evangelism.[90]

This distinction is helpful in thinking about the distinctive aspect of apologetics. As I have argued throughout, apologetics in a postconservative mode is dependent upon a more comprehensive vision of Christian faith than the kind of syllogisms that often made up the apologetic witness of propositional theology. Therefore I have argued extensively that the entirety of the Christian vision of the world and the complex practice of living the faith are the "argument" of a postconservative apologetic. In this sense, I think, postconservative apologetics will argue differently than will apologetics of a traditional conservative method.

The role of apologetics is not different than the role that it has always played, however. To echo William Abraham's comments about evangelism, if everything is apologetics then nothing is apologetics. Apologetics is intended to defend the Christian faith as the true account of the whole world, assuage the doubt imposed by competing narratives, and fortify faith in the Christian vision. The proper context for this discipline then, is within the practice of evangelism. As I have said, apologetics is often as much for those who are already Christian, the unbeliever in the heart of every Christian,

87. Stone, *Evangelism after Christendom*, 46. Cf. Abraham, *Logic of Evangelism*, 44.

88. Stone, *Evangelism after Christendom*, 46.

89. Ibid., 48.

90. Stone makes an important distinction between the evangelism as a "logic of witness" and evangelism as a "logic of production." The former measures success according to faithfulness to the Gospel narrative and hopes that the practice of evangelism will be effective at winning persons to Christ. The latter measures success according to the number of converts it wins and assumes that the method does not matter as long as persons are becoming Christian. Stone argues that the latter kind of "evangelism" is not a witness and likely is not evangelism either. See Stone, *Evangelism after Christendom*, 49–53.

as it is for the unconvinced. In this sense, every believer is always being evangelized and their catechesis is never complete. This is a correlate of the notion that evangelism is an aspect of the whole ministry of the church. Preaching, Christian education classes, small group accountability, and many other aspects of ministry have an evangelical orientation that continues to catechize the believer. But the primary aim of apologetics is to aid the ministry practice of evangelism.

As such, apologetics is not itself a practice, it is a *skill* that aids the evangelist with bringing clarity to the Christian proclamation and showing the beauty of this good vision of the world. Lindbeck rightfully identified this ministry as a skill, though he called it "intelligibility."[91] Without a faithful witness of the church to which she can point, the apologist has no ministry, because the skill which the apologist offers the church is the ability to articulate the vision of the Christian narrative and to interpret the church's embodiment of it. The apologist is to show why this story is beautiful, like a tour guide in a grand cathedral, interpreting the intricacies of the design and the history of development. As an ongoing tradition within our family, my wife and I visit cathedrals in the various cities where we vacation. We have found that the best tour guides point out those aspects of the cathedral that reveal the depth and beauty of the place: "This side chapel over here, it was built with the sacrificial gifts of a small band of immigrants from a developing nation and donated as an act of gratitude to God for bringing them here." "This small cross commemorates Pope John Paul II's visit and marks the place where he blessed our space." "That mosaic over there utilized an innovative process that required the artist to work by herself in this room for more than ten thousand hours over four years."[92] By the time we leave the best of these tours, we are able to appreciate the beauty of the place and the goodness of the lives that gave themselves over to its completion. This may be the best analogy for the skillset that the apologist brings to the practice of evangelism.

To further this analogy, without a genuinely beautiful building to tour, the guide has little to which to draw our attention. A tour of the local department store does not leave me enchanted. This is why the identification of a faithful community is so essential for both apologetics and evangelism in the postliberal mode. Stone is right to conclude that "Christian ethics and evangelism are inseparable—and to some extent indistinguishable."[93]

---

91. Lindbeck, *Nature of Doctrine*, 114–20.

92. These are all descriptions given by our tour guide at the Basilica of the National Shrine of the Immaculate Conception in Washington, D.C.

93. Stone, *Evangelism after Christendom*, 200.

Kenneson notes that the gathering of the church makes public the community that is claiming to embody this story. "For if disciples of Jesus Christ really gather to be transformed and to make themselves available to be used by God to transform the kingdoms of this world into the kingdoms of our Lord, then the *ekklesia* and the world should rightly expect to be able to see some of this transformation taking place." By gathering, the church makes itself accountable to the world for its own claims. "The *ekklesia* becomes visible and addressable, opening itself up to being probed and criticized, not only by God, but also by the world."[94] This is true in gathering because it is the church's call in being sent. The church gathers so that it can be sent in mission. "This is not to 'instrumentalize' worship as merely a means to an end, nor is it to reduce worship to a strategy for moral formation."[95] Preparation and blessing for mission is inherent in the logic of the Christian narrative and worship's place in the narrative. "The centrifugal *end* of Christian worship is integral to the Story we rehearse in Christian worship; sending is internal to the practice."[96]

CONCLUSION

I have explained a variety of ways in which the most central Christian practice functions in the life of worshippers to enable them to articulate and to embody the Christian narrative vision of the world. At the heart of the postliberal construal is the idea that Christian practices are the primary means by which a person begins to inhabit the Christian vision of the world. I have shown that several of the practices internal to worship are helpful in understanding the uniqueness of the postliberal vision.

When Christians gather for worship, the act of gathering marks them as a peculiar people. The people that gather during this time and sing, eat, pray, and listen have a different way of inhabiting the world than those who would prefer a day of leisure or those that would gather at another space on another day to worship a different God. Because those who will gather will also sing, eat, and listen (and possibly pray) in many other times and ways during the week, the formation that happens in this Sunday gathering is also battling competing narratives in the life of those that gather.

This Sunday gathering will be the most articulate example of Christian speech and vision that these worshippers will experience this week. In the center of the practice will be the paradigmatic use of Christian speech, that

94. Kenneson, "Gathering," 66.

95. Smith, *Imagining the Kingdom*, 152.

96. Ibid., 153. See also Schmemann, *For the Life of the World*, 45–46.

of the sermon. Preaching will place the believers in this gathering within an over-arching narrative of salvation history. It will also call them to live according to the narrative in a particular way. Preaching must never forsake issuing this call.

The church must always offer ways in which to embody a response to the call issued in the proclamation. While the call will vary, always within the over-arching call to live into baptism, the responses to preaching should be bodily and repeated. Standing, kneeling, confessing, and eating will signify and make concrete the response to the call. It is here that Christians will learn to love the story that has been told.

All of this gathering, listening, eating, and praying is for a purpose. "We worship *for* mission; we gather *for* sending; we center ourselves in the practices of the body of Christ *for the sake of* the world; we are reformed in the cathedral to undertake our image-bearing commission to reform the city."[97] Worship sends forth evangelists that have been formed by God's call to God's vision.

In the opening quote, Stanley Hauerwas claimed that "You really could say that everything I've ever written is apologetics."[98] In fact, the entire work of the church is an attempt to show the truthfulness of the Christian faith. And central to that effort is the church's most basic practice of gathering to celebrate the death and resurrection of Jesus on the Lord's Day.

97. Smith, *Imagining the Kingdom*, 154.

98. As mentioned earlier, I believe that Hauerwas's theology is apologetic in the narrower sense, and not only in the larger sense that I claim all of the church's work is apologetic.

Bibliography

Abraham, William J. *The Logic of Evangelism*. Grand Rapids: Eerdmans, 1989.
————. "Cumulative Case Arguments for Christian Theism." In *The Rationality of Religious Belief: Essays in Honor of Basil Mitchell*, edited by William J. Abraham and Steven W. Holtzer, 17–37. New York: Oxford University Press, 1987.
————. *An Introduction to the Philosophy of Religion*. Englewood Cliffs, NJ: Prentice-Hall, 1985.
Allen, Ronald J. *Interpreting the Gospel: An Introduction to Preaching*. St. Louis: Chalice, 1998.
————. "Theology Undergirding Narrative Theology." In *What's the Shape of Narrative Preaching?*, edited by Mike Graves and David J. Schlafer, 27–40. St. Louis: Chalice, 2008.
Alston, William. "A Doxastic Practice Approach to Epistemology." In *Knowledge and Skepticism*, edited by Marjorie Clay and Keith Lehrer, 1–29. Boulder, CO: Westview, 1988.
————. *The Reliability of Sense Perception*. Ithaca: Cornell University Press, 1993.
Anderson, E. Byron. *Worship and Christian Identity: Practicing Ourselves*. Collegeville, MN: Liturgical, 2003.
Aquinas, Thomas. *Summa Theologica*, 3 volumes, translated by the Fathers of the English Dominican Province. (New York: Benzinger Brothers, 1947).
Augustine. "On Catechizing the Uninstructed." In *A Select Library of Nicene and Post-Nicene Fathers of the Christian Church*, Series 1, Volume 3, edited by Philip Schaff, 282–314. Grand Rapids: Eerdmans, 1956).
————. *The Works of St. Augustine: A Translation for the 21st Century*, 46 volumes. Brooklyn, NY: New City Press, 1990–2014.
Ayres, Lewis. "Patristic and Medieval Theologies of Scripture." In *Christian Theologies of Scripture: A Comparative Introduction*, edited by Justin S. Holcomb, 11–20. New York: New York University Press, 2006.
Balthasar, Hans Urs von. *The Glory of the Lord: A Theological Aesthetics, Vol. I: Seeing the Form*. Translated by Erasmo Leiva-Merikakis. Edited Joseph Fession and John Riches. Edinburgh: T. & T. Clark, 1982.
————. *Theo-Logic, Vol. I: Truth of the World*. Translated by Adrian J. Walker. San Francisco: Ignatius, 2000.
Barnes, Albert. *Notes on the New Testament: Explanatory and Practical*. Christian Classics Ethereal Library, published June 1, 2005, http://www.ccel.org/ccel/barnes/ntnotes.toc.html.

Barron, Robert. *The Priority of Christ: Toward a Postliberal Catholicism*. Grand Rapids: Brazos, 2007.

Barth, Karl. *Church Dogmatics, Vol. II: The Doctrine of God, Part 1*. Edited by G.W. Bromiley and T. F. Torrance. Edinburgh: T. & T. Clark, 1957.

———.*Church Dogmatics, Vol. III: The Doctrine of Creation*. Edited by G. W. Bromiley and T. F. Torrance. Edinburgh: T. & T. Clark, 1978.

———. *Church Dogmatics, Vol. IV: The Doctrine of Reconciliation, Part 1*. Edited by G. W. Bromiley and T. F. Torrance. Edinburgh: T. & T. Clark, 1961.

Behr, John. *The Way to Nicaea*. Crestwood, NY: St. Vladimir's Seminary Press, 2001.

Berard, John, James Penner, and Rick Bartlett. *Consuming Youth: Leading Teens through Consumer Culture*. Grand Rapids: Zondervan, 2011.

Bloesch, Donald G. *Holy Scripture: Revelation, Inspiration, and Interpretation*. Downers Grove, IL: Intervarsity, 1994.

———. *A Theology of Word and Spirit: Authority and Method in Theology*. Downers Grove, IL: Intervarsity, 1992.

Brown, Montague. *Restoration of Reason: The Eclipse and Recovery of Truth, Goodness, and Beauty*. Grand Rapids: Baker Academic, 2006.

Campbell, Charles. *Preaching Jesus: The New Directions for Homiletics in Hans Frei's Postliberal Theology*. Eugene, OR: Wipf & Stock, 2006.

Cavanaugh, William. *Being Consumed: Economics and Christian Desire*. Grand Rapids: Eerdmans, 2008.

Cherry, Constance. *The Worship Architect*. Grand Rapids: Baker, 2010.

Clapp, Rodney. "How Firm a Foundation: Can Evangelicals Be Nonfoundationalists?" In *The Nature of Confession*, edited by Timothy R. Phillips and Dennis L. Okholm, 81–92. Downers Grove, IL: Intervarsity, 1996.

Cowan, Steven B. "Introduction." In *Five Views on Apologetics*, edited by Steven B. Cowan, 7–20. Grand Rapids: Zondervan, 2000.

Craig, William Lane. "A Classical Apologist's Response." In *Five Views on Apologetics*, edited by Steven B. Cowan, 232–35. Grand Rapids: Zondervan, 2000.

Davidson, Donald. *Inquiries Into Truth and Interpretation*. 2nd ed. New York: Oxford University Press, 2001.

Dehart, Paul J. *The Trial of the Witnesses: The Rise and Decline of Postliberal Theology*. Malden, MA: Blackwell, 2006.

Desmond, William. "Neither Servility nor Sovereignty: Between Metaphysics and Politics." In *Theology and the Political: The New Debate*, edited by Creston Davis, John Milbank, and Slavoj Žižek, 153–82. Durham, NC: Duke University Press, 2005.

Draper, Paul. *A Companion to the Philosophy of Religion*. Edited by Charles Taliaferro, Paul Draper, and Philip L. Quinn. S.v. "Cumulative Cases." Hoboken, NJ: Blackwell Publishing, 2010. http://www.blackwellreference.com.turing.library.northwestern.edu/subscriber/tocnode.html?id=g9781405163576_chunk_g978140516357651.

Dulles, Avery Cardinal. *A History of Apologetics*. Eugene, OR: Wipf & Stock, 1999.

———."Postmodern Ecumenism." *First Things*, October 2003, 57–61.

Edgar, William. "Introduction." In *Christian Apologetics*, by Cornelius Van Til, edited by William Edgar, 1–16. 2nd ed. Phillipsburg, NJ: P. & R., 2003.

Ellingsen, Mark. *The Integrity of Biblical Narrative: Story in the Theology and Proclamation*. Minneapolis: Fortress, 1990.

Erickson, Millard. *Christian Theology*. 3rd ed. Grand Rapids: Baker, 2013.

Eslinger, Richard L. *Narrative and Imagination: Preaching the Worlds that Shape Us.* Minneapolis: Fortress, 1995.

————. "Tracking the Homiletical Plot." In *What's the Shape of Narrative Preaching*, edited by Mike Graves and David J. Schlafer, 69–86. St. Louis: Chalice, 2008.

Fackre, Gabriel. *The Christian Story*. 2 vols. Grand Rapids: Eerdmans, 1987.

Feinberg, Paul D. "Cumulative Case Apologetics." In *Five Views on Apologetics*, edited by Steven B. Cowan, 148–72. Grand Rapids: Zondervan, 2000.

Flew, Anthony. *The Presumption of Atheism*. London: Pemberton, 1976.

Fodor, James. "Postliberal Theology." In *The Modern Theologians*, edited by David Ford, 229–48. 3rd ed. Oxford: Blackwell, 2005.

Franke, John R. *The Character of Theology: A Postconservative Evangelical Approach.* Grand Rapids: Baker, 2005.

Frei, Hans W. "An Afterword: Eberhard Bush's Biography of Karl Barth." In *Karl Barth in Re-View: Posthumous Works Reviewed and Assessed*, edited by H. Martin Rumscheidt, 95–116. Pittsburgh Theological Monograph Series 30. Pittsburgh: Pickwick, 1981.

————. "Epilogue: George Lindbeck and *The Nature of Doctrine*." In *Theology and Dialogue: Essays in Conversation with George Lindbeck*, edited by Bruce D. Marshall, 275–82. Notre Dame: Notre Dame University Press, 1990.

————. *The Identity of Jesus Christ*. Philadelphia: Fortress, 1975.

————. "'Literal Reading' of Biblical Narrative in Christian Tradition." In *The Bible and the Narrative Tradition*, edited by Frank McConnell, 36–77. New York: Oxford University Press, 1986.

————. "Response to 'Narrative Theology: An Evangelical Appraisal.'" *Trinity Journal* (Spring 1987) 21–24.

————. *Types of Christian Theology*. Edited by George Hunsinger and William C. Placher. New Haven, CT: Yale University Press, 1992.

Geivett, R. Douglas. *Evil and the Evidence for God*. Philadelphia: Temple University Press, 1993.

Gibbs, Jeremiah. "Performative Metanarrative and Postmodern Apologetics: A Case Study with St. Augustine." Master's thesis, Garrett-Evangelical Theological Seminary, 2007.

————. "Medicine Is a Good Thing: Assemblies of God Doctrine as Support and Limit of Medicine." In *Proceedings of the Inaugural Faith and Science Conference*, edited by David R. Bundrick and Steve Badger, 175–84. Springfield, MO: Gospel, 2011.

————. "Preserving Integrity: Lessons on Interfaith Prayer from the University." *Liturgy*, 26.3 (2011) 34–41.

Goh, Jeffrey C. K. *Christian Tradition Today: A Postliberal Vision of Church and World.* Leuvain, Belgium: Peeters, 2000.

Grenz, Stanley. "Jesus as the Imago Dei." *Journal of the Evangelical Theological Society* 47 (2004) 617–28.

————. *The Moral Quest: Foundations of Christian Ethics*. Downers Grove, IL: IVP Academic, 1997.

Grenz, Stanley J., and John R. Franke. *Beyond Foundationalism: Shaping Theology in a Postmodern Context*. Louisville: Westminster John Knox, 2001.

Grillmeier, Aloys. *Christ in Christian Tradition, Volume I: From the Apostolic Age to Chalcedon*. Translated by John Bowden. 2nd ed. Atlanta: John Knox, 1975.

Gunton, Colin E. *The Actuality of Atonement: A Study of Metaphor, Rationality and the Christian Tradition.* London: T. & T. Clark, 1998.

Hamilton, Adam. *Enough: Discovering Joy Through Simplicity and Generosity.* Nashville: Abingdon, 2009.

Harmless, William. *Augustine and the Catechumenate.* Collegeville, MN: Liturgical, 1995.

Hart, David Bentley. *The Beauty of the Infinite: The Aesthetics of Christian Truth.* Grand Rapids: Eerdmans, 2003.

Hauerwas, Stanley. *A Community of Character.* Notre Dame, IN: University of Notre Dame Press, 1981.

———. "On Being a Theologian." Lecture given at the 2010 Religion and Philosophy Colloquium at Indiana Wesleyan University, November 15, 2010.

———. *With the Grain of the Universe: The Church's Witness and Natural Theology.* Grand Rapids: Brazos, 2001.

Hauerwas, Stanley, and Samuel Wells, eds. *The Blackwell Companion to Christian Ethics.* Malden, MA: Blackwell, 2004.

Hebblethwaite, Brian. "Basil Mitchell: Anglican Philosopher." *Theology* 112, no. 868 (2009) 260–69.

Henry, Carl F. H. "Narrative Theology: An Evangelical Appraisal." *Trinity Journal* 8 (1987) 9–19.

Hensley, Jeffrey. "Are Postliberals Necessarily Antirealists? Reexamining the Metaphysics of Lindbeck's Postliberal Theology." In *The Nature of Confession*, edited by Timothy R. Phillips and Dennis L. Okholm, 69–80. Downers Grove, IL: Intervarsity, 1996.

Huetter, Reinhard. *Suffering Divine Things: Theology as Church Practice.* Grand Rapids: Eerdmans, 2000.

Hunsinger, George. "What Can Evangelicals & Postliberals Learn From Each Other? The Carl Henry-Hans Frei Exchange Reconsidered." In *The Nature of Confession*, edited by Timothy R. Phillips and Dennis L. Okholm, 134–50. Downers Grove, IL: Intervarsity, 1996.

Jackson, Timothy P. "Against Grammar." *Religious Studies Review* 11 (1985) 240–45.

John Paul II. *Dominae Cenae.* Encyclical letter on the mystery and the worship of the Eucharist, February 24, 1980. http://www.vatican.va/holy_father/john_paul_ii/letters/documents/hf_jp-ii_let_24021980_dominicae-cenae_en.html3.

———. *Encyclical Letter, Fides et Ratio: On the Relationship between Faith and Reason*, September 14, 1998. http://www.vatican.va/holy_father/john_paul_ii/encyclicals/documents/hf_jp-ii_enc_15101998_fides-et-ratio_en.html.

Kallenberg, Brad. "The Strange New World in the Church: A Review Essay of *With the Grain of the Universe* by Stanley Hauerwas." *Journal of Religious Ethics* 32.1 (2004) 197–217.

Kärkäinen, Veli-Matti. *Christology: A Global Introduction.* Grand Rapids: Baker Academic, 2003.

Kavanaugh, John. *Following Christ in a Consumer Society.* Rev. ed. Maryknoll, NY: Orbis, 1991.

Keller, Timothy. *The Reason for God: Belief in an Age of Skepticism.* New York: Penguin, 2008.

Kenneson, Philip D. "Gathering: Worship, Imagination, and Formation." In *The Blackwell Companion to Christian Ethics,* edited by Stanley Hauerwas and Samuel Wells, 53–67. Malden, MA: Blackwell, 2004.

———. *Life on the Vine: Cultivating the Fruit of the Spirit in Christian Community.* Downers Grove, IL: Intervarsity, 1999.

Kuhn, Thomas S. "Reflections on My Critics." In *Criticism and the Growth of Knowledge,* edited by I. Lakatos and A. Musgrave, 231–78. New York: Cambridge University Press, 1970.

———. *The Structure of Scientific Revolutions.* 2nd ed. Chicago: University of Chicago Press, 1970.

Leffel, G. Michael. "Who Cares? Generativity and the Moral Emotions, Part 2: A 'Socialist Intuitionist Model of Moral Motivation.'" *Journal of Psychology and Theology* 36.3 (2008) 182–201.

Lindbeck, George A. "George Lindbeck Replies to Avery Cardinal Dulles." *First Things,* January 2004, 13–15.

———. "The Gospel's Uniqueness: Election and Untranslatability." *Modern Theology* 13 (1997) 423–50.

———. *The Nature of Doctrine: Religion and Theology in a Postliberal Age, 25th Anniversary Edition.* Louisville: Westminster John Knox, 2009.

———. "Response to Bruce Marshall." *Thomist* 53.3 (1989) 403–6.

———. "Spiritual Formation and Theological Education." In *Theological Perspectives on Christian Formation,* edited by Jeff Astley, Leslie J. Francis, and Colin Crowder, 285–302. Grand Rapids: Eerdmans, 1996.

Linn, Susan. *Consuming Kids: The Hostile Takeover of Childhood.* New York: New, 2004.

Locke, John. *An Essay Concerning Human Understanding.* Oxford: Clarendon Press, 1979.

Long, D. Stephen. *The Goodness of God: Theology, the Church, and Social Order.* Grand Rapids: Brazos, 2001.

———. *Speaking of God: Theology, Language, and Truth.* Grand Rapids: Eerdmans, 2009.

Lowry, Eugene. *The Sermon: Dancing the Edge of Mystery.* Nashville: Abingdon, 1997.

MacIntyre, Alasdair. *After Virtue: A Study in Moral Theory.* 2nd ed. Notre Dame, IN: University of Notre Dame Press, 1984.

———. *Whose Justice? Which Rationality?* Notre Dame: University of Notre Dame, 1989.

Mackenzie, Iain M. *Irenaeus' Demonstration of the Apostolic Preaching: A Theological Commentary and Translation.* Burlington, VT: Ashgate, 2002.

Marsden, George. "The Collapse of American Evangelical Academia." In *Faith and Rationality: Reason and Belief in God,* edited by Alvin Plantinga and Nicholas Wolterstorff, 219–64. Notre Dame, IN: University of Notre Dame Press, 1983.

Marshall, Bruce D. "Absorbing the World: Christianity and the Universe of Truths." In *Theology and Dialogue: Essays in Conversation with George Lindbeck,* edited Bruce D. Marshall, 69–102. Notre Dame, IN: University of Notre Dame Press, 1990.

———. "Aquinas as Postliberal Theologian." *Thomist* 53.3 (1989) 353–402.

———. "Introduction: The Nature of Doctrine after 25 Years." In *The Nature of Doctrine: Religion and Theology in a Postliberal Age, 25th Anniversary Edition,* by George Lindbeck, vii–xxviii. Louisville: Westminster John Knox, 2009.

Mascord, Keith A. *Alvin Plantinga and Christian Apologetics*. Eugene, OR: Wipf & Stock, 2006.

Mazza, Enrico. *Mystagogy: A Theology of Liturgy in the Patristic Age*. Collegeville, MN: Liturgical, 1989.

McClendon, James Wm., Jr., and James M. Smith. *Convictions: Defusing Religious Pluralism*. Rev. ed. Valley Forge, PA: Trinity Press International, 1994.

McGrath, Alister E. "An Evangelical Evaluation of Postliberalism." In *The Nature of Confession*, edited by Timothy R. Phillips and Dennis L. Okholm, 23–44. Downers Grove, IL: Intervarsity, 1996.

———. *The Genesis of Doctrine: A Study in the Foundation of Doctrinal Criticism*. Oxford: Blackwell, 1990.

Menzies, William M., and Stanley M. Horton. *Bible Doctrines: A Pentecostal Perspective*. Springfield, MO: Logion, 1993.

Michener, Ronald T. *Postliberal Theology: A Guide for the Perplexed*. New York: Bloomsbury, 2013.

Milbank, John. *Theology and Social Theory*. 2nd ed. Malden: Blackwell, 2006.

Mitchell, Basil. "Faith and Reason: A False Antithesis?" *Religious Studies* 16.2 (1980) 131–44.

———. *How to Play Theological Ping Pong*. Grand Rapids: Eerdmans, 1991.

———. *Justification of Religious Belief*. Oxford and New York, Oxford University Press, 1981.

———. "Newman as a Philosopher." In *Newman After a Hundred Years*, edited by Ian Ker and Alan G. Hill, 223–46. Oxford: Clarendon Press, 1990.

Morris, Thomas. "Introduction." In *Philosophy and the Christian Faith*, edited by Thomas Morris, 1–7. Notre Dame: University of Notre Dame Press, 1988.

Murphy, Nancey. *Beyond Liberalism and Fundamentalism: How Modern and Postmodern Philosophy Set the Theological Agenda*. Harrisburg, PA: Trinity Press International, 1996.

Murphy, Nancey, and James Wm. McClendon, Jr. "Distinguishing Modern and Postmodern Theologies," *Modern Theology* 5, no. 3 (1989) 191–214.

Navone, John. *Toward a Theology of Beauty*. Collegeville, MN: Liturgical, 1996.

Newman, Rick. "How Sullenberger Really Saved US Airways Flight 1549." *US News*, February 3, 2009. http://money.usnews.com/money/blogs/flowchart/2009/02/03/how-sullenberger-really-saved-us-airways-flight-1549.

Nietzsche, Friedrich. *On the Genealogy of Morality: A Polemic*. Translated by Maudemarie Clark and Alan J. Swensen. Indianapolis: Hackett, 1998.

———. *Werke, Vol. 3*. Edited by Karl Schlechta. Munich: Hanser, 1954.

O'Donovan, Oliver. *Resurrection and the Moral Order: An Outline for Evangelical Ethics*. 2nd ed. Grand Rapids: Eerdmans, 1994.

———. *The Ways of Judgment*. Grand Rapids: Eerdmans, 2005.

Olson, Roger E. *Reformed and Always Reforming: The Postconservative Approach to Evangelical Theology*. Grand Rapids: Baker, 2007.

Pahl, Jon. *Shopping Malls and Other Sacred Places: Putting God in Place*. Grand Rapids: Brazos, 2003.

Pannenberg, Wolfhart. *Jesus, God and Man*. Translated by Lewis L. Wilkens and Duane A. Priebe. Philadelphia: Westminster, 1968.

Pasquarello, Michael, III. "Narrative Reading, Narrative Preaching: Inhabiting the Story." In *Narrative Reading, Narrative Preaching: Reuniting New Testament*

Interpretation and Proclamation, edited by Joel B. Green and Michael Pasquarello III, 177–193. Grand Rapids: Baker, 2003.

Patterson, Sue. *Realist Christian Theology in a Postmodern Age.* Cambridge: Cambridge University Press, 1999.

Pecknold, C. C. *Transforming Postliberal Theology: George Lindbeck, Pragmatism, and Scripture.* New York: T. & T. Clark, 2005.

Penner, Myron Bradley. *The End of Apologetics: Christian Witness in a Postmodern Context.* Grand Rapids: Baker, 2013.

Phillips, Timothy R., and Dennis L. Okholm, eds. *The Nature of Confession: Evangelicals and Postliberals in Conversation.* Downers Grove, IL: Intervarsity, 1996.

Pimentel, David. "Ethanol Fuels: Energy Balance, Economics, and Environmental Impact are Negative." *Natural Resources Research* 12.2 (2003) 127–34.

Pinches, Charles. "Proclaiming." In *The Blackwell Companion to Christian Ethics,* edited by Stanley Hauerwas and Samuel Wells, 169–81. Malden, MA: Blackwell, 2004.

Placher, William. "Is the Bible True?" *Christian Century* 113.10 (March 20, 1996) 924–28.

———. "A Modest Response to Paul Schwartzentruber." *Modern Theology* 8 (1992) 197–201.

———. "Paul Ricoeur and Postliberal Theology." *Modern Theology* 4 (1987) 35–52.

———. "Struggling with Scripture." In *Struggling With Scripture* by Walter Brueggemann, William C. Placher, and Brian K Blount, 32–50. Louisville: Westminster John Knox, 2002.

———. *Unapologetic Theology: A Christian Voice in a Pluralistic Conversation.* Louisville: Westminster John Knox, 1989.

Plantinga, Alvin. "Reason and Belief in God." In *Faith and Rationality: Reason and Belief in God,* edited by Alvin Plantinga and Nicholas Wolterstorff, 16–93. Notre Dame, IN: University of Notre Dame Press, 1983.

———. *Warranted Christian Belief.* New York: Oxford University Press, 2000.

Presbyterian Church (U.S.A.). *Respectful Presence.* Louisville: World Ministries Division-PCUSA, 1997.

Ridderbos, Herman, *Paul: An Outline of His Theology.* Translated by John Richard de Witt. Grand Rapids: Eerdmans, 1975.

Russell, Bertrand. *Why I am Not a Christian.* New York: Simon & Schuster, 1957.

Saliers, Don E. *Worship as Theology: Foretaste of Glory Divine.* Nashville: Abingdon, 1994.

Schmemann, Alexander. *For the Life of the World: Sacraments and Orthodoxy.* 2nd ed. Crestwood, NY: St. Vladimir's Seminary Press, 1973.

Schmitt, Bernd H. *Experiential Marketing: How to Get Customers to Sense, Feel, Think, Act, Relate.* New York: Free, 1999.

Sittser, Jerry. *The Will of God as a Way of Life: How to Make Every Decision with Peace and Confidence.* Grand Rapids: Zondervan, 2000.

Smith, James K.A. *Desiring the Kingdom: Worship, Worldview, and Cultural Formation.* Grand Rapids: Baker, 2009.

———. *Imagining the Kingdom: How Worship Works.* Grand Rapids: Baker, 2013.

St. John, Allen. "What Went Right: Flight 1549 Airbus A-320's Ditch into the Hudson." *Popular Mechanics,* October 1, 2009. http://www.popularmechanics.com/science/4300211.

Stone, Bryan. *Evangelism After Christendom: The Theology and Practice of Christian Witness*. Grand Rapids: Brazos, 2007.

Swinburne, Richard. *The Coherence of Theism*. Rev. ed. Oxford: Clarendon, 1993.

———. *The Existence of God*. 2nd ed. Oxford: Oxford University Press, 2004.

———.*Is There a God?* Rev. ed. Oxford: Oxford University Press, 2010.

———. *Mind, Brain, and Free Will*. New York: Oxford University Press, 2013.

———. *Providence and the Problem of Evil*. New York: Oxford University Press, 1998.

———. *The Resurrection of God Incarnate*. Oxford: Clarendon, 2003.

———. *Revelation*. 2nd ed. New York: Oxford University Press, 2007.

———. *Was Jesus God?* Oxford: Oxford University Press, 2008.

The Persuaders: Americans are Swimming in a Sea of Messages. DVD. Directed by Rachel Dretzin and Barak Goodman. Alexandria, VA: PBS Frontline, 2005.

Thomas, J.C. "Cumulative Arguments for Religious Belief." *Sophia* 21.3 (1982) 37–47.

Tracy, David. "Lindbeck's New Program for Theology: A Reflection." *The Thomist* 49 (1985) 460–72.

Vanhoozer, Kevin. *Biblical Narrative in the Philosophy of Paul Ricoeur: A Study in Hermeneutics and Theology*. Cambridge: Cambridge University Press, 1990.

———. *The Drama of Doctrine: A Canonical-Linguistic Approach to Christian Theology*. Louisville: Westminster John Knox, 2005.

———. *First Theology: God, Scripture, and Hermeneutics*. Downers Grove, IL: IVP Academic, 2002.

Volf, Miroslav. *Exclusion and Embrace: A Theological Exploration of Identity, Otherness, and Reconciliation*. Nashville: Abingdon, 1996.

Wainwright, Geoffrey. "Ecumenical Dimensions of Lindbeck's 'Nature of Doctrine.'" *Modern Theology* 4.2 (1988) 121–32.

———. *Eucharist and Eschatology*. Oxford: Oxford University Press, 1981.

Wells, Samuel. *Improvisation: The Drama of Christian Ethics*. Grand Rapids: Brazos, 2004.

Werpehowski, William. "Ad Hoc Apologetics." *Journal of Religion* 66.3 (July 1986) 282–301.

White, Nicholas P. "Plato's Metaphysical Epistemology." In *The Cambridge Companion to Plato*, edited by Richard Kraut, 277–310. Cambridge: Cambridge University Press, 1992.

Wingren, Gustaf. *Man and the Incarnation: A Study in the Biblical Theology of Irenaeus*. Translated by Ross MacKenzie. Edinburgh: Oliver & Boyd, 1959.

Wolterstorff, Nicholas. *Art in Action: Toward a Christian Aesthetic*. Grand Rapids: Eerdmans, 1980.

———. "Can Belief In God Be Rational If It Has No Foundations?" In *Faith and Rationality: Reason and Belief in God*, edited by Alvin Plantinga and Nicholas Wolterstorff, 135–86. Notre Dame, IN: University of Notre Dame Press, 1983.

———. "Introduction." In *Faith and Rationality: Reason and Belief in God*, edited by Alvin Plantinga and Nicholas Wolterstorff, 1–15. Notre Dame, IN: University of Notre Dame Press, 1983.

———. "The Migration of the Theistic Arguments: From Natural Theology to Evidentialist Apologetics." In *Rationality, Religious Belief, and Moral Commitment*, edited by Robert Audi and William J. Wainwright, 56–74. Ithaca, NY: Cornell University Press, 1986.

———. *Reason within the Bounds of Religion*. 2nd ed. Grand Rapids: Eerdmans, 1984.

————. "What New Haven and Grand Rapids Have to Say to Each Other?" In *Seeking Understanding: The Stob Lectures, 1986–1998*, 251–93. Grand Rapids: Eerdmans, 2001.

Wood, Charles M. "Review of Lindbeck, *The Nature of Doctrine.*" *Religious Studies Review* 11 (1985) 235–40.

Wright, N. T. "How Can the Bible Be Authoritative?" *VoxEvangelica* 21 (1991) 7–32.

————. *The New Testament and the People of God.* Minneapolis: Fortress, 1992.

————. *The Resurrection of the Son of God.* Minneapolis: Fortress, 2003.

Wright, R. George. "Cumulative Case Legal Arguments and the Justification of Academic Affirmative Action." *Pace Law Review* 23.1 (2002) 1–41.

Žižek, Slavoj. "The 'Thrilling Romance of Orthodoxy.'" In *Theology and the Political: The New Debate*, edited by Creston Davis, John Milbank, and Slavoj Žižek, 52–71. Durham, NC: Duke University Press, 2005.

Index

"ad hoc" apologetics, xi, 2, 29–34, 58, 87, 101, 122, 148
Abraham, William, 106, 159–60
aesthetic criteria, 46–53
aesthetics. *See* beauty
analogia entis, 51, 56–57
Anselm, Saint, ix, 17, 47–48, 90
apologetic method, xi–xiii, xv, 1–2, 6–7, 16, 18, 32, 55, 86, 106, 122, 127
Augustine, Saint, ix, 53–54, 78, 88, 112, 144–51

Balthasar, Hans Urs von, 41, 43–46, 151
baptism, 18, 80–81, 148–52, 160, 163
Barron, Robert, 65, 74
Barth, Karl, xi, xiii–xv, 6, 23, 34, 37–40, 49–51, 55–59, 65–75, 91, 123
beauty, xii–xiii, 10, 26, 33–35, 41–55, 58–59, 84–85, 97, 130–33, 138, 150–53, 159, 161
Bible, 3, 22, 93, 100, 105, 140, 143–44

catechesis, xiii–xv, 9, 18, 30, 112, 116, 123, 125–26, 137, 146–48, 160–61
Christology, 8, 60–62, 70, 73–76, 81
church, ix, xiv, xv, 3, 14, 18, 56, 59–60, 74–82, 116, 125–31, 136–38, 140–46, 149, 152–54, 158–63
coherence, 11–13, 15, 17, 19, 52, 82, 120
consumerism, 55, 130–34

cosmological argument, 102–5, 109, 111
Craig, William Lane, x, xi
creed, 82, 149, 152
cultural–linguistic, 4–5, 7–9, 13, 15, 20, 22–23, 31, 34, 115, 122–23, 138, 150
cumulative case apologetics, xiii, 27–30, 53, 87, 101–3, 106–23

deontology, 92, 94, 96
disciplina arcani, 137, 148–49
doctrine, 3–4, 7–9, 21, 29, 35–36, 52, 69, 79, 82, 96–100, 104–5, 109, 114–15, 127
Dulles, Avery, 6, 13, 19

Enlightenment, ix–x, 54, 72, 74, 76, 81, 83, 92, 94–95, 99
epistemology, x–xiii, 14, 35–36, 42–43, 99–102; totalizing, 49–50; foundationalist, 89–90; atheistic, 91–92
eschatology, 66, 143, 152, 156–57
ethics, xiii, xv, 35, 41, 45, 54–60, 62–84, 92, 143; church, 159; Christian, 55, 62–66, 69, 73–74, 78–81, 161; creation, 64, 70, 73, 82; general, 55–58, 65–66; medical, 32; postmodern conception of, 41; theological, 55–58, 71, 84
Eucharist, 5, 127, 136–37, 148, 151–54, 157

evangelicalism, x–xii, xv, 3, 7, 10–11, 30, 39, 46, 52, 93–94, 101, 125, 144, 161

evangelism, 53, 116, 126, 128, 136, 159–61

evidential apologetics, 2, 73, 89–99, 140

evil, problem of, 54, 83–84, 109

evolution, 21, 26, 52

experiential–expressivist, 3–7, 10, 20, 31, 139

fideism, 10–11, 19, 110

first-order speech, 8–9

fittingness, 41, 52–53

foundationalism, x, xiii, 2, 6, 86–92, 94, 96, 100, 101, 103, 106, 122

Frame, John, 30, 87

Frei, Hans, xi, 10–11, 30–32, 37, 100, 140, 145, 147

fundamentalism, 6, 140

God, 10, 15–18, 27–28, 46, 92–93, 127–29, 146–47, 151–63; belief in, 95–98, 106–9; call, 127–28, 151, 163; doctrine of, 38–42, 48–84, 103–4; Kingdom of, xiii, 158

Gospel, xiii, 37, 59–60, 72, 74, 79, 98, 101, 112, 115, 129, 146, 159

Grenz, Stanley, xi–xii, 3, 6, 61–63, 66, 81, 144

Harnack, Adolf, 74

Hauerwas, Stanley, ix, xv, 31–32, 34, 37, 45, 81, 163

Holy Spirit, 30, 80–82, 97–100

imago Dei, 61, 63–64, 70, 74, 78, 80, 82, 97

incarnation, 39–40, 52, 60–62, 64, 73, 75–76, 92, 99–100, 146

inductive argument, 102, 104–9, 114

internal instigation of the Holy Spirit, 97–99

intrasystematic, 8–19, 27, 36, 123

intratextuality, 10–11, 19, 31, 122–23, 144

Irenaeus, 61–62, 64, 67

Kallenberg, Brad, 31, 45

Kant, Immanuel, 41, 54–55, 59–60, 73–74, 83, 103–4

Kuhn, Thomas, 21, 26, 112, 115–20, 122

Kuyper, Abraham, 87–88, 93

language games, 17, 28, 96, 100

Lewis, C. S., x, 27

Lindbeck, George, x–xiii, xv, 1–30, 33–37, 58, 84, 86–88, 100–103, 108, 115–16, 122–23, 125, 161; catechesis and, 125–26, 146, 148; fideism and, 10–11; typology; 100

liturgy, xiv, 127, 131, 133–35, 147–52

Locke, John, ix, 90–99

Long, D. Stephen, 2, 35–45, 49, 51, 53, 61, 84

MacIntrye, Alasdair, 23–25, 29, 54–55, 117, 123, 135–36, 142, 144, 160

McClendon, James, 16, 8, 112

McDowell, Josh, 94

McGrath, Alister, 7–13, 29, 35–36

metaphysics, xii, 17, 36–41, 49, 51, 58, 76, 84, 102–3

Mitchell, Basil, 27, 93, 101–22

Modernity, 42, 49–50, 54–55, 59, 83

natural theology, xi, 2, 29–30, 37, 51, 57, 63, 70–73, 86–90, 94, 103–5, 109–10, 114, 122

nihilism, 6, 42, 46

O'Donovan, Oliver, 57, 67, 70, 72–73, 84

objective nature of truth, xii, 2, 3, 14, 40–42, 49–50, 55, 63, 66, 69, 93

ontological argument, 90, 103, 105

ontological truth, 10–19, 27, 36–37, 123

ontology, xiii, 10, 35, 39, 41–43, 48–49, 51, 53–57, 65–66, 74, 84

ontotheology, 38

Pannenberg, Wolfhart, 75–77
Pentecostalism, xi, 29, 115, 152, 156–57
Placher, William, 8, 11, 31–32, 139, 143
Plantinga, Alvin, 30, 87–103, 107–8
Plato, 39, 48–51, 58
Pope John Paul II, 36, 153–54, 157, 161
post-Cartesian natural theology, xi, 29, 86–88, 101, 103, 107, 109–10, 122
postconservative, xi–xiii, xv, 2, 35, 84, 101, 144, 160
postfoundationalism, xii, xiii, xv
postmodern, 69, 83, 94, 112; apologetic, 18, 55; deconstruction of truth, 42, 49; ethics, 41, 81; literature, xv; Reformed tradition and, 88, 100; turn, x, 47
pragmatism, 5, 16, 45, 112
preaching, 18, 98, 127, 138–54, 161, 163
presuppositional apologetics, ix, 17–18, 30, 87
probability calculus, 99, 107–8
propositionalism, xii, 3–4, 13, 31, 100, 109, 160

realism, xii, 36, 40, 93
reconciliation, 4, 143
Reformed Epistemology, 87–88
Reid, Thomas, 93–95
resurrection, 16, 40, 64, 76–77, 82, 100, 102, 105, 107, 109, 153, 163

second first language, 23–25, 29, 117, 123, 135
second–order speech, 8–9
sin, 3, 16, 27, 28, 51, 56–58, 61, 64, 83, 97, 100, 131, 141, 149–51; noetic effect of, 63
subjective nature of truth, xii, 41–46, 48–50, 66
Swinburne, Richard, 27, 98, 101–110, 114, 120

theological method, 31, 42
Thomas Aquinas, 40, 42–44, 47–48, 52–53, 67, 72–73, 86, 88–90
Tracy, David, 9, 20
transcendental predicates of being, xii, 10, 34, 40–53, 58, 84–85
Trinity, 21, 78

untranslatability, 20–25

Van Til, Cornelius, ix, 30, 87
Vanhoozer, Kevin, 6, 79–80
Volf, Miroslav, 83–84

Warfield, B. B., 6, 93–94
warrant, 14, 26, 33, 96
Werpehowski, William, 32–34
witness, 45, 49, 52, 58, 64, 69, 72, 76, 123, 125–28, 135–36, 142, 159–61
Wolterstorff, Nicholas, 30, 52–53, 72, 87–95, 100
Wright, N. T., 76–77, 142–43